LIFT UP YOUR HEART

LIFT UP YOUR HEART

by **FULTON J. SHEEN**, Ph.D., D.D.

Agrégé en Philosophie de L'Université de Louvain
Former Professor of the Catholic University of America
National Director of the Society for the Propagation
of the Faith

Garden City Books   Garden City, New York

LIFT UP YOUR HEART

Nihil obstat:

  Rt. Rev. JOHN M. A. FEARNS, S.T.D., Censor Librorum

Imprimatur:

  ✠ FRANCIS CARDINAL SPELLMAN, Archbishop of New York

GARDEN CITY BOOKS REPRINT EDITION 1952, by special arrangement with McGraw-Hill Book Company, Inc.

Printed in the United States
At the Country Life Press, Garden City, N.Y.

DEDICATION

AS HAMMERS BEAT AND SICKLES CUT
AS ATOMS BURST AND WARFARE BLUSTERS
AT RED LUCIFER'S AND HELL'S COMMAND
LIFT UP YOUR HEART!
GOD PROMISED THAT A VIRGIN'S FOOT
WOULD CRUSH THESE COBRAS OF THE NIGHT

TO
THAT IMMACULATE HEART
MOTHER OF GRACE DIVINE
THESE STUMBLING WORDS ARE WRITTEN
AND THIS BOOK IS DEDICATED
IN PRAYERFUL HOPE
THAT AS CELESTIAL TEMPTRESS
AND WITH LOYAL DECEIT
SHE
MAY BETRAY US TO HER SON
AS UNCAUGHT CAPTIVES OF LOVE DIVINE

CONTENTS

I

The Ego and I

The Ego: self one seems
The I: self one is

THE story of Dr. Jekyll and Mr. Hyde is the story of every man born of woman, for there lives within each one of us two selves—the ego and the I: the self one seems, and the self he is; a man other men meet, and a man unknown to other men. The *ego* is what we think we are; the *I* is what, in fact, we are. The ego is the spoiled child in us—selfish, petulant, clamorous, and spoiled—the creation of our mistakes in living. The I is our personality made to the image and likeness of God!

The lives of the two selves cannot be lived simultaneously. If we attempt to do so, we suffer remorse, anxiety, and inner dissatisfaction. If true freedom is to be found within ourselves, the ego must yield itself to the birth of our true person-

1

ality. But the seeming self is so familiar a companion to some persons that it cannot be easily dropped, nor is it of any use to tell them that this superficial self has no legitimate place within them. Like a plaster cast, the false ego has to be cut away, pulled off, and this is a process that involves detachment, pain, and some indignity.

When the ego dominates our lives, we blame little faults in others, and excuse great offenses in ourselves; we see the mote in our neighbor's eye, and not the beam in our own. We wrong others, and deny that there is any guilt; others do the same wrong to us, and we say that they should have known better. We hate others, and call it "zeal"; we flatter others because of what they can do for us, and call it "love"; we lie to them, and call it "tact." We are slow to defend the rights of God in public, and call it "prudence"; we selfishly push others aside, and call it "getting our just rights"; we judge others, and say that we are "facing the facts"; we refuse to give up our life of sin, and call anyone who does so an "escapist." We overeat, and call it "health"; we pile up more wealth than is necessary for our state in life, and call it "security"; we resent the wealth of others, and call ourselves "defenders of the downtrodden"; we deny inviolable principles of law, plant our feet firmly in mid-air, and call ourselves "liberal." We begin sentences with "I"—and condemn our neighbor as a bore for wanting to talk about himself, when we want to talk about ourselves; we ruin family life by divorce—and say we have to "live our own lives"; we believe we are virtuous—merely because we have found someone who is vicious.

Our sloth and laziness we call "living sensibly"; we disguise our psychological reluctance to work by praising a socialism in which the State does everything. We want so much to be loved that we forget to love. We nurse our own troubles so much that we fail to see the lovableness of others. We possess money, and think that therefore we have worth; we criticize others unjustly, with the excuse that they should know the truth about themselves; we judge our virtues by the vices from which we abstain; we boast of the tinsel wrapping on the box of our lives, and call it "glamour"; we refuse to make up our minds about anything, and boast that we are being broadminded. These are the temptations to which we are all prone when we allow the ego in us to become supreme.

Those who glorify the ego, or the seeming-self, often develop a vicarious interest in solving problems which do not concern them, as a substitute for tackling their own problem of selfishness. One wonders if the contemporary interest in movie murder mysteries, thrillers, and newspaper horror stories is not an admission that millions of men feel the need to solve important personal problems; but rather than facing the riddles of self, which are indeed difficult, they shift the problem and study baffling events in other lives, instead. The man who has horrors tormenting his own soul may like to hear of greater horrors in others, or to see them on the screen, in order that he may for a moment forget his own hell within.

In talking about other people, we often ask: "Why doesn't he recognize his own faults?" The reason is that "he" has never practiced self-introspection; his ego has obscured his I; his egotism has drowned out his personality. On the other hand, we who see the fault are sometimes—not always—unconsciously revealing our own; for how could one of us say of another, "She is jealous," or "She is catty," unless we already knew in our hearts how it felt to be jealous or catty?

Our Lord warned us: "Do not judge others, or you yourself will be judged." (Matt. 7:1.) The judgment of our neighbor is a self-revelation, and thereby a judgment on ourselves. The very touchiness and sensitiveness of some people about themselves, the violent way they react to criticism, is an indication of how much they protect their own false ego, of how little courage they have in daring to let their real self stand the light of day.

Because the ego and the I, or the superficial self and the real self, are related as the husk to the seed, it follows that the I is not revealed until the ego is removed. The apple does not become a tree until the outer, covering pulp is shed and the seed is set free to grow.

Many writings today tell us how we may deceive people by flattery or win their good favor by a broad-mindedness about virtue and vice; these are really appeals to our egotism. Their result is to make the ego more egotistic and the husk more impenetrable, effectively preventing the release of the I, or the real self. To use others as instruments of our ambition is the antithesis of loving them—and of self-growth. Those who wear a constant disguise over the true self not only reveal themselves to their neighbors, at moments of stress, as totally different personalities, but they have within themselves a bare minimum of the true self-consciousness which is necessary for life. Their sense of selfhood is so completely externalized, so dependent on others' praise, that they never feel integrated, are never able to find peace. Their emotions and their actions are at war. A constant conflict seems to rage within their breasts, between what they *ought* to be and what they *are*. Constantly busied with appearances and with their own surface emotions, such people become incapable of love in the true sense of the word; they love the *experience* of love, but they do not love any person, because they are hardly persons themselves. Frightened to look inside themselves because of the skeletons in their own souls' closets, they abhor silence and quiet; for only the peaceful of soul can live with themselves.

The difference between the person in whom the ego, or selfishness, dominates and the person in whom the I, or personality, dominates spells the difference between false gaiety and true happiness, between neurotic and normal living. The egotist can be represented thus:

The ego—the mask he will show the world—is the central interest of his life; all desires, thoughts, and affections, are valued in respect to this. The I, or the real self, which bears the Divine Image, is very weak in him and influences only a small area of the circumference of his life.

In a normal person the situation is reversed:

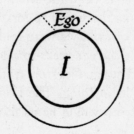

The personality (which is rooted in God) has taken over the center of life, while the ego of selfishness is so superficial as to be barely noticeable. But this does not mean that the individual personality has been lost; indeed, it is stronger and much more individual than in the case of an ego-dominated man. The I, the true personality, is what the philosophers call "subsistent"—that is, it is able to return to its own essence, to coincide with itself, to see itself as it really is, and to know itself by reflection. Each human personality is so inviolable that it stands out, against all other personalities, as unique, incommunicable, and absolutely distinct. Because of his personality, or I, every man is a precious mystery. He cannot be weighed by public opinion; he cannot be measured by his conditionings; he belongs to no one but himself, and no creature in all the world can penetrate his mystery except the God Who made him. The dignity of every I is beyond our reckoning.

But the ego is made to the image and likeness of the spirit of the world in which it lives, as the I is made to the image and likeness of the eternal God. The ego is a conformist; it is "adjusted" to its times; but the Scriptures warn: "Be not conformed to the world." The I has attained inner freedom, through transcendence of the worldly. The ego is always self-centered; the personality, because it is essentially a mystery, is willing to soar beyond the self if it can return to its source. The ego wants the world to serve it; the I wants to serve the world. Ego-centricity always leads to self-deception; for by its very nature the ego seeks to smother the I with its eagerness for effort. The ego flies from truth, because it knows that truth would be its undoing. The I, or personality, seeks truth, for it knows truth would be its flowering and perfection. Liars are always persons whose egos are fiercely prized.

In these days of socialism, with its emphasis on man in the mass, there can never be too much insistence on the value of the personality. A man's personal soul is worth more than all the collective states, for states are made to serve personality, and not the other way around. A human personality is worth more than the material universe, for a man can get the whole universe into his mind through knowledge. The good Lord Himself balanced the cosmos against a soul and asked: "What exchange shall a man give for his soul?"

The mystery of freedom is inseparable from the mystery of personality. The ego always seeks to interpret freedom as license, but the personality, or the I, understands freedom as responsibility under the law. The ego defines liberty as the right to do whatever it pleases; the I, as the right to do what ever I ought. The ego in its affections says: "I love whatever I wish"; the personality, or the I, says: "I love whatever God wishes." The ego admits no other existence than those sensate objects which can give it pleasure. The personality prizes suprapersonal values—for personality is meaningless if there is no higher world toward which it can tend. The ego meets other egos like billiard balls that hit one another in passing; the I meets other personalities in communion and fraternity, for each other I to whom the I goes out is seen, not as an object, but as another personality who is as sacred as a Thou.

The ego is not aware of other egos, except as an occasion for pleasure or ambition. The ego is like a hysterical woman who refers everything that happens to herself. It breathes in the same air that it breathes out, because it denies any other reality than itself. It sets itself up as the determinant of truth, of goodness, of morality—it acts as its own law—it denies the reality of every object and affirms only the existence of itself as the subject.

The I, on the other hand, is conscious of a vocation and of a mission. The depths of a true personality are stirred by God's call to make good use of His creative gifts—not only for himself, but for his neighbor and the world. "All are yours, you are Christ's, and Christ is God's." Above all else, because the I affirms the spirit in its consciousness of having a soul, it expects and hopes to transcend death. If man were only a thing, he would perish with things; if he were a beast, he would perish with the beasts; if he were only an ego, he would perish when people stopped talking about him; but if he is an I, because he has an immortal soul, then death itself cannot sweep away his personality.

Some egotists fight like tigers against the stripping off of their egos, but once they become convinced that there is a real self, a personality, beneath the ego, then they see the change as bringing them not loss, but gain. Our Divine Lord told us that if we wish to save our life, we must lose it; He was also stating the psychological truth that if we lose the ego, we shall find the I.

Our Lord's own followers tried to dissuade Him from sacrificing His selfless life in prophetic guidance of the way that each of us must shed his selfish life. When the Greeks came to see Our Lord, we do not know what they told Him, but we may guess that they urged Him to go to Athens, on the plea that only one wise man, Socrates, had ever been killed there and that the Athenians had regretted his death ever since. They would receive Our Lord kindly—but if He stayed on in His own country, He would probably be put to death. His answer ("A grain of wheat must fall into the ground and die, or else it remains nothing more than a grain of wheat") suggests that a death is always necessary for a resurrection. The husk must perish before the seed can generate. John the Baptist, when He saw Our Lord, said that he must decrease, but Christ must increase.

In our lives, too, the less good must give way to the best in us. The ego must decrease; the I must increase. But the I cannot increase without communion with other personalities, which involves the love of neighbor. Every neighbor, even though he be hateful in himself, becomes lovable to the full-grown I if he, too, is a child of God; thus personality flourishes by obedience to the double law of loving God and loving neighbor. When a man has overcome his ego, he thus finds that his I, or real self, is vaster than he guessed—it is an open window looking out on God and His fellow man and the whole, rich cosmos.

But there is a Divine Thou, which is more fitting as a center of life than either the ego or the I, and that is God as revealed in His Divine Nature. As the ego dies, the I is born; and as the I surrenders itself freely to God revealed in Christ Jesus, life finds a new center in Him. St. Paul expressed this experience in "I live; now not I, but Christ liveth in me." As the ego became the I through detachment from its selfishness, so the I now becomes divinized as a partaker of the Divine Nature through an attachment of interest and love. Both detachment and attachment are the work of the I, which in one instance crushes egotism and in the other, by an act of self-oblation, puts itself under the commands of the Christ-mind.

The ego has now disappeared, and even the personality has become peripheral:

When someone has thus made the orbit of his life a movement around Christ, the thoughts he thinks, the desires which
inflame him, the motivation of all his actions is centered in
Our Divine Lord. The I still remains, but, as the "Our Father"
suggests that it should be, the I is secondary—"*Thy* Will be
done on earth as it is in Heaven." Such surrender is the peak
of the I's activity—it is the I fulfilling itself by a free gift of
self-will. For the one thing that is so much our own that God
never impairs it is our freedom; the ability to sin is freedom's
temporal and negative sign, as hell is its eternal and negative sign. And since the will is always free, it is the one
supreme gift we can make to God. Such yielding of the center
of our lives to Christ is the way of supreme happiness. Our
happiness varies according to the center about which our lives
revolve. If it is the ego, there are frustrations; if it is the I,
there is a measure of natural happiness, still incomplete. If it
is the Divine, there is the joy of being one with Infinite Life
and Truth and Love.

The choice of the center rests with us: we must be satellites,
serving some center, but we may choose our sun. We cannot
remain in isolation from all centers: every person gives away
his freedom. Some give it to public opinion, some become the
slaves of their own passions; some give away their freedom to
dictators or the State, but some give their freedom away to

God. Only in the last sort of surrender does one become truly free, for only then is one united with Him Whose will is our content. Public opinion, dictators, flesh, alcohol, when we serve them, never try to set us free, but our free will is a primary concern of the Divine: "If it is the Son Who makes you free men, you will have freedom in earnest." (John 8:36.)

When the ego is strong, the I is weak; when the I is strong, God may still be weak in us if we refuse to allow the Divine to operate. But when the I relinquishes, for love, something which Love bestowed on it, then God becomes strong in the I. "Nothing is beyond my powers, thanks to the strength God gave me." (Phil. 4:13.) If an I could become so willingly weak that it reposed wholly in God, begging Him to work through it as an instrument, then, by a curious paradox, that I would be strong with the power of God.

The ego-center never loves God, for it is its own God; the I-center loves God in a limited way, knowing Him as a Power Who made the world, as a Wisdom Which planned it, and as a Love or a Divine Law of Gravitation Which would draw all things back to Himself. But the Christ-center makes the I-will identical with the God-Will, and finds no happiness but in loving God and all creatures, even enemies, in Him.

2

The Egotist—an Escapist

AN ESCAPIST is one who calls religion "escapism" so as to avoid that amendment of life which religion requires. His favorite expression is: "My conscience is at peace." But it is of a self-made and deceptive conscience that he speaks. A true conscience is not of our making; otherwise we could induce it always to testify in our defense, as alienists may sometimes testify in court for any side that hires them. Conscience cannot come to us from the rulings of society; otherwise it would never reprove us when society approves us, nor console us when society condemns. But a sound conscience stands firm, no matter whether we dislike its findings, and no matter whether those around us are opposed to them or not. Just as there is no way of knowing which keys on the piano ought to be played and which keys ought not be played, except by having a musical score outside the keys, so the very existence of conscience implies that there is outside of us a Divine Law-maker, Who legislates—a Divine Executive, Who witnesses our correspondence with the law—and a Divine Judge, Who passes sentences. At all times, we feel that there is confronting us an unseen witness in whose inner praise we rejoice, in whose inner reproof we blush with shame; and this witness is God. The very word conscience means *knowing with*—knowing with Whom but God? For conscience is the impact of Divine Truth and Goodness on our inner self.

But there are two kinds of consciences: there is the one God gave us, and there is also the one we may have made for ourselves. Guided by the first, we recognize that God has not only implanted in us a desire to make a journey to the Heavenly City, but that He has given us the map of how to get there. Following a self-made conscience, we may deny there is a destiny in life, may throw away the map, call any mood we feel the right mood. Owners of such false consciences are the ones who boast that "my conscience is at peace."

Peace is a nice word—but it, too, has a true and a false sense. True peace is a gift of God; false peace is of our own making. True peace flourishes in an increasing friendship with God; false peace is spawned in forgetfulness of God and exaltation of the self. True peace deepens in sorrow; false peace is shattered by reverses. True peace has no wants; false peace is restless and covetous. True peace has a lowly estimate of self; false peace lives in fear of being found inferior. True peace has a firm trust in God despite its own past sins; false peace shrinks from the thought of God because it will not put an end to present sins.

Dives had false peace, Lazarus true peace; the foolish virgins slept because they had peace, but it was false peace; the foolish man who kept the one talent was at peace, but his was only peace of mind; the man who built his house on sand was at peace—until the storm came. In false peace, the conscience is dead; the eye of the soul is blind; the ear of the soul is deaf; the fingers of the soul are paralyzed. False peace accompanies the false conscience we have forged with our misdeeds.

There are three steps in making a false conscience:

The conscience is dulled.

The conscience is numbed.

The consience is killed.

Stealing is here taken as an example, though any other sin would do just as well. At the first temptation to steal, the inner voice of conscience recalls the Seventh Commandment: "Thou shalt not steal." The ego answers: "This fountain pen is of no great value, and the owner will never miss it anyway; he has at least a dozen others. And in any case, I will steal only this once." This is the dulling of conscience. Next follows the stage of numbing—the voice of conscience speaks: "You *ought* not do this. You said you would never do it again. Stealing will become a habit if you do it often enough." The ego answers: "I guess I am built that way. How can I help it? Anyway, I heard one of my professors say that we were not free, but were 'determined' to be the way we are. Since I am inclined to steal, I probably inherited a tendency toward stealing from my grandfather. Also, I may have an inferiority complex due to a repression of my ego by my reactionary parents, who lived before progressive education; it is perfectly natural for me to compensate for it, by the extension of my ego in the acquisition of property."

After such a rationalization and a further theft, the last stage is reached: the killing of conscience. The voice of conscience no longer speaks out loud; it faintly whispers: "Stealing is still wrong." The ego answers: "Who decides what is right and wrong except myself? Conscience is only the vestige of an infantile dread. Why should anyone tell me what is right or wrong? How do I know there is a God? Conscience is a residue of social taboo and totem. I have heard of some primitive tribes that do not consider stealing a wrong; anyway, one has to live his own life. Stealing is wrong only if you get caught."

At the end of this trail of rationalization the "conscience is hardened as if by a searing iron" (I Tim. 4:2), and a false conscience is born. Few people can, in the first act of self-indulgence, foresee the calloused thief. Thus the little infractions of youth become the grave rebellions of maturity. For what crime is long inexcusable if one makes his own conscience the standard? If each man is to be his own judge, who will be condemned? If the ego's "right" is identified with its cupidity, then what injustice will it not espouse? Often when souls say that their conscience is at peace, it is only because they have identified conscience with the ego's interest or the ego's libidos. Instead of their desires following the dictates of conscience, conscience now follows their desires.

But is such a man's conscience really at peace? No. If the false conscience were at ease, it would not boast so much about its "peace." The healthy do not go about thumping their breasts, saying, "I am healthy": it is the sick who talk about their health. The right conscience never boasts of its righteousness, for it sees its judge in God, not self. As St. Paul said: "My conscience does not, in fact, reproach me; but that is not where my justification lies." (I Cor. 4:4.) Furthermore, it is the people with false consciences who try the hardest to es-

cape consciousness: an easy conscience ought to be an enjoy-
able conscience. How, then, explain the flights from consciousness through alcoholism, drugs, and excitement—or through
the throwing of the self on that psychoanalytic couch which
is for rent to those who will pay to hear a denial of their guilt?

Men cannot find true peace by tailoring a lax conscience
to their sins. Such men still worry, because they cannot separate their actions from an uncertain future wherein they will
have to render an account of their stewardship. Even the false
conscience, which has succeeded in gaining all that it thought
it wished, remains uneasy among its spoils.

> But, O what form of prayers
> Can serve my turn? Forgive me my foul murder?
> That cannot be; since I am still possess'd
> Of those effects for which I did the murder,
> My crown, mine own ambition and my queen,
> May one be pardon'd and retain the offence?
> In the corrupted currents of this world
> Offence's gilded hand may shove by justice,
> And oft 'tis seen the wicked prize itself
> Buys out the law; but 'tis not so above;
> There is no shuffling, there the action lies
> In his true nature; and we ourselves compell'd
> Even to the teeth and forehead of our faults,
> To give in evidence.
>   —*Hamlet*, Act III, Scene 3

Suicide sometimes becomes the last resort of those who boast
of an easy conscience; the disorder of a nature turned topsy-
turvy—with the body subjugating the soul—seems no longer

endurable. It is a psychological fact that a sense of something amiss within him makes a person strike his breast, whenever he has done wrong. The faithful do it three times when they recite the words of the Confiteor, "through my fault, through my fault, through my most grievous fault." It is as if there were something evil inside us that we should like to beat and to subdue. The executioners on Calvary left the hill striking their breasts, as if to drive out their crime. When deep despair settles on a sinful soul which has no outlet—either because it denies God or because it refuses to have recourse to His mercy —then this desire for self-infliction may reach a point where one takes his own life, as Judas did. The Judge had not yet appeared, and yet judgment had already judged: the elaborate and beautiful composite of body and soul was so disordered that the conscience now condemned it to be severed.

The sense of guilt is never completely destroyed in anyone. Conscience lives on, even when deliberately strangled or ignored. The ego may resort to many subterfuges less radical than suicide, in the hopeless effort to evade its warnings. Of these, three may be mentioned, (1) hyperactivity, (2) violence, and (3) a false sense of social justice.

Some souls try to escape the reproaches of conscience by an excessive activity, even to the point of jitters and neurotic overwork. Happy people work, sometimes very hard, in the fulfillment of their duties. But others use work as a drug to keep their thoughts off their own conscience, their inner misery. When work is done for its own delight or to provide the economic necessities, it is normal; but when it is a compulsive escape from inner guilt, it ceases to be work and becomes an addiction. Normal work takes a man outside of himself, exteriorizes his ego, unites him with reality, and atones for his sins. But abnormal activity is one of the means a fearful ego uses in the effort to lose itself.

Each period of life has its own favorite egress from the inner voice of God to the excitements of the outside world. In youth, it is the restlessness of uncontrolled passion which attracts; in maturity, it may be absorption in business, the pursuit of profit, of power, of prestige, of publicity—all of them the building of bigger and bigger barns. The Godless person, who makes sex, or the Eros, the goal of his youth, often sublimates this urge in later life to a mad pursuit of economic success. It may well be that success as a goal is merely the middle-aged substitute for lust in many souls—and both of them are escapes from the burden of choice and responsibility. The impatience associated with such excessive activity does not mean that an ambitious man or woman really wants fame or more money (for he does not stop when he achieves it), but rather that he wants to give himself an external "treat" to compensate for his want of inner peace. Such people measure greatness by what they have in stocks or press clippings, rather than by what they are.

One wonders if the violence and aggressiveness of our age are not due in part to the actions of many so-called "consciences at peace," trying to atone for their want of inner order by the repressive submission of others to their egotistic wills. Inner guilt is always accompanied by a deep sense of inferiority in the face of goodness—and an attempt is made to compensate for this by violent efforts to make the neighbor feel inferior. Class conflict, bickering, scandalmongering, hate, and persecution are exterior symptoms of consciences that are interiorly ill at ease.

The third escape from the voice of God is a false interest in social justice. There is a true and also a false passion for the underprivileged, the poor, and the homeless. It is true when the individual himself is just; it is false when the individual is himself unjust. A passion for social justice is not incompatible with an individual's injustice and his evil conscience. David stole the wife of Urias and put Urias in the front of his army in battle so that he would be killed. David justified this by saying: "Someone must die in battle." But when Nathan, the prophet, told David about a poor man who was robbed of his one ewe lamb by a rich man who desired to entertain a guest, David, with a keen sense of political justice, spoke up as a defender of the downtrodden and said in righteous anger: "He shall die." And Nathan, knowing that David had violated the laws of individual justice, said: "Thou art the man." David's remorse then became the occasion of his rebirth to both individual justice and social justice; he composed the Seven Penitential Psalms, crying out, in the agony of a soul that was beginning to find its peace: "Have mercy on me, O Lord; have mercy on me, O Lord."

A troubled, remorseful conscience which has not yet killed the voice of God—or which has not yet yielded to those charlatans who would deny the reality of sin—has always within it a token of life, as David's had. There is hope for everyone, regardless of how wicked he may be, so long as he still hates his evil. The worst thing in the world is not sin; it is the denial of sin by a false conscience—for that attitude makes forgiveness impossible. The unforgivable sin is the denial of sin. But until that sorry stage is reached—despite the failure of false starts, the short breathing spells between relapses—so long as there is real remorse, the voice of God is still being heard, and no such case is hopeless. Such a soul may already be dead to Divine Love; but in its moments of turmoil it is not dead to Divine Fear, and that can stir it into conscious life again.

Even if conscience is dead in a man, his vices live on. For it must never be thought that those who deny God and the Moral Law are outside the reach of Divine Justice. A man can deny sin, but he never escapes the *effects* of sin. A person can deny the law of gravitation, but if he throws himself off the Empire State Building in defiance of the law, he nevertheless will feel the very sad and tragic effects of that denial. So it is with the Conscience and the Moral Law. A husband and father not only denied morality, but he went into fits of laughter whenever anyone mentioned the Divine and did his best to pervert souls away from all religion and morality—yet he felt within himself the unconscious penalty of that denial. This man developed a terrific jealousy of his wife, who all the time had been very faithful and patient. Obviously, his jealousy was a projection of a sense of violated justice; though he denied any standard of righteousness for himself, he nevertheless insisted upon it in his wife. This "atheist's" contempt for infidelity was his unconscious recognition of the Moral Law; but instead of making himself conform to such a standard, he covered up his guilt by accusing his children's mother of not conforming to the Law.

A homely analogy will drive home the point: if the cap is not off a tube of tooth paste when it is pressed, the tooth paste will force a hole in the tube, at the weakest spot. In like manner, whenever there is an unadmitted violation of a moral law, the human mind is under pressure. The repressed guilt breaks forth, creating a psychosis or neurosis, at its weakest point. Defiance of morality sometimes manifests itself in pessimism, in which one becomes a constant harbinger of disaster and catastrophe, expecting defeat in every enterprise he undertakes. This overwhelming sense of pessimism is due to a consciousness of self-defeat, of which hell is nothing but an eternal expression. If anyone in the environment of such a soul is happy, he or she is made uneasy and tries to spoil this happiness by slander, ridicule, and jealousy. Such souls are already self-doomed at the center, and as their hatred of God spreads to the circumference, their inner hell begins to touch the lives of others. It is often said that people have their hell here and now; they do have hell in this life, but not the whole of it. Hell and Heaven both begin for us on earth.

Another escape hatch for unadmitted guilt is cynicism. The difference between the pessimist and the cynic is that the pessimist carries on the losing battle against life in his own soul, while the cynic tries to wage the battle in someone else's soul. His own inner defeat, the cynic projects onto others; because he is unhappy, he tries to make them unhappy by ridiculing the basis of their inner peace. His joy is to "debunk" others, because he has already "debunked" himself. Such a person tries to free himself from guilt by projecting it onto his neighbor.

Shakespeare has shown two possible effects of guilt, as psychosis and neurosis, in Macbeth and Lady Macbeth, respectively. Macbeth suffers from a fear fantasy as the result of having murdered the King of Scotland in his sleep, in order that he might assume his crown. Even before the murder his hallucinations produce a dagger dripping with blood:

Is this a dagger which I see before me,
The handle toward my hand? Come, let me clutch thee;

I have thee not, and yet I see thee still.
Art thou not, fatal vision, sensible
To feeling as to sight? or art thou but
A dagger of the mind, a false creation,
Proceeding from the heat-oppressed brain?

Following the murder, there are more hallucinations, and he hears strange voices echoing throughout the castle. Macbeth even imagines that he has seen the ghost of Banquo, whom he killed. This constant brooding on his unadmitted guilt finally produces a state of mind in which nothing seems real to him; from a Scriptural point of view, he suffers from "the hardening of the heart." In the end, when it is announced that his wife is dead, Macbeth betrays himself as a complete sceptic and agnostic and, like many of the modern pessimists, sums up life as nothing but the flickering of a "brief candle." Thus Shakespeare has revealed how an atheist attitude can be developed from a guilty act.

When Macbeth learns of his wife's suicide, he has nothing to say except to preach his pessimistic creed, which actually foreshadowed the "Nothingness" of Sartre:

She should have died hereafter;
There would have been a time for such a word.
To-morrow, and to-morrow, and to-morrow.
Creeps in this petty pace from day to day,
To the last syllable of recorded time;
And all our yesterdays have lighted fools
The way to dusty death. Out, out, brief candle!
Life's but a walking shadow, a poor player
That struts and frets his hour upon the stage,
And then is heard no more; it is a tale

> Told by an idiot, full of sound and fury,
> Signifying nothing.

If Macbeth manifested a psychosis, Lady Macbeth was a textbook case of compulsion neurosis. This is the peculiar state in which the sinner, having repressed his guilt, feels compelled to perform a certain ritual as a substitute for repairing the violation of the moral order. The normal thing for a conscience to do would have been to confess the guilt and make what reparation one could have made on this earth: in the spiritual and supernatural order, the proper means of release would have been Confession, Absolution, and Penance. But Lady Macbeth tries to calm her conscience by denying that there is any Judge who will ever call us to account. This conscious denial, however, does not save her from admitting in another form her sense of the necessity of a cleansing. For the appropriate moral cleansing, through Confession and Absolution, she now substitutes a physical cleansing in which she constantly washes her hands. It was her soul that needed to be bathed—not her body. (Pilate did somewhat the same thing when, after sentencing Our Lord to the Cross, he called for water and rinsed his guilty hands.)

Lady Macbeth imagined she saw spots of blood upon her hands; therefore she cried out, inconsolably, from time to time: "Out, damned spot. . . . Hell is murky. . . . Here's the smell of the blood still: all the perfumes of Arabia will not sweeten this little hand. Oh! oh! oh!"

The doctor in the play who saw this abnormal manifestation of guilt was an extremely good psychiatrist; for he knew that the basis of her compulsion neurosis was moral, not organic. Yet he entertained a religious hope that she might receive the mercy of God before she died: "This disease is be-

yond my practice; Yet I have known those which have
walked in their sleep who have died holily in their beds."

> Foul whisperings are abroad. Unnatural deeds
> Do breed unnatural troubles; infected minds
> To their deaf pillows will discharge their secrets;
> More needs she the divine than the physician.
> God, God, forgive us all!

There are many modern Lady Macbeths, suffering from
other sins than murder. Nowhere is there such a feverish and
cowardly escapism as in souls like hers, which seek madness
rather than face themselves as they really are. They construct
a thousand and one crosses more crucifying than the Crucifix.
At the very moment that they call religious people "cowards,"
they know in their hearts that they are the real cowards,
fearful of giving up the evil in their own lives.

Perhaps what we call worry, anxiety, fear, substitution is
always, at bottom, remorse. This remorse can be the starting
point for the recovery of true peace. As a broken bone hurts
us because it is not where it ought to be, so a conscience, too,
is painful when it is not where *it* ought to be—in a right relationship to God. This inner hell, instead of being fled, should
be approached. To get away from the self, one must first of
all get into the self. Remorse is the negative presence of God
in the soul, as grace is the positive presence of God. Remorse
is incomplete, for it is self-disgust divorced from God; but
remorse can become sorrow, and then hope, the moment the
soul turns to God for help. God is saying to the uneasy soul:
"Peace is not along the way that you are traveling; if it were,
I would not have troubled you." Unrelated to God, the emptiness and loneliness of a guilty conscience beget despair. But

once related to God, the misery of remorse becomes repentance from sin. As soon as the soul turns to the Redeeming Saviour, the burden of guilt disappears—just as a patient forgets his pain in the joy of seeing the physician who can cure him.

In considering our virtues, we can be deceived, mistaking frugality for temperance and avarice for detachment; but remorse never deceives us. As repression of guilt begets our inner unhappiness, so release of it through Confession creates our inner joy. An ancient German author wrote: "The anguish of Our Lord can only set you free, if first your heart becomes it own Gethsemane."

Even those who live in a false peace, founded on false maxims ("Everybody's doing it"; "The Kinsey report shows we can't"; "We need new ethics to suit our habits"), know that there are things they would be ashamed to do if their associates learned of them. Yet if everything a false-peace conscience does is good, why not let everybody see it? If there is no fixed wrong, there should be no sense of shame.

False consciences may sometimes stop deluding themselves if they recall that one day we shall all be judged by God; His judgment will not be based on the verdict of the conscience we made for ourselves, but on the conscience God gave us— the conscience of our youth, before it was perverted by sin; the conscience as it was before we warped it by a false education; the conscience which considered as wrong the sins we now justify; the conscience before it was polluted by license and mixed with selfishness; the conscience before it became "broad-minded" and gave to right and wrong an equal value. This conscience will drag up from our unconsciousness all its hideous, leprous mass of sins in judgment.

As the businessman at the end of a day takes out the list of debits and credits from his cash register, so the slips of conscience will be pulled out at the end of our life for the final reckoning. God will not judge us so much as we shall judge ourselves. Our conscience will speak and say: "I am the conscience God gave you! Behold thyself in it as a mirror. What gravitation is to the stars, what instincts are to the animal, that I was to you, a law laid down to help you in your course. I warned you often; I shouted; I whispered; I murmured; I kept you awake at night; I made you afraid to wake in the morning. I troubled you in your pleasures; I gave you no rest in your sins; I filled you with a sense of fed-upness and satiety and emptied you of inner peace. To escape me, you tried to find peace in a second or third marriage or a fourth or fifth drink. You were analyzed by your psychiatrist, but never synthesized; you were taken apart, but never put together. You said your conscience was at peace, but it was the false peace of which the Saviour spoke, the deadly peace of the devil's palace with all its armor; you tried to stop worrying when you should have worried; you should have mistrusted yourself when you were most certain you were without blame. But I, your conscience, never tired; I would not let you escape, though you fled from me; I would not desert you, though you deserted me. With remorse, reproach, uneasiness; in shame, disquiet, bitterness, fear, anxieties, I kept you always restless."

This conscience need not wait until the moment of God's judgment to awake. It can rouse itself now—can start worrying and begin living. But before a conscience can be made true again, it must first cease to be afraid of God.

3

Why the Ego Dreads Betterment

WHAT makes us afraid of God? If He is Love, should we not embrace Him? If He is Life, should we not be one with Him? If He is Truth, should we not follow Him? In theory, yes; but in practice, it does not work out that way. For there are some who say that this God is not a God of Love but One of Wrath. And others are afraid to give this God their finger, lest He seize their hand. Goodness and Truth can act as a reproach to our feelings, making us afraid of God. All egotists are frightened people in their hearts; they fear Goodness, and they dread the Truth.

FEAR OF GOODNESS. Everyone has experienced this fear in the physical order. It is not the goodness which we fear, but the pain which is its price. One dreads the pulling of a tooth or an operation, because the good effects we want will not appear until we have passed through a moment or so of suffering. The good of being free from future pain cannot allay our fears of an increase of present pain. Socrates observed that "people are afraid of letting themselves be cut and cauterized for their healing." In like manner, spiritual goodness can be feared because it will demand a painful uprooting of what is evil. Evil can get so deeply into a man—into the fibers of his muscles, the cells of his blood, the fissures of his brain—that he revolts against the very thought of its removal from him by Perfect Goodness. As some get used to living in dirt, so others get used to sin; and as some dread cleaning their homes, so others dread Confession.

This dread of Goodness is present at many levels of the spiritual life. Wherever there is something to be surrendered—whether it be downright sinful, such as pride, lust, avarice, or something only mildly selfish—the soul shrinks back from having to make those ethical and moral sacrifices which religion demands. God is feared because He is Goodness, and Goodness will tolerate no imperfection in us. If God were broadminded about whether we choked our neighbor—or were tolerant about divorce and entering into a second or third marriage—then no one would fear that doddering old grandfather, God. But the soul shrinks from a God Who cannot be deceived. It fears Him, not because He is *not* good, but because He is *too* good, because He is Goodness Itself. The soul fears, not because it is unloved, but because it is loved by Perfection. The fear of losing a lesser good keeps one from loving the Perfect Good: "A dread lest having Him, I must have naught beside." As the human lover likes to see his beloved perfect in manner, speech, and appearance, so the Divine Lover wants to see all our souls perfect as the Heavenly Father is perfect, and this expectation frightens us.

God loves us too much to leave us comfortable in our sins. Because the violinist wants the best from his violin, he tightens its strings in penitential disciplines, until they can give forth the perfect note; if endowed with consciousness, the violin would probably protest the sacrifice it had to make in preparation for the perfection it was destined to attain. We are like the violin.

If Our Lord were liberal about our sins and took them lightly, He would never have been sentenced to the Cross. He had at least five good chances to leave us as we were: He could have courted the Pharisees or wooed the Herodians; He might have disclaimed Divine Authority before Pilate, or spoken to the wicked Herod, or, finally, come down from the Cross instead of paying the penalty of death for sin. It is no wonder that, in the face of that persistent, resolute Goodness, the bystanders at the Cross pleaded: "Come down, and we will believe." They wanted a Cross without a Crucifix; a Teacher, but not a Saviour; a Pulpit, and not a Confessional Box; a Communion, but never a Sacrifice.

Self-made rationalizations always justify the egotist's flight from Goodness—as St. Augustine said: "I want to be chaste, dear Lord, a little later on. Not now!" The price of goodness frightened him. And when Our Divine Lord told St. Catherine of Siena that His Goodness chastened and purified souls, she said: "And *that* is why you haven't any friends." A rich ruler one day came to Our Lord and asked: "Master, who art so good, what must I do to win eternal life?" He was hoping for a pat answer, a less exigent formula for living, such as a merely human man might give him. Our Lord answered: "Why dost thou call Me good? None is good, except God only." In other words, "My Goodness is Divine Goodness. You will have to

derive your own goodness from that Source, too." When Our
Lord told him to sell all he had and follow Him, the Gospel
says, "The answer filled him with sadness, for he was very
rich." (Luke 18:15.) Goodness demands that we be perfect,
and nothing less will ever satisfy God. The thought of how
much change in us this will require is always frightening. We
dread the pain more than we want the cure that it will bring.

FEAR OF THE TRUTH. People are afraid of God because
He is Divine Truth; this fear condemns them to spend their
lives in mediocrity, indifference, and unbelief. St. Paul touched
on this in writing to the Galatians: "Have I made enemies of
you, then, by telling you the truth?" (Gal. 4:16.) There is
a difference between our flight from God as Goodness and as
Truth. Goodness is feared, but it cannot be wholly hated,
because even in rejecting perfect Goodness, one still loves an
imperfect good; fear is aroused because we suspect that the
greatest Good of God will wrest from us some lesser goods
we love. Truth, however, is not so much feared as it is hated,
for truth is hurtful and repugnant to the ego. Unable to bear
what is called the "awful truth" about himself, man conceives a hatred against truth itself—against the true explanation of the universe. Even though he disguises it with the
polite veneer of agnosticism, or by the despair which always
follows arrogance, or by a violent cynicism and hatred of all
life, such a man is fleeing truth for fear of the demands that
it might make on him.

Truth can be hated for any one of three reasons: First, because of our intellectual pride, which refuses to admit that a
position, once taken, can be false. That is the pride of those
egotists who become angry when contradicted or when

proved false: they are so attached to their own point of view that they will not listen to another, and will refuse even to inquire into religious truth, lest the falsity of their own ideas might be revealed. This leads in time to prejudice and bigotry, which blinds the mind to Truth through hate.

Truth can also be hated because its acceptance would require our giving up our evil ways. "We desire not the knowledge of Thy Ways." (Job 21:14.) Many a person who calls himself happy, and yet identifies his happiness with carnal pleasures or egotistic desires, sees in the bearer of truth a threat to his so-called happiness; therefore he hates him. As the alcoholic will hate the truth that alcoholism has ruined his health and that therefore he must give it up, so one can hate the truth which is in the Christ, His Church, because it demands a way of life contrary to the present way of sloth and sin.

Truth can also be hated when it implies that another Mind knows the truth of our sins, is not taken in by the false face of piety which deceives the world. This explains why so many people hate the Doctrine of the Last Judgment or refuse to believe in Hell. The Truth that God knows what they are is so repugnant to them that their minds may even construct a crazy creed to suit their crazy lives. The good never deny the truth of Hell; but the evil often do so, in order to quiet their uneasy consciences.

In each of these instances Truth is hated because the egotist wishes to be a law unto himself and thus to escape responsibility, or else because he wishes to continue an evil life which Truth condemns, or else because he wishes that nobody else knew the truth about him. The penalty of such an attitude is great and terrible. The more souls hide from Truth, the more Truth is hidden from them; the more they fear Goodness, the less beautiful Goodness comes to seem.

Nobody would ever admit, in so many words, that he feared Goodness or hated Truth, for these things are admirable in themselves to all of us. But the mind resorts to a rationalization to justify its rejection of the true. All nonreligious or antireligious people are escapists; being afraid to inquire, to seek Truth, or to pursue virtue, they rationalize their escapism through indifference or mockery, ridicule or persecution. The most popular form of covering up hatred of Truth and fear of Goodness is indifference, which the intelligentsia (or those educated beyond their intelligence) call agnosticism; they deny that Truth exists. By a cultivated indifference to the distinction between truth and error, they hope to render themselves immune from any responsibility for the way they live. But the studied refusal to distinguish between right and wrong is not, in fact, indifference, or neutrality—it is an acceptance of the wrong. Pilate, the first pragmatist, sneered, "What is Truth?" and after doing so, he crucified It.

Mockery and ridicule of religion form another device by which the fear of goodness and the hatred of truth inside one's heart are projected onto the Goodness and Truth existing outside one's heart. The virtuous, the devout, the religious in offices and factories are often scoffed at and ridiculed. By dragging down the goodness of others, the scoffers hope to justify their own want of goodness. But he who makes fun of divine Goodness or Truth has already uprooted it from his own soul. Herod's posterity survive today; being confronted with an accusing Truth, they calm their consciences by robing Christ in the garment of a fool. Evil cannot stand the sight of Goodness, because it is a judgment on evil, a reproach to unrepentant wickedness; so it is always met with abuse and vilification. Look for the religion that is persecuted by the spirit of the world, and one will find the religion that is Divine. If Our Lord had not been perfect Goodness, He would never have been crucified.

The third type of escape from Truth is atheism, which is so violent in its hatred that it would destroy both Truth and Goodness if it could. Until the present century, only one or another aspect of the Truth was ever generally denied at a time; now the opposition is to total Truth. The Lord's warning is fulfilled: "The time is coming when anyone who puts you to death will claim that he is performing an act of worship to God." (John 16:2.) To be in sin and to dread sin can be the path to Goodness; but to be in sin and to dread Goodness and hate Truth is demonic. St. Augustine, who fought against Divine Truth in his youth, ought to know why men hate Truth, if anyone does, for he hated it for so many years. And his answer is this:

"Men love Truth when she enlightens; they hate it when she reproves. They love Truth, when she discovers herself unto them, and hate her when she discovers them. Whence she shall so repay them, that they who would not be made manifest by her, she both against their will makes manifest, and herself become not manifest to them. Yea, thus doth the mind of man, blind and sick, foul and ill-favored, wish to be hidden, but will not that aught should be hidden from it."

One wonders if in all literature there is clearer evidence of how men fear Goodness and hate Truth than in the history of John the Baptist. Our Divine Lord praised John's goodness, saying: "There is no greater than John the Baptist among all the sons of women." (Luke 7:28.) One day this good man was invited to preach at the court of Herod to an audience that was rich, much divorced, and much remarried. The sermon was brief. Pointing a finger at the King, the Baptist thundered forth a truth: "It is not lawful for thee to live with thy brother's wife." A minute, and John was in chains. A few months later Herod, intoxicated with wine and Salome's sensuous dance, promised that he would grant any request asked him by this beautiful stepdaughter. Well coached by her mother, Salome said: "Give me the head of John the Baptist." Evil will always kill goodness, when it has become a reproach; virtue is a dangerous career.

Knowing that some people are afraid of God, because He is Truth and Goodness, it is now clear why others say that God is the God of Wrath. They say this because of the way they live. There is no wrath in God; what looks to us like wrath is only the projection of our own inner sense of guilt onto our God. When a boy is caught stealing jam, his first words to his mother are: "Now, Mummy, don't get mad!" There is no wrath in the mother, but the boy attributes wrath to his mother, knowing he deserves a punishment. In like manner, God seems an angry God to the sinner. To live a life contrary to the Divine Will and the purpose of existence will create in us a feeling of being opposed and frustrated—as we are, but by our own evil wills. The sense of "wrath'" is anticipated hell. As Grace is the seed of glory, so sin is the seed of hell. It is this projected sense of deserved doom which makes the criminal at the bar of justice hate the judge, and makes the sinner hate his God. For everyone knows God—everyone. We know either the God of Wrath or the God of Mercy.

The way to change one's idea of God is to change his behavior. Once Goodness and Truth are sought, not fled, the soul can by-pass self-accusation and will no longer feel the need to project its own self-condemnation onto others or onto God. The moment one abandons the act of sin, his philosophy of the universe and the psychology of his soul undergo a change. God, Who a moment before seemed Wrath, now appears as Mercy; the change is not in God, but in the soul. As St. Paul says: "Once you were all darkness; now, in the Lord, you are all daylight. You must live as men native to the light; when the light has its effect, all is goodness and holiness and truth; you have to make it clear, what conduct it is that makes favor with God." (Eph. 5:8–11.)

Moses and Cain each hid his face from God. Moses hid his face because he could not bear to look upon such Goodness; Cain hid his face because he could not bear to have Divine Goodness look at him. The sinner cannot bear to have the eyes of God upon him, for he does not want to know how wicked he is. But God cannot change His nature to make up for our perversity; it is the ego which must change its ways.

If an egotist really understood the psychology of the human mind, he would never be heard to say that God is wrathful—for such a statement publishes his sinfulness. As a brown-colored glass can make the water in it seem brown, although it it not, so the Love that waits for us, passing through our sinful lives, may seem like wrath and anger. A change in our behavior removes all the unhealthy fear of God.

Truth must be sought at all costs, but separate, isolated truths will not do. Truth is like life; it has to be taken in its entirety or not at all. The truth of religion must be recognized as covering the whole of life, or it is no religion. The inquiry into religion does not mean knocking at the door of truth in the hope that no one will answer or that we shall be handed out just enough to let us live our lives on, undisturbed. We must welcome truth even if it reproaches and inconveniences us—even if it appears in the place where we thought it could not be found. "The stone the builders rejected is made the head of the corner." Truth implies commitment; it makes demands, imposes obligation. It must be sought and searched for, without a selfish bias, for it is not our making, and its authority is greater than our preferences. Truth-seeking means study, instructions, and discipleship. We cannot escape our obligation to find the truth by saying, "I will not think about God and religion," because this statement is already a decision and a rejection. To refuse to think about living is to vote for death. Such an attitude is particularly dangerous, for the opportunity to see the Way may not be held open indefinitely; and such a flight from Truth develops a tension and an uneasiness in the soul which may have disastrous mental effects. Nothing is more harmful to a man than his resistance to Grace.

Egotists flee truth to many points of the compass. A favorite refuge is in clatter and confusion. Every sinner loves what is noisy, because it distracts him from his real self. Hell is full of noise and is probably full of clocks that emphasize the time that never passes. Silence is helpful because it forces the egotist to reflect, to shift his terror from the Goodness he dreads facing to a terror of his own condition; it changes his fear of Truth into a fear of the truth of his own dissolution. Silence isolates us from the crowds that love to pool their misery; an unhappy civilization is always gregarious. Quiet tears one away from the misleading approval of the mob and from the rationalizing slogans of the crowds. Nothing is so good for the soul as a spiritual retreat where, in the requiem of prayers and contemplation, the soul makes itself receptive to new insights and energies which come directly from God. Windows are opened and new lights let in; a strong wind of resolution blows across the soul, driving away the dust that had too long covered it. In silence, one awakens from his sleep; all souls are sleepwalkers, their eyes shut against the noble lives they ought to lead. As a sleepwalker will not awaken to every sound but will often respond when his name is called, so the soul in silence hears the Divine vocation and awakens: for the Shepherd calls His sheep by name.

Since the soul dreads Goodness because of an inordinate attachment to a created temporal good, it follows that peace comes only by tearing the self away from what is evil. There is a cohesiveness about evil that is broken up only by effort: so much do the will and its sin become welded together that a soul will say, "Let me alone, I made my bed, and I will lie in it." Rupture of the egotistic from sensate pleasures is more painful than the surgeon's knife—and more blessed in the happiness it later gives. But we all feel an aversion to the transformation which must be accomplished at the root. Yet a nibble here and there of self-discipline may scintillate the nerves and fill us full of vanity, but it brings no enrichment of the personality. No habit of sin is unbreakable with the help of God's Grace; habit patterns only condition the will—they do not determine it. At any moment, under the impulse of Grace, the will can reject old habits and say: "I shall accept Truth regardless of its consequences."

When egotism is conquered and the I is integrated, all knowledge becomes correlated like a pyramid, in which one science is seen as subordinated to another science; chemicals are subservient to plant, plants to animals, the universe to man, and man to God. Peace is the tranquillity of order—of true order. It is easy to understand why so many minds of this century have flocked to the authoritarianism of the Nazi, the Fascist, or the Communist in their desperation for an ordering principle. Having no true picture of reality, but recognizing the need of *some* guiding principle outside their confused, bewildered, and frustrated minds, they throw themselves into the false ordering of dictatorship.

Surrender to a system is the destruction of freedom. We may not safely put our trust in any man-made system or in any man. We need God's truth—and yet we need it brought close enough for us to touch and love. Only once in history was Truth ever made personal—in Him Who said: "I am Truth." (John 14:6.) The Ideal and the Personal were here identified. Truth ceased to be a theory or a code and began to be a Person we might learn to love. And that same Divine Truth passed into His Mystical Body, where it is available today: "He who listens to you, listens to Me; he who despises you, despises Me; and he who despises Me, despises Him that sent me." (Luke 10:16.)

Surrender to His Truth is thus an escape from authoritarianism—which is always alien to the best spiritual interests of the individual. Identification with Divine Truth spells freedom. Only he who knows the truth about an airplane is free to fly it. So with life: to know the truth of what I am—the truth of why my body and soul are in conflict—the truth of how they can be reconciled—the truth of how to find Divine strength to overcome sorrow and sin and Divine knowledge to overcome my mistakes—would mean I could be free to live.

Goodness is not be be feared, because Goodness is Perfect Love. The sinner has nothing to lose but the chains of self-love which chafe and torture him. It is true that Love costs something: it cost the woman Our Lord met at the well her five husbands and a passing lover. But when she gave them up, she also gave up her distress of mind and, in the new-found ecstasy of the spirit, she called Our Lord the "Saviour of the World."

Those who now hate Truth and fear Goodness are not far from the Kingdom of God. They are fighting against it, and yet they know that theirs is a losing battle. The more violently men hate truth, the more they think about it. The more they fear the Goodness that demands perfection, the more they know it is what they really seek. As Our Lord told Paul: "This is a thankless task of thine, kicking against the goad." (Acts 9:6.) The goad was a nail on the end of a shaft, which pricked the donkey when he pushed backward and refused to go forward. We, like Paul, draw back from the prodding of God toward a more glorious destiny that lies ahead.

It makes no difference what the past has been, nor how many falls nor relapses there we may have had. When a sheep falls into a mud puddle, it tries to get out and bleats for rescue; when a pig falls in, it relaxes and stays there. We need the courage of the sheep. All human beings are in the mud; for who of us is clean in the sight of God? But if a man takes one step out of that mire, He will advance toward us as a Blazing Fire to make us clean.

Every human being feels within himself the terrible para-dox of not wanting God and of wanting Him, as well. Many avoid God because God is not concerned with having, but is pure Being. God owns nothing—as we might own a book, or a house, or a boat. At Sinai He defined Himself as One Whose nature it is to exist: *I am who am.* It is His nature to be, with no succession, no becoming, no future. Because He *has nothing*, He can give only Himself, and His charity is Infinite. Most of us are satisfied with what we *are*, but not satisfied with what we *have!* We shrink therefore from God, knowing that He wants to enrich our being, rather than our having—that He wishes to elevate our nature, not to submerge and lose it in trifles. He has called us to the superior vocation of being His sons, of partaking of His nature, and of being related to Him as branches to vine. Few of us completely want that elevation; it is our petty desire to *have more*, not to share the glory of *being more*. We want the poor shadows, not the light—the sparks, and not the sun—the arc, and not the circle. As the desire for the world and things increases in us, God makes less and less appeal. We hold back, our fists closed about our few pennies, and thus lose the fortune He holds out to us. That is why the initial step of coming to God is so hard. We cling to our nursery toys and lose the pearl of great price.

But there is another side to the paradox. Besides fearing God, we also want God. Mixed with our lack of trust in Him, there is also a longing for Him. Even while we flee from Him, we hope we shall not escape. The flight from God causes fear in us, but there is also a longing to be captured by Him. There is a greed for God which is never sated.

For although the soul quickly reaches a point where it is fed up with sensate pleasures, it can never have a glut of the spirit. A light that is too bright can blind the eyes, but an idea that is universal can never hurt the mind: the more we love God and know Him, the more we want Him. The passion for God grows in direct ratio and proportion to intimacy with Him. That is why the greatest agony of religious souls is the feeling that they are so far away from Him. It is not their stomachs, but their spirits that are starved; they want to possess the Infinite, but their minds are too small. They cup their hands, but they cannot contain His ocean. To love Him and not to *be* one with Him is the greatest of all human tragedies. God always keeps something back that we may want Him more.

Life is difficult for most of us because we have not read God's meaning, written in His universe. He gives us the power to have, and He promises us happiness through the right use of creatures. He intends that each thing be used as a sacrament, a channel, a steppingstone to Him—a reminder of how much He is to be loved. Every fine human love He meant us to take as a foretaste of Infinite Love, and if the human heart thrills us, so much more should the Divine Heart set us aflame. God gives us little snatches of His goodness in creatures, that we might want the Whole.

But some of us want only the swatches and the samples, and not the whole cloth of Divinity. We reject the Divine reality and live only for its reflections in the pool. God "deceives" those who think they will find any happiness apart from Him. Though He drops hints of happiness through *creatures*, He fulfills that happiness only in Himself. And anyone who lives solely for the world, turning it into an end instead of a means, must end in cynicism and despair; for creatures cannot give what they promise, unless they are used as scaffoldings to the heavenly mansions. No man is deceived who uses this world as a steppingstone to the next. As Christ fed the multitude in order to lead them to an understanding of the Eucharist, so He gives love of the flesh as a vestibule to love of the spirit, love of science as a vestibule to love of theology, and love of beautiful things to make us love Beauty in Him.

Freedom can thus lead us to God, or away from Him. Man can choose creatures against the Creator, or he can choose creatures *for* the Creator. But though we are free to rebel against the Divine order, we are not free to escape the effects of such rebellion: ennui, boredom, frustration, melancholy, and despair. Yet even here, God does not abandon us—He leads back to Himself, for it is possible to come to him through a series of disgusts. In our emptiness we are really looking to Him to fill us. We may deny the water, but we may never deny the thirst; we may deny God, but we are seeking Him even in our denial.

As God is a "deceiver" in making the world point to Him, rather than to us, so from another perspective God is a deceiver because He at first seems forbidding; but once He is embraced, He becomes a veritable passion. There is nothing that so much frightens the soul as the vision of a Cross: looking at a King who was cypress-crowned and robed in the purple of His own Blood, we fear that He may bring us only mortification, and death, and sacrifice. But this is a holy deceit. Once we accept Him, we find that we were truly deceived. It was only the skin of the heavenly fruit that seemed bitter; the meat ravishes the soul. He seems to bring bondage, but actually it is freedom. His Law would seem to be the Crucifixion, but it is only a prelude to the Resurrection.

If we live far off from God, we are afraid to accept gifts from Him, as children are loath to accept gifts from strangers; but when there is a union in spirit, gifts are accepted and there is no feeling of embarrassment or fear. At first glance, God seems to be taking away our happiness; but in the moment of surrender, we discover that He deceived us. He has merely taken away the dross to give us the gold of His Eternity.

4

When the Ego Lets Itself Go

IF THE ego is given its way, with no moral discipline to lift it to the I-stage, the personality degenerates through seven stages. These represent the rebellion of the ego against its proper expansion into the larger I, the person oriented to God. No soul need ever take all these seven downward steps; they can be checked at any moment by human resistance in co-operation with the energy which God supplies. The seven steps of the intensification of egotism are solicitation, pleasure, consent, act, habit, necessity, and death.

The first stage is suggestion, or the *solicitation* to do what is evil. If the suggestion be to commit a sin involving sex, as adultery or fornication, it can come into the mind through what is seen, or heard, or touched, imagined or remembered. Inasmuch as every human being has a Divinely given impulse to propagate the human species, the temptation to this evil has already some emotional predilection on which to work. The sexual passion itself is not wrong; the exercise of it in the duly ordained ways of God not only is right and good but can be a means of Grace. Because the impulse is so strong, it responds with rapid intensity to any suggestion entering the mind and allowed to stay there. The particular temptation which is presented, like the forbidden fruit, is always delightful in prospect—for no sin ever presents itself under the guise of evil. Evil is always willed because of the good elements, real or imagined, which accompany it. But our minds are also aware of the fact that this act or that would involve us in a sin. Our task, then, is to resist it—as we can. It does not matter how violent the temptation may be, nor how long it lasts: there is sin only when there is consent of the will. If we should yield, the chances are that we will excuse the act as the result of our "temperament" or give it a name which carries no reproach, calling it a "human need." We tend to claim full credit for our virtues; our faults we blame on environment or on some provocation beyond human endurance. Yet, in more honest moments, we know that it is a superficial view that we take of ourselves, that we are not all we should like to be. It is then that we ask: "Why am I not better?"

The "I" to whom this question refers is our real self, the fully human personality which is the proper captain of our soul, under God. Too often, however, the I is not in command. It has retired, lashed the rudder it should control, and now allows the blind and witless ego to take over.

Those who do not understand the psychology of human nature often assume that evil acts are embraced because evil itself appeals to us. This is not true—if sins were seen for what they are, no man would ever sin. One can go through the catalogue of man's rebellions and discover that every solicitation to evil has always wrapped itself in the garment of virtue. The caresses by which the lustful seduce each other are disguised as love; curiosity passes itself off as a desire for knowledge; laziness calls itself a love of quietude and rest; wastefulness presents itself as generosity; enviousness, as a legitimate wish to excel; cruelty, as a love of justice; and pride, as loftiness of spirit. The first downward step comes when we deceive ourselves, accepting a lying label which makes an evil thing seem good to us.

The second stage in the psychology of egotism is excitation of the passions; there is a feeling of pleasure, of wellbeing or enchantment. The suggestion of evil now goes into high gear, as the impact of the suggestion is felt on the body itself. In this stage we have a perfect example of the psychosomatic interdependence—the *psyche* being the mind, and the *soma* being the body. These two are as closely united as the subject and predicate in a sentence. No sooner is a solicitation to evil made welcome in the mind than there is a physical response—a stirring of passion or a thrill. If it is a question of a sin of the flesh, this arousing of the passions has very marked organic reactions, which intensify its allure. So long as the temptation was purely mental, it had little appeal; but at this stage, when the emotions are aroused, there begins the warfare St. Paul described as the "flesh lusting against the spirit." It is very important, however, to remember that at this stage—as in the earlier stage of mere suggestion—there is no sin whatever involved. An unavoidable physical reaction or the arousing of passions in response to a stimulus one did not invite is not blameworthy. For the basic principle of moral life must constantly be kept in mind: one sins *only* through the consent of the will. St. Benedict was once so strongly tempted to impurity that he ran into the bushes to be pricked by thorns in order, through pain, to overcome this solicitation to evil—and even when temptation has reached this stage, there is still no sin, because there is no consent. But the stage in which the body begins to feel the enchantment of the allure is the immediate vestibule to the third stage, at which the crucial question is to be answered: "Will the will consent, or will it resist?"

The third stage of degeneration into sin is *consent:* the will always has, in itself and in cooperation with God's help, the power to repel the evil that attracts, thus turning the experience into merit. But since here we are concerned with the psychology of egotism alone, we are assuming that the will *does* consent. A temptation to impurity, at this point, is like a spark which has fallen from a burning hearth onto a carpet; if one were eager to save the house, he would immediately extinguish the spark. But if one believed in thoroughgoing "self-expression"—and were accustomed to the belief that resistance to any impulse is wrong—then he would take steps to encourage the spark. He would begin igniting papers from it, and throwing wooden bric-a-brac and curtains onto the flame, until finally it reached a point where the whole house was in danger. This gathering up of inflammable material to spread temptation is an act of the will, and itself represents, to some extent, consent to the sin that is still to be accepted or repelled.

Those who are bent on living a moral life and doing what is conducive to spiritual happiness are often troubled at this point as to whether or not they have consented. It is a generally safe rule to say that if—in spite of the violence of the temptation and the intensity of luxuriant sensation—there is a disgust, disappointment, and shame at being thus tempted, then there is no consent. Sometimes, however, the refusal to sin is not clear, in which case the consent is imperfect; this is the case when one does not reject the temptation as soon as it is perceived as evil, or when one momentarily hesitates, or when it is resisted in a halfhearted way.

In the case of the egotist, we assume that consent is full and entire. This happens when the will lets itself be drawn to taste willfully of the evil, despite the protests of conscience which recognize its true nature. Once the will gives its imprimatur and elects the evil, then the act of the will moves into the fourth stage of *action*.

Evil now passes from the will to the deed, from the desire to the execution, from the wish to the transaction, from the passion to its exploitation. In the case of sins of impurity, the consent proceeds to realize its evil desires in one or the other forms of lust. When there has been only a single such sin or several intermittent sins, the voice of conscience is still very strong; and the disgust, and emptiness, and boredom which one feels after the deed is the voice of the conscience telling the soul that happiness does not lie in that direction. Remorse of conscience is very much like an aching tooth; it is there to remind its owner that things are not with him as they ought to be. One of the most merciful acts of God is the stirring up of an uneasy conscience—just as one of the most destructive acts of man is the dismissing of conscience as a "guilt complex" or a residue of childhood miseries. Sometimes the egotist who finds his conscience an uncomfortable housemate seeks out a psychoanalyst of the Freudian school, who will explain away his moral uneasiness through a denial of God and conscience and the moral law. If, however, such a sinner falls into the hands of a more scientific psychiatrist, he will be told to re-integrate himself into the moral order and thus recover peace. But if the egotist is basically in rebellion against God, he often develops an abnormal hatred and bigotry of any adviser or any institution that reminds him of the violated order. He seeks out only those who will allow him to continue with his sin; he asks of them only that they cure the remorse which is sin's sequel.

The fifth stage of *habit* is reached when there is a repetition of the sinful acts, so that rebellion becomes habitual. The evil is now routine, a kind of second nature, so accepted a part of the egotist's way of life that it can almost completely stifle the summons of Divine Love in the conscience. The will has now become so weak that—almost upon the first presentation of a stimulus of the flesh—it allows the body to seek to satisfy itself. As a habitual smoker automatically reaches out his hand whenever a cigarette is offered him, so the habitual sinner, so accustomed to crushing his conscience and his will, is in almost constant search of a satisfaction for his passions.

The act which was at first a frail cobweb binding a man now becomes, by repetition, as strong as a steel cable. Every habit is either an acquired power or an acquired weakness; a moral man has good habits, and an evil man has evil habits. As a path is made by the passing of many footsteps, so road-ways to future evil become easier to follow for the man who adds footprints today to the traces of yesterday's passage.

The sixth stage is reached in *necessity*, when the egotist feels himself "determined" to indulge in his excesses over and over again. He may psychologically justify his weakness by denying that he has free will; because a man's philosophy is made by the way he lives, it would be interesting to make a statistical study of the moral activities of those who most learnedly deny freedom of the will in lectures and in books today. Generally they are the individuals in whom the will has become so weakened, through one or another breach of morality, that they find its denial a philosophical convenience to themselves.

But even at this sixth stage there is no genuine determinism of the will to sin; the egotist has still some vestige of freedom and therefore some resistance left. The will itself, left to its own resources, cannot lift itself out of the morass—but it can do so in cooperation with God's Grace, which is never lacking. The determination to evil, which seems almost automatic, might be better called a hardening of the heart. It is a disturbing thing for the soul in such a plight to feel God in pursuit of it—but it is a worse thing for the soul if it can persuade God to leave off the pursuit. This the sinner often tries to do. The favorite expression of the egotist at this level is "Let me alone!" whenever any spiritual or moral suggestion is made to him; if God takes such an egotist at his word, then there occurs what is called the "delivering-up to a reprobate sense." As St. Paul wrote:

"God abandoned their lustful hearts to filthy practices of dishonouring their own bodies among themselves. They had exchanged God's truth for a lie, reverencing and worshipping the creature in preference to the Creator; and, in return, God abandoned them to passions which brought dishonour to themselves. Their women exchanged natural for unnatural intercourse; and the men, on their side, giving up natural intercourse with women, were burnt up with desire for each other; men practising vileness with their fellow-men. Thus they have received a fitting retribution for their false belief.

And as they scorned to keep God in their view, so God has
abandoned them to a frame of mind worthy of all scorn, that
prompts them to disgraceful acts. They are versed in every
kind of injustice, knavery, impurity, avarice, and ill-will;
spiteful, murderous, contentious, deceitful, depraved, back-
biters, slanderers, God's enemies; insolent, haugthy, vainglorious; inventive in wickedness, disobedient to their parents;
without prudence, without honour, without love, without
loyalty, without pity. Yet, with the just decree of God before
their minds, they never grasped the truth that those who so
live are deserving of death; not only those who commit such
acts, but those who countenance such a manner of living."
(Romans 1:24,23.)

When the egotist is given over to a reprobate mind and left
alone, the Lord allows him the desire of his heart. He gets
exactly what he wants—and yet he hates himself for wanting
it. The sense of despair which the egotist feels is the beginning
of his hell. So long as the egotist felt the tension between what
he was doing and the feeling that it was wrong, there was
hope. But when the tension has ceased, God seems, at least for
the moment, to have left him alone, as he wished. But in
truth God never abandons him until his final rejection of
Grace at death. The egotist in his false peace may boast that he
has quite "outgrown" the thoughts of God and judgment and
religion and that he will now enjoy his freedom. With this
decision, he enters into that stage of evil of which Nietzsche
boasted: "Evil, be thou my good." If he feels frustration, and
boredom, and despair, he refuses to see these things as the
result of having already drunk too deeply from the cup of sin,
but seeks to cure them by drinking its dregs. He may acknowledge his boredom—but he fancies that a greater boldness in

evil will stimulate his interest in life. Regarding such egotists, Our Lord reminded the good that it was useless to speak to them of things Divine: "Do not cast your pearls before swine."

As time goes on, the heart of such an egotist becomes more callous, and the tender sensitiveness of his soul is dulled. Faults multiply to a point where, having ceased to fight against evil, he now begins to fight against God. Such is the psychological explanation of atheism in the modern world. For the new atheism is not like the old, theoretical atheism, which prided itself on being intellectually compounded of a little science, anthropology, and comparative religion. The new atheism is not of the intellect, but of the will; it is an act of free and eager rejection of morality and its demands. It starts with the affirmation of self and the denial of the moral law. The new atheist does not "know there is no God," as he tells us. There is no man in the whole world who *knows* there is no God; but the modern atheist *wishes* there were no God. He is not really intent on denying God; he seeks to destroy Him. His life is a refusal of God in action. Today's atheism is not passive, like the old-fashioned atheism, which allowed believers to exist alongside of it; it is now militant, active, political, proselytizing, and communistic. The bourgeois atheist said, "I do not believe in God"; the newer atheist, whose belief was born of the hardening of his heart, says, "I believe in the *anti-God*." But even in the case of such an advanced case as his, it must never be thought that hardening of the heart is hopeless; as long as any man has life, there is hope for his soul. An egotist may have led a most wicked and perverse, most voluptuous and atheistic existence—and yet if, at any moment, he turns to God and asks for His forgiveness, he will be saved.

Such complete hardening of the heart, persisted in, can damn a soul. But every individual in the world has some milder indication of the malady. He may have fallen into a sin against charity or against justice; though it was not his intention to persist in it, but only to give himself a little longer time to enjoy his sinful delights, nevertheless he may have deferred penance. He wanted to be better, but a little later on. He was thus trifling with God; yet God endured that warding off of Him. So long as there is smoking flax, and so long as there is a broken reed that daily tries to lift itself, the Good Lord will provide the needed energy. The eye of any sinner, if he turns it to God, can become dim with tears, and the stiff neck can bend in adoration and prayer. The hardened heart may relax its defenses against God at any stage, early or late, and He will enter it. The thief who cursed and blasphemed Our Lord on the Cross was the same thief who, a few moments later, asked to be remembered, and to him there came the quick assurance of the Saviour: "This day thou shalt be with me in Paradise."

But if the egotist persists, rejecting Divine Love to the last, he arrives at the final, seventh stage of *eternal death*. Biological death is the disintegration of our component physical parts; and spiritual death is the eternal disintegration of the mind and soul. The ego wished to be left alone, and in hell it is alone; it hates its own aloneness, and it loathes its own ego. Even in this world egotists find it very hard to enjoy the "being left alone" for which they clamor. They have to escape from their lonely egotism in alcoholism or in soporifics, or they lose themselves in crowds. If it is so hard to live with our own egos in time, then to live with the ego for eternity is hell. The fires of hell will be enkindled from within the self. The unhappiness, the misery, the self-torture that the egotist feels is already a self-burning; hell may be described as a place where the ego eternally burns in its own solitude. Egotism is anti-love, and hell is the place where there is no love; there is only one thing that the egotists have in common with one another in hell, and that is the hatred that they bear for one another. This hatred will there be intensified, because each egotist will see in the other that which he hates within himself.

St. James, in rapid review of these seven stages of sin, says: "When a man is tempted, it is always because he is being drawn away by the lure of his own passions. When that has come about, passion conceives and gives birth to sin; and when sin has reached its full growth, it breeds death." (Jas. 1:14.) Thus the love of God, which was meant to draw us to Himself, actually becomes the basis of the egotist's eternal self-torment. The rain which nourishes the grain can also rot the grain. The sun that warms and nurtures the harvest in one crop can scorch it in another; the same food that nourishes a person in one state of health can sicken and endanger him in another. Knowledge which illumines one mind can make another man a monomaniac. The sun that shines on wax softens it; the sun that shines on mud hardens it. Love either cherishes or consumes; it draws us to heaven, or flight from it delivers us to hell. For hell is not an experience that begins in the next life; it continues there, but it begins on earth. The despairing and the bored have already had their first knowledge of hell in the final stage of egotism enthroned.

5

The Philosophy of Pleasure

BECAUSE pleasure is the supreme goal of all egotistic living, it is fitting that we should know something of its laws. The very fury with which modern men and women seek pleasure is the strongest proof that they have not found it; for if the streets of our city were filled with clanging ambulances, and the hospitals were jammed to capacity, and nurses were running about madly, there would be a strong suspicion that health had not yet been found. Pleasure as a life goal is a mirage—no one reaches it. But it is possible to enjoy stable, refreshing pleasures, provided that one knows their laws.

The first law of pleasure is that it is like beauty: it is conditioned by contrast. A woman in white, if she has any esthetic sense, would rather stand before a black curtain than a white one. Similarly, every pleasure, to be enjoyed, must come as a sort of treat, as a surprise. The kind of pleasure that evokes laughter is an example: incidents that are not funny on the street are hilarious in Church because of their contrast with the seriousness of the ritual—a man with his hat on the side of his head in the street does not provoke laughter, but a Bishop with a miter on the side of his head does.

The condition of having a good time is that one shall not be always trying to have a good time. There is no fun in life, if everything is funny; there is no pleasure in shooting fire-crackers, if every day is the Fourth of July. Many people miss pleasure because they seek nothing else, so removing the first condition of enjoyment, which is contrast. In the liturgy of the Church, there is a constant contrast between joy and sacrifice, between fast and feast. Even during the seasons of Lent and Advent, when there is penance and pain, the Church inserts a Laetare and a Gaudete Sunday, on which we are called to rejoice. She does this, first of all, to remind people that penance is not perpetual; and, secondly, to prevent them from getting into a psychological rut.

The second law of pleasure is that no pleasure ever becomes our permanent possession until it has passed through a moment of pain. No one ever gets his second wind until he has used up his first wind; one never enjoys reading the Latin classics until he has survived the tedium of grammar and declensions; to swim is a thrill, but only after the shock of the first cold plunge. Even the joys of eternity are conditioned by this law; for unless there is a Good Friday in life, there will never be an Easter Sunday; unless there is a crown of thorns, there will never be the halo of light; and unless there is a cross, there will never be the empty tomb. In our temporal concerns, too, the law prevails. In marriage, it is only after the first misunderstanding has been survived that people begin to discover the beautiful joy of being together.

The third law of pleasure is this: Every quest for pleasure is fundamentally a striving for the infinite. Every pleasure attracts us because we hope, by savoring it, to get a foretaste of something that will exceed it in intensity and joy. One bird, one star, one book should be enough to fill the hunger of a man, but it is not: we find no satisfaction in anything, because our appetites are formed for everything. Like a great vessel that is launched, man moves insecurely in shallow waters, being made to skim the sea. To ask man to stop short of anything save the infinite is to nullify his nature; our greed for good is greater than the earth can gratify. All love of poetry is a cry, a moan, and a weeping; the more sublime and true it is, the deeper is its lament. If the joy of attaining something for which we longed ravishes the mind for an hour, it reverts, by evening, to the immensity of its still-unfulfilled desires.

Our hunger for the infinite is never quieted; even those disillusioned by excess of pleasures have always kept in their imagination a hope of somewhere finding a truer source of satisfaction than any they have tried. Our search for the never-ending love is never ended—no one could really love anything unless he thought of it as eternal. Not everyone gives a name to this infinity toward which he tends and for which he yearns, but it is what the rest of us call God.

The pursuit of pleasure is thus a token of man's higher nature, a symptom of his loneliness in this world. Torn between what he has, which surfeits him, and the far-off Transcendent, which attracts him, every worldly man stands in grave danger of self-hatred and despair until he finds his true Infinite in God. As Pascal put it: "The knowledge of God without a perception of man's misery causes pride, and the knowledge of man's misery without a perception of God causes despair. Knowledge of Jesus Christ constitutes the middle course, because in Him we find both God and our own misery."

Until a man has discovered the true Infinite, he is invariably led from subjectivism—the setting up of his ego as the absolute —to hedonism—the philosophy of a life given solely to sensate pleasures. When a man starts with the assumption that his selfish wishes must be held supreme, that nothing beyond the ego is significant, then it follows that the only standards by which he will be able to judge the worth of any experience are its pleasurableness and its intensity. The more he feels something, the truer and more admirable it will be. There is a fallacy, however, lurking behind the hedonist's assumption that the motivation of every action is pleasure, for if this were the case, no hedonist would be moving about today; he would have lain on the ground and refused to stir the first time he fell down and hurt himself as a child. A baby with barked shins does not get up and try, again, to toddle, out of a search for pleasure, but because his drive to develop human capacities overcomes his desire for the pleasure of lying supinely on the floor. Pleasure is actually a by-product of duty, and it evades direct pursuit. It is like the bloom on the cheek, as Aristotle has told us; the bloom is not something men try to develop but is the by-product of a healthy organism.

The proper attitude toward life is not one of pleasure seeking, but the cultivation of a Divine sense of humor within our human limitations. And what is humor? It is said that one has

a sense of humor if he can "see the point" and that he lacks a
sense of humor if "he cannot see the point." But God has made
the world in such a way that He is the point of everything we
see. The material is meant to be a revelation of the spiritual;
the human, a revelation of the Divine; and the fleeting experiences of our days, a revelation of Eternity. The universe,
according to God's original plan, was made transparent, like
a windowpane: a mountain was not to be just a mountain, but
a symbol of the power of God. A snowflake was not just a
snowflake, but a clue to the purity of God. Everything created
was to tell something about God, for "by the visible things
of the world is the Invisible God made manifest." According
to this plan, every man was to be a poet, a humorist, a man
endowed with a sense of the invisible, infinite values in everything.

Such was God's drama, of which man was to play the lighthearted role of Lord of Creation. When the lines were given
to the first man to speak, he made a botch of them. That slip
which destroyed man's role in Creation was sin; and sin is a
disproportionate seriousness. Sin was the act by which man
refused to see creatures for what they were—steppingstones
to God, a means to an end—and began, instead, to clutch at
them as ends in themselves. That is what sin is, still. As a man
loses his sense of humor when he cannot see the point of a pun,
so he loses his sense of humor in its entirety when he ceases to
see the point of the universe, which is that all things are
revelations, symbols, reminders of God Who made them. To
take things seriously as ends in themselves is to overrate them,
to treat them with a solemnity that is not warranted.

The awful seriousness of the pagan centuries lay like a pall
over mankind: all the genius of the Greek playwrights could

not conceal the deep despair that filled the cramped hearts of
men who found no greater meaning in the world than its
own brittle beauty of color, line, and rhythmic harmony.
Truth was the noblest master any pagan poet or philosopher
had found to serve—but truth, when seen, appeared as loveless
and impersonal.

The pagan's sad despair heard, on the stillness of a winter
breeze, the cry of the Babe. The great ones of the earth did
not hear the cry, for they were occupied with the concerns
of self. There were only two classes of people who heard that
cry: shepherds and wise men. The shepherds represented
those who know that they know nothing; and the wise men
stood for those who know how little learning teaches us. The
two kinds of simplehearted pilgrims saw a Babe, and they saw
It with a Divine sense of humor. They saw God through a
man. It was the Word, Who had become Emanuel, God
with us.

And when the Babe grew in age and grace and wisdom, He
went into the public lanes and market places and began to
teach a new doctrine to men: the doctrine of the Divine Sense
of Humor. It could all be summed up in these words: "Nothing in this world is to be taken seriously—nothing except the
salvation of a soul. The world, and the things that are in it,
will one day be folded up like an Arab's tent; you are not to
live exclusively for this life." It came as a shock to men who
were taking the world seriously to hear Him, the God-Man,
thunder out: "How is a man the better for it, if he gains the
whole world at the cost of losing his own soul? For a man's
soul, what price can be high enough? The Son of Man will
come hereafter in His Father's glory with His angels about
Him, and He will recompense everyone, then, according to

His works." (Matt. 16:26,27.) He refused to take fishermen as fishermen seriously—to Him they were "fishers of men." A wedding garment was not important in itself, but as a symbol of charity; a mustard seed was relevant as foreshadowing the Church; grass and lilies were tokens of Divine Providence; sheep and goats, of the just and the wicked; and the poor—the poor were Himself.

Things were to be held lightly by Christians, for true values could not be found by anyone who stopped short at things or took their surface meanings seriously. And still, today, there are the two possible outlooks on the world; either that of the hedonist, who is solemn about this world, considering it the only one that he will ever have; or that of the Divine sense of humor, which permits a man to "see through" this world to the other world that he will have hereafter. The Christian can be careless of his life and property. A child who has only one ball which cannot be replaced will be chary of using it. There will be a seriousness characterizing his play. But if he is told that he will some day be given another ball which will never wear out, he can take the first ball more lightly, can enjoy it without hoarding it.

Only those people who believe in transcendent reality can pass through this life with a sure sense of humor. The atheist, the agnostic, the sceptic, the materialist—all these have to take themselves seriously; they have no spiritual vantage point on which they can stand, look down upon themselves, and see how laughable they are. There is nothing more ludicrous than pretentiousness, and unless self-knowledge comes to puncture it, the absurdity will grow. Yet, if our self-exaltation is deflated without a recognition of the Mercy of God, Who can lift up the sinner, then it may beget despair: God is required for gayety.

There is only one place in Sacred Scripture where God is said to laugh: "He Who dwells in Heaven is laughing at their threats, the Lord makes light of them." (Ps. 2:4.) We become laughable through our incongruities and our affectations: a boy of twelve who shaves, a girl of nine who dresses up like her mother will provoke laughter because they are posing as being something they are not. So, when the materialist or atheist sets himself up as God, denying any dependence on a Creator, repudiating his need of a Saviour to forgive his faults and sins, then he becomes so ridiculous as to provoke the laughter of God Himself. And the pride of the scoffer is the thing that makes him doubly ridiculous: two people on ice can fall, but if one of them is wearing a silk hat, he will look funnier than the man who is dressed humbly. Self-exaltation humiliated and dignity punctured amuse us—and they may even amuse God.

But while God laughs at the atheists, the saints and those who have a Divine sense of humor laugh at themselves. Their faith has taught them that this life is only a vestibule to the next and that everything in it is a kind of sacramental, leading the soul to God. They envisage the world as a scaffolding, up which souls climb to the Kingdom of God; when the last soul shall have climbed up it, the scaffolding will be torn down and burnt with fervent fire—not because it is base, but because it will have done its work of bringing us back again to God. If God matters enough to us, His thumbprints are what make the visible world precious to us. If He chooses to remove some particular created thing, it cannot matter very much—for He Himself remains. When Job lost everything he had, he still maintained his Divine sense of humor as he said: "The Lord gives, the Lord takes away, praised be the Lord." St. Francis viewed the universe with the same lighthearted wisdom when he claimed the moon for his sister and the sun for his brother, felt a creaturely kinship with fire and wind and water, and then, as he died, saluted death as a "welcome brother." Most of us become very provoked at mosquitoes—but St. Rose of Lima chose them as her favorite pets; they never harmed her, and she used to bid them sing to her as she prayed.

It may well be that on the Last Day, when the Good Lord comes to judge the living and the dead, He will give a very special gift to those who have not taken the world too seriously but have made every material thing in it a steppingstone to Heaven. To those who have not taken either themselves or the world too seriously—to those who have the Divine sense of humor—He will show His smile.

6

How God Breaks into the Ego

DESPITE egotism, despite men's fear of Goodness and their hatred of Truth, God has His own way of getting inside a soul. For there are only two kinds of people in the world:— those who have found God and love Him, and those who are looking for Him. Among the latter are included those who are labeled Communists and bigots, unrepenting sinners and libertines, tyrants and their willing slaves. In general, there are three classes of such men who divide the world: the pre-Christians, who have not yet heard of the fullness of Christ; the post-Christians of our Western civilization, who once possessed Him but now abandon Him; and finally the anti-Christians, who would destroy His memory from the earth— and whose energy for the anti-Christ often puts Christians to shame. "The best lack all conviction, while the worst are full of passionate intensity." But *all* these groups are men who are seeking God.

Of men engaged today in such a search, one thing is notable: that they are not going to God through nature, but through themselves. The modern man is not so much impressed with the ordering of the physical universe, which draws our minds to a Transcendent Cause, as with the disorders and frustrations of his own soul. The classic rational arguments for the existence of God no longer appeal to men— not because the arguments have become irrational, but because minds are not trained today to obey the rules of formal logic in the search for truth. But God has other ways of drawing souls to Himself, if they will not seek Him down the road of reason; He can still make them feel His presence by their own loneliness and emptiness.

Those who have not found the fullness of God in His revelations find themselves frustrated. Men were made to know God, to love Him, and to serve Him; if they cannot do this, for lack of faith or for some other reason, they are living unnatural lives. They are like jungle lions condemned to the cramped life of a cage in a city zoo—or like a tree that is warped by being planted in a soil unsuited to its healthy growth. The climate of man's soul is God; he cannot flourish in another atmosphere. Souls who do not find Divine Life to complete their incomplete existence, Absolute Truth to steady the waverings of their mind, and Perfect Love, which is the goal of all their lesser loves are bound to feel let down and incomplete, to ask: "Is life worth living?"

This mental condition is reflected in the philosophy that men began to embrace at the end of World War II. Thought then became pessimistic—if for no other reason than because it had been born in catastrophe. The Stoics of classical times met the external catastrophes of their age by idealizing the men who grit their teeth in the face of disaster; so the new Stoics of our time (who are sometimes called Existentialists) meet the internal catastrophe of the modern mind by a cry of anguish, a moan from the heart of the philosopher who has no God. Mystery and paradox—which have always made the universe baffling to man—have now moved inside of man's own mind, so that he is a contradiction to himself. It is this shift of interest from the cosmos to man, from the universe to the human mind, from man as a problem to the problem of man which creates a great task for the apologist for the Divine. In the face of it, either he can try to make the modern man move his sights beyond himself to nature, where he can appreciate the customary arguments for God's existence; or else the apologist can start with man as he is, locked inside himself —frustrated, despairing, cynical, and atheistic.

Our Lord appears always to have taken this second short cut to the souls of those He joined to Him on earth. It seems to be His way to start with men just as they are: the Grace of God does not ask that we all be fitted into a mould before He will consent to work on us. As an example, we find Our Lord talking to a woman at the well—a woman who came at high noon to draw water, as no one would choose to do under the hot sun of the East. She came at this unusual hour, it seems, because she was an adulteress; the other women would not permit her to join them either in the cool of the morning or at night. How did Our Lord set about converting her? What possible common denominator would there be between Divine Innocence and this woman of the five divorces? There *was* one thing in common—the thing that had sent her to the well

—a common love of a drink of cold water in the heat. All men
are equal in thirst.

Starting with that primitive, pedestrian fact, Our Lord
lifted the woman's mind to a desire for other fountains of
peace and joy, and through a series of brilliant thrusts He
brought her first to call Him, "Jew," then "Sir," then
"Prophet," then "Messias," and finally "Saviour of the
World." One thing is certain: Our Lord started with *her*
problem, with *her* thirst, *her* emptiness, *her* frustration, and
her need. When she tried to shift the talk away from the uncomfortable topic of moral regeneration, by a theoretical
question as to which hill one ought to worship on, Our Lord
answered her: "The Kingdom of God is within you." Within
a few moments that thirst of hers for water became a thirst
for making Christ's name known and loved.

This method of starting with men as they are was also used
by St. Paul. Visiting the proud intellectual center of the world
—Athens—Paul, like all good apologists, looked about him for
something good to link to Goodness. There was not very
much that was good in that city, with its Pantheon full of
golden gods and silver deities; there was not much in paganism
to commend itself to Paul, as his eye fell on one graven image
after another. But finally he hit upon a common denominator
with his Christ. It was only an inscription carved at the base
of an altar, but it was enough to supply the inspiration for his
discourse as he began:

Men of Athens, I perceive that in all things you are very
religious, for when I went about and observed the objects
of your worship, I found among other things an altar
upon which was the inscription:

TO AN UNKNOWN GOD

That God Whom you know not, is the God Whom I preach to you. (Acts 17:22.)

So Paul, then, started with men as they are. As the Saviour had turned His gospel on the word "thirst," Paul turned his on the word "unknown." He assumed that the men of Athens sensed in themselves a capacity for worship not yet realized in their idolatries—he preached to them the God that is not made with human hands: the God Who made the world, the God Who sent His own Son to the world to save it, the Son who brought to men a chance for resurrection from the deadness of sin and the corruption of life.

In this spirit, the true lover of God may well say to the people of the twentieth century: "I perceive that you are religious men, for walking through your streets, I find more than one statue to the unknown God. You, too, are looking for a God Whom you know not. I see a statue to Marx—who promises the brotherhood of man, but who cannot give it, because he denies the fatherhood of any God. I see a statue to Freud—who offers peace of mind, but who cannot give it, because he denies all belief in God and all need for redemption from sin. That brotherhood of man, that peace of soul which you know not today you can find in the Fatherhood of God and in the Redemption of Our Lord."

Today's atheists and egotists are hungry, thirsting, starving, famished, frustrated souls—as pagans always are. They are often bigoted, prejudiced, fed-up with the world; they may be locked up inside their own minds, prisoned with their fears and their anxieties; they may be still filled with illusions because of their youth, still at that stage of life where false pleasures have not let them down. It makes no difference what they are. But if a man in this or in any century is conscious of a heavy burden—the weight of his own weary self—then the Divine Invitation can be heard: "Come to Me all ye who labor and are heavily burdened and find rest for your souls." (Matt. 11:28.)

But how can the man who longs for peace be sure that the God Who solicits is real? How dare a man begin to believe in God? How shall he rescue his imprisoned self?

There are two breaches in our walls; two cracks in our armor; two hidden entrances to the soul through which God can enter. These are so much a part of our nature that we cannot alter them: when God made us he built them, like trap doors, in our natures. Even when our intellects bar God's passage by the false obstructions to belief that unsound thinking has erected, He is able to penetrate to us through the secret doors we have not known how to bolt.

The first of these trap doors in the soul is the love of goodness. As we chase after every isolated tidbit that attracts us by its good, the soul is really in pursuit of the Whole and Infinite Goodness of God. Every quest of pleasure, every love of a friend, every approval of a good child, every comparison of good and better, implies some Goodness beyond all these good things, for none of them completely fills our hearts. Every lesser good we approve intimates our longing for utter Goodness, for God. To say that we want good things but not Goodness, which is Godness, is like saying that we love the sunbeams but we hate the sun, or we like the moonlight but despise the moon. The substance of the sun does not reach our room with the sunbeam, but some participation of it does; and, in like manner, no part of God is in the good apple, the good friend, but a participation of that Goodness is always there. No one can love the good without implicitly loving Goodness, and to that extent God creeps into the soul in its every wish and every joy.

Even the evil that we do is done because it seems to be good to us in some aspect. No one sins except from a desire for goodness; the sinner is simply mistaken in his choice of good, as the stomach is mistaken in its choice of good if it tries to live on a diet of pickle juice. But a man could not embrace even nihilism if it did not seem good to him. Drunkenness seems good to the alcoholic, money to the miser, and carnality to the lecher. Everything that God made is good: fire is good, although it burns houses, and water, although it drowns the swimmer. The most perverse atheist can love Godlessness only because such an idea seems good.

Because of this human predilection for what is good, no life is made up entirely of actions that are intrinsically wicked. The murderer savors the true goodness of a good dinner; a thief responds to the virtue of a child; a gangster feeds soup to poor people out of honest generosity. Good deeds are mingled with evil deeds. No one is forever persecuting, sinning, blaspheming; sometimes a hardened sinner is engaged in planting a rose, nursing a sick friend, fixing a neighbor's tire. There are considerable hidden reserves of natural goodness in everyone; they live on stubbornly in company with his predominant passion, even if that is turned toward evil. Because there is something in us that escapes infection, we are never intrinsically wicked, never incurable, never "impossible." Those who see our good deeds admire us; and those who see only our bad deeds hold us low: that is why there can be such divergent judgment about a man. Even when the will is perverse—even when a creature is enthralled and captivated by one great sinful adhesion, which makes his days a flight from God toward lust or power—even then there are some few good and commendable acts which contradict his general attitude. These isolated acts of virtue are like a clean handle on a dirty bucket; with them, God can lift a soul to His Peace.

The second trap door by which God enters a soul in flight from Him is by its ennui, its boredom, its satiety, its fed-upness, its loneliness, its melancholy, its despair. No matter how many evils we may have chosen, we have never exhausted the possibilities of choice—the human is still free—its power of choice is never exhausted. Every libido, every passion, every craving of the body is finite, carnal, and its cravings, when satisfied, fail to content us. But in the life of the weary sensualist, there is still one choice that has never been made, one great chord that has not yet been struck. He has not tried the Infinite. Statements like "I have seen life" and "I have tried everything" are never true, because the men who speak this way have not explored the greatest adventure of all. The rich man still asks: "What lack I yet to make me happy?" He knew, as all sensation seekers know, that gratifying every whim still leaves the deepest appetites unsatisfied. There is always still something to be had—something we need badly. We know, but we do not know everything; we love, but not forever. We eat, and we still hunger; we drink, and we still thirst: "The eye is not filled with seeing, neither is the ear filled with hearing." (Eccles. 1:8.)

Despite our efforts to find contentment in the temporal, we fail. For as the fish needs the water and the eye needs light, as the bird needs air and the grass needs earth, so the spiritual soul needs an Infinite God. Because God, for Whom we were made, is left out of its reckoning, the soul feels an emptiness, a boredom with what it has, a yearning for what it has not. This ennui is the negative presense of God in the soul—just as sickness is the negative presence of health in the body, and hunger is the negative presence of food in the stomach; a lack in us points to the existence of something capable of filling it. Through this trap door of our emptiness, God enters. If we do not admit Him at first, He will intensify the dissatisfaction and the loneliness, until finally He is accepted as our souls' Guest and its Eternal Host.

Such are the two secret entrances by which God insinuates Himself into the life of the atheist and the egotist who would keep Him out. He enters through the good that is loved and the infinite that is missed—in the sinner's craving for goodness, and in his emptiness without it; in his good deeds performed among a series of evil deeds, and in the dissatisfaction his soul feels with the finite satisfactions of life. He gives us His joy each time we do something good; He fills us with anxiety every time we do something evil. When we do good, God begins to work in us as a Gift; when we are bored and dissatisfied, He begins to work in us as a Longing.

Every satiety is accompanied by a desire. This accounts for the feeling we have that we are not only pursuing, but being pursued—not only seeking the Infinite, but being sought by It. The Good Shepherd is always in search of the lost sheep.

There are thus two main roads by which our own experiences can lead us to the God our natures need to know: Our happiness in the created goods of the world can draw us to their Creator. And our unhappiness, because no created thing gives the infinite joy we try to wring from it, can also lead us to the True Infinite. These experiences constitute the first dim stirrings of the soul to God. There is a primitive awareness of Sovereign Goodness in His handiwork on the one hand, and the longing for a Merciful Redeemer to free us from sin and anxiety on the other.

St. Francis de Sales gives us an analogy of mother partridges; these birds often steal the eggs of other partridges in order to hatch them. When the chick which has been hatched under the protecting wing of the thievish partridge first hears the cry of its true mother, it immediately abandons its false parent and flees to the true one. Apparently the baby partridge is drawn by some affinity in its nature, so that it is never satisfied until it finds the mother bird. God puts some such affinity for Him into our natures—a nostalgia for Him which renders us dissatisfied with the thieving enticements of flesh, wealth, and power, until we finally respond to our inborn need and fly to His loving embrace. But we are not guided by instinct as the partridges are. Reason and free will are our human faculties, so that the return to God is, for us, the result of a free choice.

Whether we respond or not to God's summoning of our souls, notice that the first impetus always comes from Him. He seeks us before we dream of seeking Him—there is God-priority everywhere. God knocks before we invite Him in—He loves us before we respond. We are all recipients before we are donors: our life was given to us; our education was given to us; our graces are given us, too.

The Divine Invader, then, cannot be kept out of our lives, since His love is a stowaway in every joy and every misery. But although we cannot prevent His entering our souls, we can prevent His staying. God, Who wishes to dwell in us, can always be evicted by a single word of dismissal. And so it is important to consider the way to respond to God's visitation—which we cannot prevent, but can cut short. The first necessity of our cooperation with God is the consciousness that it is He Who is present; the will to know Him causes our recognition of His presence. If we lack this readiness to know Him, we are like those who smell, and perceive no fragrance; taste, and know no sweetness; touch, and enjoy no ecstasy. It matters little to an ignorant person whether he meets a wise man or a dolt, if he has no will to learn. We must prepare the soul to welcome God before we can apprehend His presence. The man who loves good things will not recognize God until he wants Goodness even more than he wants the created good things; the man who is bored with life will not recognize the Divine Physician until he wants to be healed, at any cost.

St. Thomas tells us that what begins as the action of God on our souls becomes our cooperation, if we will it to be so. Or, in the language of St. Bernard: "There is a moment of inseparability, a common action on the part of God and the will, not entirely caused by God's action in the soul, not entirely by free will, but springing completely from the first and the second. Divine action and human responsibility go hand in hand." Once the will stirs itself to do something which before this it had refused to do, or against which it had a prejudice, or for which it had no taste, it never reverts to the former condition: it is summoned to new heights. What was before a vague affinity for good can now become a passion for Infinity. "But as many as received Him, He gave them power to be made the sons of God, to them that believe in His Name." (John 1:12.)

There is no escaping God; there is only the possibility of greeting Him with hate instead of love. For we cannot keep God out of our lives. The atheist must use God's name every time he explains his unbelief, as the prohibitionist must talk about liquor to be a prohibitionist; the persecutor must breathe the name of His Divine Son whenever he gives a reason for his hate; the Communists, who deny His existence, must each day date their anti-Christian publications as so many hundreds of years after His Birth. Those who are less extreme in their rejection also confess Him in every unsatisfied desire, in every longing for love, in every disappointment with it. The miser who wants to have more, the student who wants to know more, the libertine who wants to thrill more are dimly, feebly, gropingly reaching out their hands to Him when they long for an infinite plenitude of the things they prize.

There is not a single soul at which God has not knocked thousands of times. His knock may not be recognized because we have so little familiarity with Him; we recognize externally only the knock of those we know. But as the sun is always illumining, so God is always acting on the soul. His knock may come as fear, frustration, emptiness, anxiety, despair, pessimism concerning one's own ability to overcome difficulties—or as a faint suspicion that there may be something in the talk about Eternal Life and Beauty, after all. His summons may also come in satiety after sin, in self-disgust, in discontent with life, in disappointment, or in suffering.

Sickness is frequently the time when God is first admitted to the soul; for in physical disorder there is often a mental reordering, a canvassing of life, a stock taking of values. Sickness, moreover, forcibly deprives one of his sinful pleasures, and the soul then discovers how well he can get along without them, how much happier he really is. In the quiet of the sickroom a patient comes to an overwhelming sense of how much time he has wasted on trivial things—how his energies have been dissipated—how his mind could have been illumined if it had not spent itself in the chitchat of the cocktail hour (which probably represents the lowest level of conversation in the history of mankind). But God does not always need to lay us low through sickness in order to penetrate our souls. Every misfortune and setback in life is a hint from Him that contentment is not found along the way the egotist has chosen. If souls in such moments would turn from their complaints, their bickering, their revolt and would open the door to God's Grace, instead, they would find such a peace and contentment as is a true foretaste of Heaven. The great tragedy of life is not what the soul suffers, but how close it can come to happiness without finding it. Those who reject God are like a prospector who misses the gold that his successor will discover. But the fault it not on God's side—it is on ours. The principal reason why we drive God's actual Grace out of our souls is because we are unwilling to detach ourselves from our egotisms to meet the moral requirements which a union with God eventually demands.

Many people nowadays want God, but on *their* terms, not on *His*. They insist that their wishes shall determine the kind of religion that is true, rather than letting God reveal His truth to them. So their dissatisfaction continues, and grows. But God finds us lovable, even in our rebellion against Him. He does not love us because we are lovable of and by ourselves, but because He has put His own love into us. He does not even wait for us to love; His own love perfects us. Letting it do this, with no resistance, no holding back for fear of what our egotism must give up, is the one way to peace which the world can neither give nor take away.

PART TWO: *The I-Level*

Knowledge of the I

MAN is the only creature in the visible universe who can know himself—can turn around and observe his own thoughts, as it were, in a mirror. A stone, a tree, an animal—such things cannot turn back in their thoughts to identify themselves, nor can they contemplate themselves or stand off and regard themselves as an object. But the human spirit can penetrate itself; it can be not only a subject but also the object of a thought; it can admire itself, be angry with itself, and even despair of itself. This capacity for self-reflection, which animals do not have, makes man superior to the animal but also makes him subject to mental disorders when the soul does not fulfill the high destiny to which it is called—when it refuses to use the human faculty of unprejudiced examination of the self and its acts. To surrender this activity is to move down from the human level to that of the animal; to replace the I with the ego; to enter into the realm of mental eccentricity.

We are all conscious beings, but very few of us are really self-conscious. We are aware of the existence of the objects around us, but are not fully aware of ourselves. We know the ways in which we resemble other human beings and conform to their habits of dress and thinking, but we rarely think of ourselves personally and uniquely, in our differences from other persons, and as we stand, alone, in our relationship to God.

Everyone else knows our faults and failings, but we can close our eyes to them. We are indignant when we hear ourselves accused, even though we have a sneaking suspicion that what we are told may be true. Our neighbors' defects of character we carry before our eyes, but our own are carried out of sight in a sack on our backs. Every man *can* know himself, but often a man knows everything except himself, and therefore he knows nothing. The artifices, the pretenses, the make-believe, the masks that others wear, all these we see through—but we are blind to our own, to those we ourselves put on in order to deceive the world, if some dominant fault has dogged us.

In extreme cases, the I, in panic, flees from any chance of self-knowledge to deliberately sought unconsciousness, as in the case of alcoholism. There is a vast difference between the individual who gets drunk because he loves liquor and the one who does it because he hates or fears something else so much that he has to run away from it. The first becomes the drunkard, the second the alcoholic. The drunkard pursues the exhilaration of liquor; the alcoholic pursues the obliteration of memory. Very few women ever become alcoholics because they like alcohol; they become alcoholics because they violently dislike something else. That is why, in some instances, the cure of alcoholism implies the facing of the very problem one is seeking to escape. And this procedure is impossible without self-knowledge.

The flight from the responsible I sometimes, however, takes the form of what theologians call a "conversion to creatures." This is an excessive externalization of the personality—an effort to drown and lose the self in outward events and things. It involves a loss of that inwardness which is essential for happiness; no man is safe in his contentment if he derives his pleasures wholly from the things outside of him, for they may change at any time or be taken away. If we want nothing, need nothing that the outer world can give or withhold, then, and only then, happiness lies within our own control.

But no one can attain such freedom or self-possession unless he first knows himself and has faced his failings as they are. Self-knowledge is a peeling off of the false ego which we wear, in order that we may discover the true I and lift ourselves to the second, or higher, level of living. But self-knowledge is by no means the same thing as psychoanalysis. In self-knowledge we accept responsibility for the mental and moral states we have created; in psychoanalysis, the self is merely a spectator of the things which events and instincts have made him do. In psychoanalysis, the patient inspects his own mental condition as he might study a chemical process or the habits of a colony of mice. In self-knowledge, we see ourselves as persons whose decisions and choices have landed us where we are now. Psychoanalysis is idly curious about the goings-on of this mysterious "self" on which it does research, with no sense of personal guilt for any of its actions; the basic assumption of such a technique is that every patient has been immaculately conceived and is therefore free of any tendency toward sin. The psychoanalytic patient may even become proud of his complex and tortured mental state and may ask the doctor: "Did you ever hear a case as bad as mine?" But self-knowledge, honestly obtained, begets humility. After psychoanalysis, there is no moral obligation to change one's habits or to mend one's moral ways: conduct in opposition to the will of God is blandly accepted and justified. But self-knowledge makes us face the fact that some of our attitudes and habits are evil and must therefore be abandoned. Our sins are not glossed over by self-knowledge; they are faced, admitted, and regretted before God.

Self-knowledge can lead us to the real self, the human I, only if we accept a standard outside of ourselves, for if we make our own characters the measure of perfection, we shall never escape from self-deceit. Our watches cannot be called either fast or slow if there is no other timepiece against which to check them; in the same way, we cannot measure ourselves against ourselves. There has to be a standard, outside our own minds, which is more reliable than any of our moods.

Nor can we accept the generally admired code of conduct of our age as the extrinsic standard of behavior—for this is always an expression of the way that people are *living* in a particular place and century, but not of the way they *ought* to live.

The proper way to judge a thing is by its purpose: and the purpose of man is to be happy—not in his body alone, but in the highest reaches of his personality. But man has been so made that complete fulfillment can be attained only if he has Perfect Life without Death, Perfect Truth with no admixture of error, Ecstatic Love without satiety—in other words, the Supreme Happiness of God. It is God, then, Who provides the only scales and yardstick in the universe against which man may measure his own capacities and failings. In the physical order it is the sun which lights the darkness, and in the spiritual order, too, darkness prevails until we seek the only light that can fully illumine our life's purpose and destiny, and that is Christ, the Light of the World.

When we begin to use Christ as our measuring stick, we begin, for the first time, to see our lives as the inadequate things they are. A picture in a poor light may seem perfect; a strong light will bring out its defects. Standing in our own shadow, we used to appear good to ourselves; but as we bring ourselves nearer to the Light of God, revealed in Christ, His Divine Son, we see how much we have failed to be all that creatures ought to be, and thereby we discover the true secret of our unhappiness.

When Our Lord said, "One of you is about to betray Me," every one of the Apostles asked, "Is it I Lord?" None of us is assured of his innocence before Divinity; but when the ego is its own judge, who is ever a failure? The Divine Standard is a Light to those willing to see their failings; it can also become the object of a great hate, when one is unwilling to change his ways. The Crucifixion was the inevitable consequence of the Sermon on the Mount. He who preaches purity of heart to a sensuous generation, and meekness to an age of power, will not be tolerated. Only the mediocre can survive.

True self-knowledge is always God-regarding, as St. Augustine showed us in his prayer:

Lord Jesus, let me know myself, let me know Thee,
    And desire nothing else but only Thee.
Let me hate myself and love Thee,
    And do all things for the sake of Thee.
Let me humble myself and exalt Thee,
    And think of nothing but only Thee.
Let me die to myself and live in Thee,
    And take whatever happens as coming from Thee.
Let me forsake myself and walk after Thee,
    And ever desire to follow Thee.
Let me fly from myself and turn to Thee,
    That so I may merit to be defended by Thee.
Let me fear for myself, let me fear Thee,
    And be among those who are chosen by Thee.
Let me distrust myself and trust in Thee,
    And ever obey for the love of Thee.
Let me cleave to nothing but Thee,
    And ever be poor for the sake of Thee.
Look upon me that I may love Thee,
    Call me that I may see Thee,
And forever possess Thee.

That is the goal—and the first long step we take to reach it
lies in a truthful and pitiless examination of the self. Self-
knowledge demands the discovery of our predominant fault—
of the particular defect which tends to prevail in us, affecting
our sympathies, our decisions, desires, and passions. The predominant fault is not always clearly seen, because it acts as a
Fifth Column in our souls. A man who by nature is gentle and
kind may easily have his spiritual life ruined by the hidden
fault of weakness toward ethical and moral issues. Another
person, who by nature is courageous, may have as his pre-

dominant fault a bad temper—or fits of violence which he calls "courage." The existence of a predominant fault does not indicate that there is no good quality in us; yet our good qualities may possibly be rendered ineffective by this hidden defect. The quickest way to discover the predominant fault is to ask ourselves: "What do I think about most when alone? Where do my thoughts go when I let them go spontaneously? What makes me most unhappy when I do not have it? Most glad when I possess it? What fault irritates me most when I am accused of it, and which sin do I most vigorously deny possessing?"

The predominant fault varies from person to person; it can be any one of seven capital sins and their correlated failings, which will be treated in the next chapter. The seven capital sins are the seven pallbearers of the soul. We hate to acknowledge any one of them as being our own, for we see their ugliness; self-knowledge is not easy, because self-love cannot endure humiliation. It hurts us to tear off a layer of our conceit. If a thought suddenly crosses the mind, "How rotten I am," the ego is alert to drive it away. When the real self—the I—sees itself in God's Light as it really is, the ego vanishes.

But the ego does not want to vanish. That is why some people try to avoid the painful process of self-knowledge on the ground that it develops an "inferiority complex." Of all the towering nonsense in the modern world, nothing is greater than this dread of an inferiority complex—the roots of such a fear are always pride. Pride tells us: "I am not as proud or bold or self-assertive as I might be if my conscience were quieted by self-deception. I know that I am not so learned or so beautiful as my neighbor, and this fact hurts me, makes me miserable. I had better forget it." But the acceptance of our natural imperfections is desirable: we cannot all be giants. To accept both our talents and our lack of talents as God's will is true humility. It is realism to say, as John the Baptist did: "I must decrease." He saw his true inferiority when he was confronted by Divinity—yet Our Lord said that he was the "greatest man born of woman."

The real self must be accepted for what it is: perhaps it *is* not learned, nor beautiful nor charming. But what of that? The real self can have its own wisdom and its own beauty if it yields to God, for "the beauty of the King's daughter is from within."

It is further objected that self-knowledge brings despair, as it reveals our true defects. There is no doubt that such despair *is* likely if we view ourselves apart from God revealed in Christ. A materialistic psychoanalysis necessarily makes one pessimistic about human nature: the soul naturally shrinks from the discovery of a disease which cannot be cured. Atheists shudder at the prospect of going down into the pit of their real selves, for there is no exit for them toward happiness. Not having the humility to face the fact that their real selves are guilty, they deny the very existence of guilt, although seeing their sins would be the essential condition of their cure. Self-knowledge is never despairing to those who acknowledge the power of God. Who fears to reveal sickness to a physician who can cure him? Who fears to reveal his guilt to a Saviour Who redeems? Self-examination to the Christian is the digging of a foundation. The deeper the foundation, the higher the building will finally soar; the more humble the soul, the greater his exaltation when God touches him.

As Cardinal Newman wrote:

Do you desire to be great? Make yourselves little. There is a mysterious connection between real advancement and self-abasement. If you minister to the humble and despised, if you feed the hungry, tend the sick, succour the distressed, if you bear with the forward, submit to insult, endure ingratitude, render good for evil, you are, as by a divine charm, getting power over the world and rising among its creatures. . . . The more they abase themselves the more they are like to Him; and the more like they are to Him, the greater must be their power with Him. . . . When a man discerns in himself most sin and humbles himself most, when his comeliness seems to him to vanish away and all his graces to wither, when he feels disgust at himself, and revolts as the thought of himself seems to himself all dust and ashes, all foulness and odiousness, then it is that he really rises in the Kingdom of God.

Self-knowledge has many advantages for the soul aware of God. The sense of loneliness and isolation disappears, for now one no longer understands love as the satisfaction of the ego, but as expansiveness toward God and neighbor. Mental health begins to improve; there is no more need of erecting defenses to protect an indefensible egotism, no dread of the revelation of the true self—a kind of fear which is sometimes the cause of mental breakdowns. The superficial self ceases to whisper, "Life is passing, you have not lived," for now, for the first time, one discovers *why* he is alive. Self-knowledge evaporates our moodiness. Formerly our emotional reactions were determined wholly by the outer world—a rainy day, a nasty job, an unwelcome guest completely upset our peace because we were not self-possessed. Now by concentrating on

God, we can impose His atmosphere on the outer world. Saints are happy in situations when others are in despair; they are so emancipated from life's accidentals, so rooted in God, that, like the ocean, they remain calm in the depths although the waves may roar at the surface.

Self-knowledge does away with boredom. To live on the level of the superficial self is to feel empty, because the soul knows it has greater capacities than any which are being realized. With the discovery of the real self, the I, one does not resort to the search for shallow satisfactions any longer. Boredom came from lack of purpose; now the purpose of life is clear to see. Self-knowledge also makes us more active; a false view of life paralyzes action. But when the goal of life is found, we cease to build up defenses, and we become less sensitive, more other-regarding. The real self soon becomes an apostle of love to others, now that he no longer has to hide his shameful self from them. As soon as one becomes keen to his own failing, he is immediately made sensitive to the needs and losses of others and feels them as his own. Excuses no longer have to be made for self—there is no more effort to delude others into thinking of us as better than we are. Thus, we are free to begin to live a life of consecration.

Self-knowledge unravels the knots in our natures, gives the soul room to stretch, removes the compression from the outside which had troubled us, and allows expansion from the inside out. For too long the ego has been stuffing the soul with hates, jealousies, and envies—as one might throw old paper boxes and wrappings into a cellar, creating a fire hazard that endangers the house from below. But our repressed sins are not like the rags, papers, and bottles we throw into the cellar; they are living, squirming, crawling things that come to the surface on sleepless nights. One tries to forget them, but they are always there. There is no place for us until we admit them to our consciousness, seeing how one sin is linked to another, and how, at the bottom of them all, is our self-will. Now we admit that the ego has been setting itself up as a god, crowding the real God out. If a box is filled with sand, it cannot be filled with salt; and if the character was filled with ego, it could not be filled with God.

> If thou couldst empty all thyself of self,
> Like to a shell dishabited
> Then might He find thee on the ocean shelf
> And say: "This is not dead,"
> And fill thee with Himself instead.
> But thou art all replete with very thou
> And hast such shrewd activity
> That when He comes He says: "This is enow
> Unto itself: 'Twere better let it be
> It is so small and full, there is no room for Me."
>
> —T. E. Brown

After the self-knowledge has been completed in what is known as the examination of conscience, then the soul is ready for the Confession. Here it gathers up the bundle of sins and defects, prides and egotisms and lusts which constitute the rubbish of its life and throws them onto the fire of Calvary, to have them burned and purged away. Anyone who on a Saturday afternoon has entered a large city Church with rows of confessionals on either side has seen, protruding from the little curtains of the confessionals, feet—big and small, male and female. These feet, which look like wriggling little worms, belong to persons who have learned the difference between the ego and the I, and who have finally come to disown their sins by owning them, and to fill themselves by emptying themselves. The only part of them which is revealed to the world is the lowliest part, as a kind of symbol of the absence of pride the act requires. As Paul Claudel has suggested, instead of putting the best foot forward, the penitent puts his worst foot forward. Every penitent who has completed his self-knowledge before he entered the box has said, "I may fool others, but what a fool am I if I fool myself. And what a sinful fool, if I imagine I can fool my God!"

8

The Seven Pallbearers of Character

EGOTISM—an inordinate love of self—is the basic cause of all sins and of all unhappiness which lacks a rational cause. There are also other effects of self-love, so numerous that no psychologist has ever listed them in their completeness. Fear, for instance, is an isolation from our fellow men, a feeling that we are surrounded by foes bent on the destruction of our ego. Procrastination is the act of an ego refusing to face its responsibilities in order to enjoy its ease. Worrying about other people and "bossing" them result when the ego is trying to maintain itself as a center of the cosmos. The bore is the egotist struggling to increase his prestige, either by telling about the books he has read or the women he has wooed. Cursing is an art of the ego in rebellion against the God Who challenges its superiority or renders the ego uncomfortable. Freakishness in dress is the behavior of an ego in wild pursuit of attention. Defiance of the ordinary standards of society results if the ego sets itself above the rest of men. In the spoiled child's tantrums the youthful ego draws attention to itself. Hurry, hustle, bustle, and two telephones on every desk are the outward sacraments of an ego bent on impressing other people with its own superiority. The telling of stories at the expense of someone else reveals the ego in jealousy or in envy.

At the root of every such disorder is self-love, the error in living which hatches out a brood of seven major effects of egotism. These—the seven pallbearers of character—are Pride, Avarice, Envy, Lust, Anger, Gluttony, and Sloth. It is against these seven major forms of egotism that self-knowledge is directed.

Pride is too great admiration of oneself. The ultimate stage of pride is to make oneself his own law, his own judge, his own morality, his own god. The Evil Spirit first promised Eve: "You will be as gods." A man makes himself a god by the exaltation of his own will against God's Will; from this rebellion flows contempt of others' rights, excessive love of personal advancement, the desire to be in the spotlight, and intolerance of opinions that differ from our own.

In the modern world, pride disguises itself under the prettier names of success and popularity. We are encouraged by quack psychologists to "trust ourselves" instead of trusting God. False confidence in the self is encouraged—although the only formula for a man's true contentment lies in his saying to God: "Thou alone art the Way, the Truth and the Life." The modern man's desire to serve the best liquor, his woman's ambition to be the best dressed, the college sophomore's hope of being the most studiously unkempt—these are symptoms of an egotistical vanity which makes its owners dread not being noticed. Criticism, backbiting, slander, barbed words, and character assassination are acts of egotism intent on elevating the ego on the carcass of another's reputation; each depression of another's ego is made an elevation of one's own. The more important the egotist feels himself to be, the more irritated he becomes when he does not receive worship; those who flatter him are called wise—those who criticize him are condemned as fools.

Today, a whole civilization has entered into a conspiracy to "make friends and influence people," by diplomatic self-deceit. All appeals to moral betterment are dubbed as "interference"; all intimations of truth are denounced as "intolerance"; talk about a law above our whims is hissed at as "authoritarian." Excuses are always at hand; everybody is wrong but the egotist. And yet it is a paradoxical truth that all egotists really hate themselves. Their excesses in drink and promiscuity, their violent aggressions against those who cross their self-will, their consciousness of an ever-widening chasm between their dreams and their realizations—these things react on their consciousness as cynicism and doubt, and on their unconsciousness as fear, dread, anxiety, and worry. The false self-love begets a violent self-hatred—an urge to sabotage the self, to punish it for not being perfect, for not living up to the ego's maniacal vision of the self as godlike and infallible. A man can hate himself in two ways: either by hating the vanity, conceit, and self-glorification which do injury to his soul—and this is the way of purification—or by hating whatever in him interferes with his pretense of being God—and this is the way of self-destruction, one of the clearest foretastes of hell that exists on earth.

Egotism, if not arrested, becomes the source of an inordinate love of honors and praise, which the egotist seeks by virtue of his clothes, jewels, family background, notoriety, and bank account. The egotist instigates applause by boasting, ostentation, pompous display, and studied affectation; he justifies all the sham of his existence with a boast: "It is the only way you can get ahead in this world."

Pride has seven evil fruits: *boasting*, or self-glorification through one's own words; *love of publicity*, which is conceit in what other people say; *hypocrisy*, which is pretending to be what one is not; *hardheadedness*, which is a refusal to believe that any other opinion is better than one's own; *discord*, or refusing to give up one's own will; *quarreling* whenever others challenge the wishes of the ego; and *disobedience*, or the refusal to submit one's ego to a lawful superior. Very often conceited people regard getting their own will as a more important gain than obtaining the thing which is withheld: it is the victory they value, not the spoils. That is why they will refuse to accept a gift that was not given to them at once when they first expressed their desire: they would rather punish the friend who did not instantly yield to them than have the object he withheld. In arguments they do not want to know the truth, but only to vindicate their own self-importance, to reaffirm their own opinions.

Avarice is a perversion of the natural right of every man to extend his personality by owning the things which minister to the needs of his body and his soul. Its disorder can come from desiring wealth as an *end* rather than as a means, or through the *manner* in which wealth is sought, with its disregard of others' rights, or in the way in which the money is *used*—to increase one's capital without limit, instead of using the excess to minister to the needs of others. Avarice readily leads to other evil practices which are adopted to preserve wealth, such as fraud, perjury, dishonesty, perfidy, and harshness in dealing with others.

Avarice never calls itself by this name; it wears such flattering tags as "thrift," "security," "big business," and "drive." (Since each sin disguises itself by a similar semantic dodge, one has to look for each under its modern name. The real self, or the I, is discovered as soon as the superficial self discovers sin beneath its modern dress.) There are two kinds of wealth: real and artificial. Real wealth is limited. There are just so many potatoes that a man can comfortably eat, and so many suits that he can wear. But artificial wealth—in the shape of stocks and bonds and credit—is unlimited and is therefore infinite. That is why love of abstract wealth can become an insatiable craving which completely destroys the development of the real self.

Avarice is a sign that one does not trust in God but feels the need to be his own Providence. "So much for the man who would have none of God's help, but relied on his store of riches, and found his strength in knavery!" (Ps. 51:9.) Unless corrected, avarice leads to several other serious defects of character: it causes an insensibility to the suffering and the needs of others; it creates anxiety and restlessness in the soul, which is continually bent on the pursuit of "more"; it leads to violence against others in the cause of protecting wealth; to lying, that the owner may acquire more; to perjury, that he may protect his hoard; and to treachery, as in the case of Judas.

Excessive love of luxury and ease is another sign of nakedness of the soul. The less character a person has, the more he needs to supplement it by external show: furs, diamonds, jewels, yachts are so many vain attempts to make the poverty-stricken ego rich. *Having* is confused with *being;* the egotist imagines that *he* is worth more, merely because he owns something that has worth. This is the one sin which is most apt to provoke contempt when we see it in others, and pride when we practice it ourselves. It is a psychological fact that the avaricious man who disguises himself as "devoted to business" is extremely difficult to spiritualize. He lives under the illusion that he needs nothing, because the only needs he admits are those which supply the body. "And Jesus looked around, and said to His disciples, With what difficulty will those who have riches enter God's Kingdom!" (Mark 10:23.)

Envy is sadness at another's good, as if that good were an affront to one's superiority. As the rich are avaricious, so the poor are sometimes envious. The envious person hates to see anyone else happy. The charm, the beauty, the knowledge, the peace, the wealth of others are all regarded as having been purloined from him. Envy induces ugly women to make nasty remarks about beautiful women, and makes the stupid malign the wise. Since the envious person cannot go up, he tries to achieve equality by pulling the other down. Envy is always a snob, is always jealous and possessive. To the envious, all who are polite are castigated as "high-hat"; the religious they dub "hypocrites"; the well-bred "put on airs"; the learned are "high-brow." Envy begins by asking, "Why shouldn't I have everything that others have?" and ends by saying, "It is because others have these virtues that I do not have them." Then envy becomes enmity; it is devoid of respect and honor, and, above all, it can never say, "Thank you," to anyone.

Envy is related to pride, which also can endure no rival or

superior. It is related to jealousy, as well. Jealousy consists in an inordinate love of self, mixed with the fear that we may be robbed of our complacency by others! We are envious of another's good, we are *jealous* of our own. Some egotists who suffer from these twin sins become carping critics of whatever good is done by others. They have to see that it is good, but they are angry that they did not do it themselves and that they did not receive the honor it receives. Hence they seek to nullify its value by depreciation. Jealousy is psychologically very dangerous—it has led to suicide when the jealous person realized that there was no hope of catching up with his competitor.

Envy begins its course by seeking to lower the reputation of another, either secretly, by talebearing and gossip, or overtly, by detraction. These succeeding, the term of envy is reached when there is joy at another's misfortune and when there is grief at another's success. When envy attacks another's spiritual progress or apostolic success, it is a grave matter. Much journalism today is founded on envy; it seeks to stir up conflicts, to arouse controversy, to contradict, to foster antagonisms, to belittle. This is due, in part, to the general feeling of discontent and unhappiness in most souls. Misery loves company. The inner conflicts of the envious seem diminished when the weaknesses of well-known men are spread before them. Readers who enjoy columns of scandals and gossip unconsciously seek to drag others down to the level of their own behavior. The truly charitable person is reluctant to hear of evil; and the saint, when he hears it, keeps it to himself and does penance for it.

One of the most effective ways of counteracting jealousy and envy in ourselves is to say a prayer immediately for the

intention of the person we resent. By referring our enemies to
God and by spiritually wishing them well, we crush the
psychological impulse toward envy. A second means is to try
to emulate those who provoke our envy: the Church holds up
the good example of the Saints, not to depress us, but to im-
press us—not to discourage us in our failings, but to encourage
us to greater efforts. "Let us keep one another in mind, always
ready with incitements to charity and to acts of piety." (Heb.
10:24.)

   Lust is an inordinate love of the pleasures of the flesh. It is
the prostitution of love, the extension of self-love to a point
where the ego is projected into another person and loved
under the illusion that the Thou itself is being loved. Real love
is directed toward a person, who is seen as irreplaceable and as
unique; but lust excludes all personal consideration for the
sake of sensate experience. The ego mislabels lust with modern
tags, pretending that such a sin is required for "health" or for
a "full life" or to "express the self." The feverish attempt to
give a scientific warrant to this vice is in itself an indication of
how great a natural reluctance man normally feels for seeing
this breach of the moral law as the sin it actually is. Men and
women are bored and discontented today; they turn to lust to
make up for their inner misery—only, in the end, to find themselves plunged into a deeper despair. As St. Augustine says:
"God does not compel man to be pure; He only leaves those
alone who deserve to be forgotten."

   Lust is a shifting of the center of personality from the spirit
to the flesh, from the I to the ego. In some instances, its excesses are born of an uneasy conscience and of a desire to
escape from self toward others; sometimes there is a contrary
desire to make the ego supreme by the subordination of others

to itself. In its later stages, the libertine finds that neither release from self nor idolatry is possible for long; the soul is driven back to self and, therefore, to an inner hell. The effect of lust on the will is to develop a hatred of God and a denial of immortality. Excesses also deplete the source of spiritual energy to such an extent that one finally becomes incapable of calm judgment in any other field.

Lust is not sex—for sex is purely biological and is a God-given capacity; nor is it love, which finds one of its lawful expressions in sex. Lust is the isolation of sex from true love. There is no passion which more quickly produces slavery than lust—as there is none whose perversions more quickly destroy the power of the intellect and the will. Excesses affect the reason in four ways: by perverting the *understanding* so that one becomes intellectually blind and unable to see the truth; by weakening *prudence* and a sense of values, thus producing rashness; by building up self-love to generate *thoughtlessness;* by weakening the will until the power of decision is lost and one becomes a prey to *inconstancy* of character.

The effects on the will are as disastrous as the effects on the reason. In those who are repeatedly given to excesses, there is apt to be a hatred of God and religion and a denial of immortality. The hatred of the Divine comes because God is seen as an obstacle to self-gratification. Lechers deny God because His Omniscience means that their behavior has been observed by the One bound to reproach it. Until such men abandon their egotistic animality, they must insist on being atheists, for only the atheist is able to imagine that he is unwatched.

A related effect of lust is the denial of immortality. As the egotist lives more and more in the flesh, the thought of Judgment becomes more and more distasteful to him; to quiet his

fears, he embraces the belief that Judgment will never be. The
acceptance of immortality would carry a responsibility which
the lecherous ego is afraid to face—one which would force him
to transform his whole life, if he did face it. Any mention of
a future life is apt to drive such a person into a fury of cynicism; the reminder of the possibility of Judgment increases
his anguished anxiety. Every attempt to save such a man is
regarded by him as an attack upon his happiness.

A belief in God and immortality would make the lustful ego
want to be an I; but when he is not ready to give up his vice,
he must refuse to dwell on such thoughts as these. It would be
well for apologists of religion to learn, in dealing with egotists
who are for the moment lost in the sloughs of lust, that a
willingness to change behavior must precede a change in
religious belief. Once a lecher gives up the evil, he will seek the
Truth, for now he need not fear it.

Lust has nothing to do with the lawful expression of sex in
a legitimate marriage. True married love is the formation of
the "we," is the extinction of ego-centricity. In married love
the I seeks the complete development of the Thou, of the
personality opposite the I. There is no moment more sacred
than that in which ego is surrendered to another personality,
so that the need to possess disappears in the joy of loving the
other person. Such lovers are never alone, for it takes not two
but three to make love, and the Third is God. One ego loves
another ego for what it gives, but an I loves another I for what
it is. Love is the joining of two poverties out of which is
created a great wealth.

Divorce, infidelity, planned un-parenthood, invalid marriages are so many travesties and heresies against love—and
whatever is the enemy of love is the enemy of life and
happiness.

Anger is a violent desire to punish others. Here we refer not to righteous anger, such as that of Our Lord when He drove the buyers and sellers out of the Temple, but the wrong kind of anger, which expresses itself in temper, vindictiveness, tantrums, revenge, and the clenching of the fist. Anger's disguise in the egotist's eyes is the desire to "get even" or "not to let him get away with it." In the press and on the platform anger calls itself "righteous indignation"; but underneath, it is still a mania to exploit wrath, to malign, and to foment grievances. Anger is very common among those with bad consciences; thieves will become far angrier when accused of theft than any honest man; unfaithful spouses will fly into a rage when caught in infidelity; women guilty of jealousy and malice "take it out" on their employees in the home. Those who displease such egotists are repulsed violently, and the good who reproach them by the pattern of their virtue are viciously maligned.

There are various degrees of anger; the first is touchiness—undue sensitiveness and impatience at the least slight. Because the coffee is cold at breakfast, or because the morning paper is late, the impatient ego nags and grumbles. The second stage is a flaring up of the temper, with violent gesticulation, blood boiling, redness of the face, and even the throwing of things; all of these are indications that the ego will brook no interference in the fulfillment of its selfish desires. The third and final stage is reached when there is physical violence directed against another—when hatred seeks to "get even" either by doing harm to another person or else by desiring his death. Many a man does not realize how much diabolical anger there is in him until his ego is aroused. Anger prevents the development of personality and halts all spiritual progress—not only because it disturbs mental poise and good judgment, but because it blinds to the rights of others and disturbs that spirit of recollection which is so necessary for compliance with the inspirations of grace.

Anger is always related to some frustration of the ego. It is particularly difficult to cure in others because it is rooted in self-love, although no egotist will admit that this is the cause. He would rather have his body hurt than his ego humiliated by such a meek acknowledgment.

Gluttony is an abuse of the lawful pleasure that God has attached to eating and drinking, which are a necessary means of self-preservation. It is an inordinate indulgence in the pleasures of eating and drinking, either by taking more than is necessary or by taking it at the wrong time or in too luxurious a manner. Gluttony disguises itself as "the good life," or as "the sophisticated way," or as "gracious living." An over-stuffed, double-chinned generation takes gluttony for granted, rarely considering it a sin.

The malice in excessive love of eating and drinking comes from the fact that it enslaves the soul to the body and thus tends to weaken the moral and intellectual life of man. There is not today as much excess in eating as in drinking—modern man does not emulate the pagan Romans who used to tickle their throats after eating a meal in order that, having disgorged, they could once again enjoy the pleasures of the table. The excess today is more apt to be in drinking, as the high incidence of alcoholism so well testifies. Medical authorities bear witness to the fact that hard drinking causes deterioration of the intellect and personality. Memory, judgment, concentration are all affected; personal pride and social judgment vanish. Among the moral effects are despair, a weakening of the will, and the materialization of life.

Sloth is a malady of the will which causes neglect of one's duty. In the physical realm it appears as laziness, softness, idleness, procrastination, nonchalance, and indifference; as a spiritual disease, it takes the forms of a distaste of the spiritual, lukewarmness at prayers, and contempt of self-discipline. Sloth is the sin of those who only look at picture-magazines, but never at print; who read only novels, but never a philosophy of life. Sloth disguises itself as tolerance and broad-mindedness—it has not enough intellectual energy to discover Truth and follow it. Sloth loves nothing, hates nothing, hopes nothing, fears nothing, keeps alive because it sees nothing to die for. It rusts out rather than wears out; it would not render a service to any employer a minute after a whistle blows; and the more it increases in our midst, the more burdens it throws upon the State. Sloth is ego-centrical; it is basically an attempt to escape from social and spiritual responsibilities, in the expectation that someone else will care for us. The lazy man is a parasite. He demands that others cater to him and earn his bread for him; he is asking special privileges in wishing to eat bread which he has not earned.

There are various degrees of laziness: indolence: a careless execution of work, the performance of a job not because there is pride in the work but merely to get paid for it; procrastination: the endless postponing and putting off of tasks until a tomorrow which never comes; listlessness: an aversion for effort in any form. Sloth can bear not only upon manual and mental labor but also upon spiritual progress. It makes one negligent in his works of piety, inclines him to shorten his prayers or to neglect them altogether; it may even degenerate into a hatred of things spiritual. Sloth becomes spite, when it leads to resentment against those who advocate our spiritual development; distraction, when it prompts the heart and mind to turn from the spiritual to the temporal; faintheartedness, when it seeks to avoid doing those things which are spiritually or morally difficult.

Self-examination always bears on one or another of these seven basic egotisms. It is hard to bear—the ego is reluctant to have itself examined. We tend to cheat ourselves through flattery: David begged God to search his heart, knowing that if he did it himself he would overlook serious sins. But self-knowledge is rewarding, for these two things go together: self-revelation and God-revelation. The more a person discovers himself the way he really *is*, the more he feels the need of God, and the more God manifests Himself to such a soul. He becomes singlehearted, easy to understand. The less a person knows himself, the more complex he is: a mind into which self-analysis has never penetrated has a thousand unrelated motives and concerns. Its complexity is due to a want of inner penetration and the failure to bring all things to a focus in a single human goal.

Character grows by leaps and bounds as soon as one has ferreted out the master egotisms and removed the disguises of the superficial self. Self-knowledge is really the reversal of criticism from those around us to ourselves. Observing the neighbor's faults raises our ego; as we depress the ego and face our own predominant fault, the neighbor who before seemed hateful takes on a new lovableness. By losing our own pride and vanity, we gain a world of friends.

9

Putting the Ego in Its Place

AFTER one has discovered the basic defect of the character through self-knowledge, the next step is to put that knowledge into practice by self-discipline. Self-knowledge is diagnosis of the disease; self-discipline is the operation by which the malady is cured. But self-discipline is not only an eradication of evil—it is also a guarding of all the roadways to the real self, lest the enemy again make a foray by another and unsuspected route. For sins, even when they are seen as such, still retain some of their false glamour. This is one of the psychological weaknesses of man which makes virtue difficult for us.

From the beginning of time, the remorseful have asked themselves these questions: "How can I love vice and hate it at the same time?" "Why do I love alcohol and hate being an alcoholic?" "Why do I love being in love and hate the lust that follows?" The answer is: every sin has a double element, material and formal. The material element in sin is its content, or the stuff of which it is made, and this is always good; there is nothing in the visible universe that is intrinsically wicked. "God looked at the world and saw that it was good." Alcohol, flesh, sex, gold, wine—all these things are good and therefore are desirable. All reality, having been created by God, is beautiful, and permeated with Divine reflections of His attributes.

The formal element in a sin is its evil and perverse abuse of a good thing. It is this distortion and exaggerated love of something which makes us misuse it for an evil end; it turns love of flesh into lust, love of alcohol into drunkenness, and love of wealth into avarice. Because man, through an original abuse of his freedom, is now on a lower level than that for which he was created, he has a tendency to pervert all things, as he once perverted and disordered himself.

Sinners look only at the material element of a sin and find it good—as it is. Then, when they have abused its goodness, they turn against God because the effects of this misuse have brought them misery. They forget that God does not forbid the right use of things, but only their abuse. Sinners point to saintly people who enjoy the same good things without ill effects—failing to understand that the saintly use them according to right reason and the Will of God. What the sinner loves in sin is the *matter* of sin, which is good; what the sinner hates in sin is the unhappiness, remorse, melancholy, and sense of defeat which comes from the *perversion* or *abuse* of what is good. He loves sin in the concrete; he hates it in the abstract. This accounts for the psychological feeling of tension and conflict inside of every sinner. The ego wants one thing; the I, another. The ego wants reality to yield to him and to let him enjoy things to excess, without the ensuing remorse.

Because of this inner contradiction, two effects follow: the *first* is a constant anxiety in the soul of the sinner. He loves and hates—he desires and despises. Driven on to further sins by passion or bad habits, he is in a constant agony of self-disgust. As Ovid described it: "I see and approve the better things of life; the worse things of life I follow." St. Paul also mentioned this tension: "The evil which I will not, that I do; the good which I will, that I do not." The soul craves for the Infinite and, seeking it in the wrong place, is disappointed when it gets the finite. It demanded gold, and it received tinsel. This inherent disproportion between one's anticipation of pleasure in a sin and its actual realization intensifies the anxiety; no sin ever realizes its promises. Man tries to escape inner dissatisfaction by more and more pleasures, more and more riches, more and more power—but these things make him hungry and fail to satisfy. The result of increasing wants is an increasing dissatisfaction. Advertising tries to stimulate our sensuous desires, converting luxuries into necessities, but it only intensifies man's inner misery. The business world is bent on creating hungers which its wares never satisfy, and thus it adds to the frustrations and broken minds of our times.

The *second* effect of this contradiction of both loving and hating sin is a worldliness which expresses itself in a hatred of religion; by "the world" here we do not mean the physical world, but the spirit of the world, which gives the primacy to matter, flesh, and time. Of this spirit, Our Lord said: "I am not praying for the world." (John 17:9.) In some cases, the spirit of the world so completely possesses the egotist that it determines his desires, his judgments, his point of view, and his philosophy. Afflictions cast him down; prosperity alone rejoices him. If a desire for holier things enters the heart, it is dethroned before it can begin its reign. The world is in his

soul, but it does not fill it, for his soul was made for something
else.

Very few people realize why they do not always strive
for the higher and the best, nor how they "happened" to fall
into a serious moral lapse. "I cannot understand why I did it,"
they say. The answer is that since human nature lost its original, unspoiled friendship with God, it is deflected from its true
center. The insubordination and rebellion of the will against
Love led to an insubordination of the ego against the I, of the
lower against the higher self—just as, in a machine, when the
main wheel breaks down, all the little wheels, too, cease to
function. The desires and the appetites of man became scattered, disparate, each seeking its own satisfaction regardless of
the welfare of the whole man or of society. Our passions are
constantly threatening rebellion against our reason and our
will. But the will remains in control despite the passions; the
reason of man still has validity despite the rebellion of the
flesh. Man is not intrinsically corrupt.

There are four wounds in human nature which make goodness an effort for us. One wound is in the intellect and reason,
which is somewhat darkened by the Fall and arrives at truth
only with an effort; another wound is in the will, which can
now pursue the highest good only by resisting the appeal of
the lower. The two other wounds are of the passions: one
inclines us to do the easy thing; the other inclines us to avoid
doing what is hard. This means that we are bound to have
temptations to do what is wrong; but the temptations themselves are not sinful, unless our will yields to them. A person
cannot help having a temptation toward lust, any more than
he can prevent the rumbling of his stomach when he is hungry; but he can refuse to commit adultery in the first instance,

or gluttony in the second. The one point to be kept in mind is that no amount of *libido*, or passion, no external force, and no inner prompting to sin can make the human action of man anything but free. We are never tempted beyond our strength. Every moral failure is ours alone, because our choices are our own.

The damaged ego falsely identifies its fulfillment with the *sensate*, and seeks its perfection in what it has, rather than in what the person is or can become. To check the ego's errors, there must be a reversal of attitudes that will reestablish a balance between inner spiritual development and external activity. The ego must be tamed; the old self must be purged; the true I must be released. As St. Paul told the Ephesians: "If true knowledge is to be found in Jesus, you will have learned in His school that you must be quit, now, of the old self whose way of life you remember, the self that wasted its aim on false dreams. There must be a renewal in the inner life of your minds; you must be clothed in the new self, which is created in God's image, justified and sanctified through the truth." (Eph. 4:22,24.)

Self-discipline is necessary because the body and soul, the flesh and the spirit, the ego and the I, each make their demands. The higher self can never emerge unless the ego, or the lower self, is tamed. But self-discipline should not be misunderstood: self-discipline does not require the Puritan's detachment from the evils of the world for the sake of earthly prosperity. Such an attitude has, in history, produced two separate and untouching interests in a society: one was Church on Sunday, and the other was the factory, run six days a week for profit. This division eventually ended in secularism and the complete elimination of the spiritual.

Nor does self-discipline mean Stoicism, or the killing of our passions; for the passions are not wrong—it is only their abuse that is wrong. Passions of and by themselves are not moral, but a-moral, neither good nor bad; the morality depends on the way in which they are used by the intellect and will. Our Lord did not kill the passion of Magdalene, but He transformed it into apostleship, a passion for God; He did not kill the hateful energies of Paul, but directed them into new channels of love and the apostolate.

Self-discipline never means *giving up* anything—for giving up is a loss. Our Lord did not ask us to give up the things of earth, but to exchange them for better things. "For a man's soul, what price can be high enough?" (Mark 8:23.) All exchange involves a decision as to which things we can get along without and which we cannot get along without. We can get along without a dime, but we cannot get along without a loaf of bread, so we exchange the money for the loaf. Some souls find that they can get along without possessions, but they cannot get along without the joy of being free from material cares in order to possess God alone—so they exchange one for the other, and this is done through the Vow of Poverty. Others find they can get along without their own will, but they cannot get along without union with the Will of God—so they exchange one for the other, and this is accomplished by the Vow of Obedience. Others find they can get along without the thrill of the flesh, but not without the ecstasy of the spirit—so they exchange one for the other, and this passionless passion, this inner tranquillity, results from the Vow of Chastity. If asceticism were a genuine giving up, it would be a loss, a reduction of our natures, a narrowing of our lives. But since it is an exchange, it is a realization—a liberation of the true essence of personality from the false attachments to which the ego is prone. Some men are not willing to make even the smallest exchange; they are like the rich young man in the Gospel who "went away sad because he had many possessions." A cowardly patient can refuse to have the operation needed to cure himself of his illness, because he dreads the pain that is the price of health. Knowing of our timidity in undertaking a war against the ego, Our Lord affirmed that the peace He would give would be quite different from the false complacency we dread surrendering: "Peace is my bequest to you, and the peace which I give you is Mine to give; I do not give peace as the world gives it. Do not let your heart be distressed, or play the coward." (John 14:27.)

Self-discipline does not mean self-contempt or destruction of personality, but it rather aims at self-expression in the highest sense of the term. A train is not "self-expressive" when it refuses to follow the roadway laid out for it by an engineer and jumps the track to its own self-destruction. A train is "self-expressive" when it keeps its pressure within determined limits and follows the tracks. A man is not self-expressive when he satisfies his lusts like the beasts; he is "self-expressive" when he orders his passions according to reason and the promptings of the Holy Spirit.

A stream which is divided into many channels has little depth. A mind that has no single purpose in living becomes tired and bored. It is this frittering away of life's energies by many little loves which destroys character. Self-discipline integrates us by deepening the channel of our lives. As St. Thomas Aquinas says: "Man's heart adheres the more intensely to one thing, the more it is withdrawn from others." This gathering of the soul into one focus through self-discipline not only perfects the personality, but it gives a new importance and enjoyment to all other activities of life by arranging them into a pyramid or hierarchy of values, according to their true importance.

Self-discipline is not motivated by a hatred of the world, nor of society, nor of the common good of mankind. It is not indifferent to the world, as Stoic asceticism used to be, nor does it aim at extinction of the self, with Hindu asceticism. Rather its purpose is the salvation of the world through the salvation of souls—betterment of the world through the regeneration of hearts. These Stoic and Hindu asceticisms have this in common: they both end in indifference. One is indifferent to the welfare of society; the other is indifferent to the human personality. The first really glorifies the ego in isolation from its fellow men; the second kills the I for the sake of the great "universal unconsciousness." But true self-discipline makes such a divorce of personality from society impossible. Our Lord said: "For their sakes do I sanctify Myself." Even the Trappists, who leave the world, do not enter upon a life of penance to save themselves, but to save the world. Disinterested, self-sacrificing love transmutes renunciation of the world and service of the world. A heart that surrenders pleasures for the love of God burns with a love for all the men whom God has made. In such detachment the I, working toward the heights, which is God, becomes more lovingly united to the world—as the tree that grows higher must strike deeper roots into the earth.

The purpose of self-discipline is, thus, not to destroy freedom but to perfect it. Freedom does not mean our right to do whatever we like, but to do whatever we ought; a man does not become free as he becomes licentious, but as he diminishes the traces of original sin. Self-denial is a denuding of the ego—it seeks to make the I free to follow God. The more the ego knocks off the chains which bind it to things outside itself, the freer it is to be its own, its I. As the drunkard is liquor-possessed, so the saint is self-possessed. There is a potential nobility or even divinity in all of us, as there is a potential statue in a crude block of marble. But before the marble can ever reveal the image, it must be subjected to the disciplinary actions of a chisel in the hands of a wise and loving Artist, Who knocks off huge chunks of formless egotism until the new and beautiful image of Christ Himself appears.

Self-discipline, then, is not an end in itself but a means to an end. Those who make self-discipline the essence of religion reject some of God's creatures as evil; generally they become proud. But detachment, properly practiced, is only a means of attachment to God. When there is no love of Him, there is no true self-discipline. St. Paul tells us that philanthropy, sacrifice, alms, even martyrdom, if embraced for any reason except love of God does not deserve an eternal reward. "I may give away all that I have, to feed the poor; I may give myself up to be burnt at the stake; if I lack charity, it goes for nothing." (I Cor. 13:3.)

In the romantic order, a youth reveals his love for a girl by a surrender of other women's friendships and a concentration on the beloved. In the spiritual order, the soul reveals its love of God by a detachment from creatures and an attachment to the Creator alone.

In sharp contrast to this way of self-discipline for love of God is the concentration on the ego, or autoeroticism, the beginning of all unhappiness. The present tendency of our age to seek security without effort and to eat food it has not earned

can be very destructive of personality: anything which keeps
the ego safe from hourly efforts, anything which spares it the
task of resistance to sloth, is dangerous to character. Asceticism or self-discipline is necessary to crush selfishness—and it
is not as unnatural as some would believe. As one mounts up
the hierarchy of creation we see an increasing disposition for
change. The chemical element known as H_2O is capable of
only three forms: water, ice, and steam. The plant order has
greater adaptability, a wider potentiality than the chemical.
And animals, because of their powers of locomotion, manifest
a greater capacity for adaptation than anything in the lower
orders of creation. But man himself has the greatest potentiality for conversion of anything in the universe. Not only
can he move about the world freely on the horizontal plane,
but it is even possible for him to mount from the stage of
slavish self-love to the level of a controlled personality and,
finally, to the heights of the Christ-centered life.

But because there is in man a bias toward evil, a downward
pull, a carnal law of gravitation, he has constantly to walk,
even to remain where he is. By merely letting himself go, man
degenerates; neglect, carelessness, self-indulgence, and sin all
result in the loss of self-control. The egotist's unconsciousness of his inner loss of unity—his ignorance of the fact that
his higher faculties have been subjected to the lower—does
not alter the truth. Many a person prides himself on his health
while a hidden and unsuspected cancer undermines his life.
Knowingly or unknowingly, each of us is threatened by this
downward pull of the ego, and all the powers of the mind and
body must cooperate in resistance if the I, or person, is to
remain intact.

This reordering of our natures demands sacrifice in proportion to the former misuse of any sense of the body or power of the mind. There is in modern society a greater potentiality for sacrifice than there has been in many decades. A negative, but none the less certain, sign of it is the readiness with which the youth of Europe in this century flocked to Communism, Nazism, and Fascism, systems which demanded a heroic self-surrender for the sake of the collective. The totalitarian systems show us what great sacrifices modern man will make for even a false ideal. These authoritarian parties demanded much more than ego discipline—they even required the surrender of the person into the collectivity of a race, state, or class. That millions of young people could be found ready to surrender their characters and wills and reasons to a "cause" is an indication of how much men nowadays welcome any reaction against the old liberalism, which allowed every man to do as he pleased. The instinct of the young people of Europe was right; the way in which they satisfied it was wrong. Under the American appearances of materialism and pragmatism, there is also hidden a readiness for sacrifice of another and higher kind; it manifests itself in the disgust of the young with the excesses of ease and comfort their elders enjoy, and in the increased number of those who seek complete detachment from the world and of a life of contemplation in a monastery, such as the Trappists.

This latent readiness for sacrifice in man has profound roots in our natural knowledge of God. We see God as opposed to the clutter of "things." Human reason actually knows more about what God is not, than about what He is; natural theology describes God in terms of eternity, which is the negation of time; in terms of immensity, which is the negation of space; and also by eliminating all imperfections from such

universal concepts as justice, truth, beauty, and love. Supernatural revelation gives a more positive insight into the Divine
Nature, but even on the plane of reason alone, man sees that
by the negation of certain things in this world, he comes closer
to God. There is a parallel between the knowledge of God by
negation and our movement or action toward God by self-
discipline. Man senses the paradox that if he gets closer to the
nothingness from which he came, he will grow closer to the
supreme Principle of Life, and Truth, and Love, Who created
him. God made man from nothing. Therefore, to the extent
that man by an act of humility *nothings* himself, he begins to
recover and to find himself in the God Who made him. As
the ego, which is the affirmation of his false divinity, vanishes,
the I, which was created by Divinity, begins to appear and to
show its readiness to be divinized by a participation in the
Divine Nature, which is called Grace.

In studying painting, we view the work of masters rather
than of dabblers—and so in studying self-discipline, the great
artists of the spiritual life will have more to tell us than the
psychologists. St. Augustine is one such master; he was afraid
to surrender his ego, which had disintegrated by love of the
flesh. As he put it:

"I do not press on to enjoy Him; and so—though Thy
beauty caught me to Thee—I was anon torn away from Thee
by my own weight and fell back with sorrow to the lower
sphere. That weight was carnal custom. Yet Thou didst live
on still in my memory; and I never doubted that there was
One to Whom I might speed, though I was not yet such as
could speed to Him . . . . I could not keep my gaze on Thee.
My weakness threw me back and I was cast back upon my accustomed ways of life, bearing with me naught but a loving
memory."

After having had an intellectual conversion from Manichaeanism, a moral conversion from a life of egotism, and a spiritual conversion to Christ, the convert sees life as a battle between the two loves of men: the love of ego and the love of God. Or he may, with St. Augustine, see the world as divided into two cities:

"Two loves therefore have given origin to these two cities—self-love in contempt of God unto the earthly; love of God and contempt of oneself to the heavenly. The first seeketh the glory of men, and the latter desires God only, as the testimony of the conscience, the greatest glory. The former glories in itself, and the latter in God. The one exalteth itself in its own glory; the other sayeth to God, 'my glory and the lifter up of my head.' The one boasteth of the ambitious conquerors led by the lust of sovereignty; the other, everyone serveth his neighbor in charity . . . . The one city is seated in worldly possessions; the other in heavenly hopes; both coming out of the common gate of mortality, which was opened in Adam, out of whose condemned progeny, as out of a putrefied lump, God made some vessels of mercy, and some of wrath; giving due pains unto the one, and undue grace unto the other, that the citizens of God upon earth may take this lesson from those vessels of wrath never to rely on their own election, but hope to call upon the name of the Lord."

Hugh of St. Victor gives another metaphor for the resistance of the ego to the Grace of God:

"Damp wood kindles slowly under fire, but a strong breeze will fan it into flames with black clouds of smoke. Little by little the smoke is dissipated, as the moisture drys up, and the blaze spreads freely over the whole crackling pile . . . till the wood is wholly changed into the likeness of fire . . . then the crackling ceases . . . nothing is to be seen save the

victorious fire, glowing in the profound peace of great silence
. . . . First fire and flame and smoke; then the fire and the
flames, but smoke no more; last of all, pure fire, with neither
flame nor smoke. As is the damp wood, so are our carnal
hearts . . . touch them with the spark of the fear of God, or
Divine Love, and the great clouds of evil passions and rebellious desires roll upwards. Then the soul grows stronger; the
flame of love burns more hotly and brightly; the smoke of
passion dies down; and the purified spirit rises to the contemplation of Truth. Last of all, triumphant contemplation fills
the heart with Truth; we have reached the very source of the
sovereign Truth and been enfolded thereby, and neither
trouble nor anxiety cut the heart more. It has found peace and
rest."

St. Thomas in his cold and profoundly philosophical approach teaches the same lesson by inquiring into the true
nature of man. After having eliminated as our proper goals the
love of wealth and honor, sexual license, and other forms of
selfishness, he affirms that the true end of the I, or personality,
is the contemplation of truth. But this is impossible to see
without giving up our ego-centric habits and turning away
from the worldly distractions which veil its discovery.

"Hence the last end for men is the contemplation of truth.
This alone is distinctive of his nature, and no other corporeal
being shares it with him. Nor is there any end beyond it, for
the contemplation of truth is an end in itself. Hereby man is
united in likeness with the superior spirits, because this alone
of all activity is common to God and the angels as well . . . .
And to this end, all other human activities seem directed. For
perfect contemplation, we require bodily health, which is
secured by all such artificial contrivances as are necessary for

life. We require freedom from the perturbation of the passions—a goal attained by the moral virtues and by prudence. We require freedom from external perturbation—a freedom at which the entire organization of civil government aims. So, if you look at the matter rightly, all human occupations appear to be directed to the needs of those who contemplate truth."

It cannot be stressed too much that in this passage the great thinker, speaking of self-discipline, does not regard either the body or the passions themselves as evil; it is only the abuse of these passions which he condemns. Bodily passions and temporal goods, though they do not constitute the whole of human perfection, are genuinely a part of it. Even in its glorified state after the resurrection, the body will be necessary for the well-being of the soul, and the glory of the soul will overflow the glory of the body, so that it, too, may have its heavenly inheritance.

10

Self-Discipline

As self-love or egotism is the root of all unhappiness, so the elimination of it is the beginning of joy. Because ego-centrism isolates one from society, the discipline of the ego restores fellowship. To associate with our fellows, we must accept the conditions friendship lays down—and the first of these is that we cease to live solely for our own selfish pleasures. Nothing in the natural order is more certain to increase happiness than the doing away with self-love. Granted the necessity of asceticism, the problem of putting it into operation arises.

Self-discipline can be applied as a remedy to six different possibilities of evil: (1) the occasion of sin, (2) the dominant passion, (3) the external senses, (4) the internal senses, (5) the intellect, (6) the will.

1. *Occasions of sin* mean those places, and persons, and

circumstances which constitute the environment favorable to the development of self-love. For the alcoholic, it might be a bar, a certain home, or a boon companion; for the erotic, a certain person; for the scandalmonger, a gossip who always has scandal to trade. As a wise and cautious traveler, looking ahead, avoids obstacles in his path, so does the man who is on the way to heaven deliberately avoid those things which interfere with the development of his character and union with God. Many a soul who once had faith and lost it, and many men who no longer have well-integrated personalities in the natural order, can trace their loss of peace of soul and peace of mind to evil companionship or to an environment which robbed them of their heritage. Sacred Scripture warns us that "he that loveth danger shall perish in it."

2. By the *dominant passion* is meant some violent movement of our sensitive appetite toward a sensate good. Not bad in itself, it is so strong in us that, uncurbed, it may occasion sin. These passions are numerous. *Love* is a yearning for a person or thing which delights and pleases us; and when we love, we crave either possession or unity. *Hatred* is only love upside down. All hatred is born of love, because we hate that which in any way endangers our love. For example, we hate disease because we love health, and hatred is, at bottom, an eagerness to rid ourselves of whatever displeases us. *Desire* is an urge or quest for an absent good, and it is born of love for another good, which may be a thing or a person. *Aversion* is the passion which makes us shun or repel some proximate or approaching evil, and *joy* is the passion of satisfaction which arises from the present possession of any good. *Sadness* is grief over an evil or a disaster which is present. *Courage* or *daring* is the passion which makes us strive after

some lovable good, whose possession is difficult or arduous. *Despair* is the passion which arises in the soul when possession or union with the loved object seems impossible. Finally, *anger* is that passion which violently repels what hurts us and incites in us the desire for revenge.

It need hardly be repeated that all of these passions, when well ordered, are God-given. Our Blessed Lord experienced many of them. Not only did He love us with His Whole Will and His Whole Heart, but He also wept over the city of Jerusalem and shed tears at the death of Lazarus; He aroused Himself to righteous indignation and anger when He drove the buyers and the sellers out of the Temple; He felt fear and anxiety when He went into the Garden of Gethsemane, and yet all of these passions were so disciplined that they were used to purchase our salvation.

The dominant passion differs from individual to individual. Egotism often takes advantage of this fact to flatter itself that it is not vicious, because it does not have the disordered passion of its neighbor. The dominant passion is always the one to which we are most naturally inclined, and also the one whose discipline we resist the most. Because it impels the ego to inordinate affections, it is always the source of much disquietude.

It must be repeated that, as the love of drink is good, but not drunkenness, and as the imagination is good, but not planned murder, so the passions are good, because they are made by God. But the use of a passion is not good when it is directed toward an evil end, or even toward a good end with too much vehemence. When the emotions are regulated by right reason, they beget courage, bravery, and zeal. Nothing worth while is ever accomplished without passion—and the basic passion of all is love. But if our passions have taken command of us, they constantly clamor to be satisfied and make us very unhappy; for the more they are satisfied, the more they become dissatisfied. When the passions are regulated and tamed, are made subservient to virtue, they become like a horse with a bit in his mouth. Love of ownership can thus be restrained by an occasional practice of frugality and generosity, lest our money possess us instead of our possessing our money; the passion for applause will be tamed by the practice of humility and anonymity, in which we seek to have good deeds known only by God. The passion for the body will be tempered by a consciousness that its highest destiny is to be a Temple of God; not only will it have its occasion for pleasure and feasting but, since it is God's, it will bend its knees in reverence, fold its hands in prayer, and bend its head in adoration.

3. Since the *external senses* offer another danger to us, the man of God will mortify his eyes from those things which might lead him into temptation. As he turns his eyes from a too brilliant light lest it destroy vision, so he diverts his eyes from evil, too, lest he find it too attractive. As the worldling turns a deaf ear to words that hurt his egotisms, so the saint will refuse to listen to anything that flatters his egotism, or incites strife against his neighbor, or provokes enmity and suspicion. The well-regulated I will deny itself not only what is unlawful, but even some things that are legitimate, in order to remain complete master of itself. The extra cigarette, the second cocktail—sometimes even the first—are denied, in order to preserve the spiritual freedom of the soul. If, at the end of each day, a person could look back on three tiny acts of self-denial, he would already be on the way to a happy inner life. St. Paul

said: "You must deaden, then, those passions in you which belong to earth, fornication and impurity, lust and evil desire, and that love of money which is an idolatry." (Col. 3:5.)

Since it is through the external senses that ideas enter the mind, it follows that our state of mind is the result of our own choices as to what things we will allow inside. Every impression is a preparation for an expression. The basis of our ideas has entered the mind through the senses, and the basis of our actions has been absorbed in the same manner. Our Divine Saviour recommended that we avoid the future sin by barring its entrance to the mind through the senses. "He who casts his eyes on a woman so as to lust after her has already committed adultery with her in his heart. If thy right eye is the occasion of thy falling into sin, pluck it out and cast it away from thee." (Matt. 5:28.)

This principle of self-discipline is not the hygienic one, which prevents only the physical effects of evil; Our Lord concentrates on the elimination of the evil at its source, before it ever gets into the mind or will. If a man wishes to concentrate while reading, he must shut out the disturbing sounds about him. So if he is to integrate his personality, there must be such a deliberate closing out of those sensations which cannot contribute to his well-being. St James, speaking of the harm the tongue has done through detraction, scandalmongering, and lies, writes:

"How small a spark it takes to set fire to a vast forest! And that is what the tongue is, a fire. Among the organs of our nature, the tongue has its place as the proper element in which all that is harmful lives. It infects the whole body, and sets fire to this mortal sphere of ours, catching fire itself from hell. Mankind can tame, and has long since learned to tame, every

kind of beast and bird, of creeping thing and all else; but no
human being has ever found out how to tame the tongue; a
pest that is never allayed, all deadly poison. We use it to bless
God Who is our Father; we use it to curse our fellow men,
that were made in God's image; blessing and cursing come
from the same mouth. My brethren, there is no reason in this.
Does the fountain gush out fresh and salt water from the same
outlet? What, my brethren, can a fig tree yield olives, or a
vine figs? No more easily will brackish water yield fresh."

4. The *internal senses*, too, can trouble us. The imagination
and memory need to be rid of their bad habits. Daydreaming,
which leads to laziness, the entertaining of images which, if
carried into action, would be sinful, the recalling to our
memory of the wrongs our neighbor did us—eliminating these
will prepare for the emergence of character. If left untamed,
our thoughts can choke the real self. There are some who
think they have "lived" when they have tasted the dregs of
life. The contrary is true; the innocent, who have kept their
memory of the past free from evil and their imagination free
from fears, are those who really live. As Charles Péguy wrote
in his "Innocence and Experience":

It is innocence that is full and experience that is empty.
It is innocence that wins and experience that loses.

It is innocence that is young and experience that is old.
It is innocence that grows and experience that wanes.

It is innocence that is born and experience that dies.
It is innocence that knows and experiences that does not know.

It is the child that is full and the man who is empty,
Empty as an empty gourd and as an empty barrel;

Now then, children, go to school.
And you men, go to the school of life.
Go and learn
How to unlearn.

5. The *intellect* has to be curbed, as well. The direction our passions take will depend on our ideals. If we lack a goal in life, our passions run us; thus even the higher faculties need discipline. A detached spirit will not waste time on the slack reading of foolish romances or in gathering useless information, but it will aim at truth. As Plato wrote in the *Phaedo:*

"When the soul is dragged by the body into the region of the changeable and wanders and is confused, the world spins around her and she is like a drunkard. But when she contemplates in herself and by herself, then she passes into the other world, the world of purity and eternity and immortality and unchangeableness which are her kindred; and with them she ever lives, when she is by herself and is not let or hindered; then she ceases from her erring ways and being in communion with the unchanging is unchanging. And this state of soul is called wisdom."

The intellect is disciplined by serious reading and by a profound study of human nature in those around us. This implies a spirit of mind which fosters altruism and love of neighbor: knowledge is always to be put at the service of love. As St. Augustine said: "Let knowledge be used in order to erect the structure of love." Purification of the intellect is rarely practiced today. No one would allow garbage at his table, but many allow it served into their minds. Unless a mind watches closely over what goes into it, it will not be long before his hodgepodge of journalistic information has come to seem an absolute, and he will consider himself a great thinker without having even read the greater thinkers of our race. Soon the false ideas will pass into act, for it makes a tremendous amount of difference what a man thinks about. The movies, the newspapers, advertising, and the radio pour into the intellect confused and contradictory ideas which will produce confused lives unless the intellect, in the light of Faith, keeps many of them out. Anyone who has lived without a newspaper or radio for thirty days has experienced peace from not having to read the news of discord, strife, war, murder, and divorce. A little effort to form sound reading tastes will convince the mind that it was made to know Truth, as the eye was made to see light, and that the ultimate in Truth is Charity. As St. Bernard wrote: "There are those who wish to know for the purpose of knowing a great deal, and that is curiosity; some that they may know, and that is vanity; some that they may sell their knowledge and this is base gain; some that they may be edified, and this is prudence; some that they may edify and this is charity."

6. The *will* particularly needs to be disciplined, for it tells the body what acts to perform. The intellect gives the target, but the will shoots the arrows. The disciplined will shows its strength in the way it governs the passions, emotions, and senses. Weak wills are usual among those who have no ideals, no goal in life, those whose decisions are wholly capricious, who are influenced by human respect and the bad *example* of others, who decide by what everybody else is doing.

The will is the governor of the soul and body. It is the seat of all motivation and, therefore, the root of character. For motive determines the goodness of our acts. Two men can do exactly the same thing—for example, give alms. But one will do it because he gets his name in the paper, and the other because he sees Christ in the poor; the amount given may be the same, but the motivation which came from the will was very different. So it it is with dieting and fasting. There is no material difference between a woman losing ten pounds by fasting and ten pounds by dieting, but there is a world of difference in the effect on the character. Dieting is done for the sake of the body; fasting is done for the sake of the soul. Dieting is done for the ego; fasting is done for charity, and to tame the body that the soul may be freer in its flight toward God.

It requires great effort to make the will supple and responsive always to the highest ideals. Some people fail because they lack sufficient knowledge of what life is all about; never having disciplined their intellects to the way of truth, they are without markers on the roadway of life. Others start self-discipline too rigidly and with overeagerness, and fail as a result of too much hurry and the ensuing discouragement of finding that full sanctity is not achieved at once. (It is a generally accepted truth in religious societies that those postulants who complain about the want of opportunities for sacrifice are generally those who do not persevere.) Others fail in their attempt to discipline the will because their ego is so strong that they cannot bear the thought of any failure. But any will can be trained; if there is genuine humility after a fall, and a renewed prayer for God's grace, then self-possession begins to be a habit, and the most difficult things become easy, in time. There comes a renewed sense of power and self-mastery and self-control, and the delightful realization that one at last has true freedom. One is no longer other-controlled, but self-controlled. Freedom is not so much a birthright, as it is an achievement. We are born with freedom of choice, but the way we use our choices makes us slaves or free men. Inner freedom of this kind is the last thing a man attains, and it is what St. Paul calls the "glorious liberty of the children of God."

As physical life is the sum of forces that resist death, so spiritual life is the result of constant purification of those sinful impulses that would drag us down. Unless the I is constantly at the helm, we become idolizers of comfort, obsessed with the fear of ever doing anything unpleasant.

Purification rids us of the dead weight of evil habits and the ballast of the flesh. The soul then becomes more and more free, and derives a greater pleasure than it ever guessed was possible. As St. Thomas says: "Men must have pleasures. If they will not have the joys of the spirit, then they will degenerate into pleasure of the body." Unless there is some other interest to compensate for the loss of a surrendered pleasure, minds become cynical and bitter with an increasing desire to be coddled, respected, honored, and made the center of attention. Egotists find it hard to change, because the egotist refuses to postpone satisfaction. Overfed, overupholstered, double-chinned, he refuses to accept a few moments of pain through self-control—and thus misses a joy in this life and an eternal life beyond. A life of detachment, looked at from the outside, seems a *living death*, but once begun it is found to be a *dying life*; for each new death of selfishness, like the seed falling to the ground, brings forth a corresponding life. There are no short cuts to spirituality; pain and purification go hand in hand, for sin is not easily discarded. Purification never means crushing our wills in order to become will-less; but the will, detached from the dead weight of sin, more readily flies to union with the Will Divine. When one gets down to rock bottom, one soon discovers that the principal reason souls do not come to God is not only because they are ignorant, but because they are also bad; it is their behavior which creates the biggest obstacle to belief, however vigorously they deny it. "You will not come to Me to find life." (John, 5:40.) Associated with this reluctance toward sacrifice is an unwillingness to renounce pride and a refusal to immolate the heart. This absence of humility and sacrificial love stands like a wall between the soul and God; when it hears the Divine Command, it pleads to God, Who was similarly rejected by the man who bought a farm, "Have me excused, O Lord."

But this reluctance is not universal. Many weary souls would come to God if the faith were presented to them the hard way instead of the easy way: by an appeal to self-sacrifice, rather than an appeal to understanding. There is a far greater readiness for sacrifice on the part of the modern mind than some members of Christ's Mystical Body perceive. The good qualities of the modern soul have been under-estimated, and many would be surprised at its reaction, if shown the pierced Hands and Feet of Christ and asked: "How did They get that way?" There is a greater yearning for sacrifice in the hearts and minds of men than at any time in the last five hundred years. Whence came the heroism of soldiers during the war—at a time when we all were supposed to have been softened by luxury and ease—if it was not because this potential for sacrifice was always there in the depths of their hearts? The world is now tired of a broad-mindedness which is as cold as a miser's heart and as spineless as a filet of sole; it wants to catch fire, to feel the burning heat of its passions, and, above all, to love even to the point of death. When pagans receive the gift of Faith, they often surpass the so-called devout in self-denial and in love of God.

Because the joys of union with God cannot be experienced

without willing pain, and because the soul without Faith has a capacity for sacrifice, Divine Truth should be presented to modern men as the Saviour made His appeal—by a summons to sacrifice. He asked His followers to sell the field to gain the pearl of great price and to leave their nets and boats to become fishers of men. Everyone without Faith is in pain; where there are no broken bodies, there are agonized minds, restless, fearful, and anxious. Our generation may well be the most unhappy that has lived during the history of Christianity. Suffering is universal; and suffering is never far from sacrifice. A toothache in a saint is no different from a toothache in an evil man—what makes the difference between suffering and sacrifice is the love of God. Sacrifice without the love of God is only suffering; suffering with the love of God becomes sacrifice. The Trappist monk who gets out of bed at two o'clock in the morning to pray for the sins of the world is undergoing the same discomfort as the victim of insomnia who gets up to take a stiff drink; but what a difference in the attitude of the soul! It may well be that modern souls are already suffering enough—perhaps too much—but the pain is all wasted. Either they do not turn it into merit by offering it to God, or they complain with defiance and rebellious protests: "Why should God do this to me?" A wedge must be driven between their actual pain and their potential sacrifice by bringing to them some understanding of a Love, Who suffered everything, so that we might never say: "He does not know what it is to suffer." Like the young man who obeyed the Commandments but refused to give up his possessions, Our Lord may say of them that they are not far from the Kingdom of God.

To convert a pain into a sacrifice demands the surrender of

the intellect and the will to God as a first condition. The
intellect must become docile to Divine Truth, less intent on
saying: "Now, this is *my* idea of religion." The will must see
all that happens to it as coming from the hands of an all-loving
Father Who could only desire the complete happiness of His
children in eternity—although not necessarily in time. For, as
He said: "In the world ye shall have tribulations." (John
16:33.)

The oblation of the soul becomes the condition of changing
an agony into sacrifice, and this is not easy. It costs something
to come to God, as it cost God something to come to us.
When God asks for sacrifice, some complain; when a trial
comes, they rebel; when a temptation assaults, they surrender.
Indeed, belief is a yoke, as the Saviour said, but it is a yoke that
is sweet and a burden that is light. At the moment when one
must decide between the selfish ego and the Divine "Thou,"
when the finite within and the Infinite without wrestle as
Jacob with the angels, there is an agony of soul; but when
it is over, the soul has passed from agony to joy, from emo-
tionalism to Faith. The true believer can become a hero by
even a single decision, for in cooperation with God's Grace he
can pass from darkness to light.

The burden of bringing Divine Light to the unhappy
egotist is a task for the faithful. A few sacrificial leaders who
would spend themselves, and be spent, for the cause of Christ
would do more good to the world than thousands of dis-
courses on civil rights. Too many today are substituting action
for prayer, are trying to change other people instead of changing themselves. Some are like Peters who are bidden to pray—
and then when the enemy comes into the Garden turn, instead, to action; they draw out a sword to hack off an ear,

which the Good Lord later has to replace to make up for their stupidity.

All souls have, in themselves, the purchase price of joy; it is the present agony, misery, boredom, and ennui of their hearts. But like a child before a store window with a copper penny in his hand and the delirious vision of the candy within, they may miss the delirium of the sweets, because they refuse to give up the dirty coin. The coin is self-will, egotism, and selfishness. The candy is peace, and love, and joy.

II

Emergence of Character

EVERYONE in the world is defeated in one area of life or another. Some fall away from their high ideals; others bemoan their failure to marry or, having married, lament because the state failed to realize all its hopes and promises; others experience a decline of virtue, a gradual slipping-away into mediocrity, or a slavery to vice; others are subjected to weariness, a failure of health, or economic ruin. All these disappointments are voiced in the mournful regret: "If I only had my life to live over again!" But it is of the utmost importance that, in facing our defeats and failures, we shall never yield to discouragement; for discouragement, from a spiritual point of view, is the result of wounded self-love and is therefore a form of pride.

We all have to accept failure; we do not all have to lament it. It is interesting to contrast the Christian's proper attitude toward defeat with the pagan's; the unbeliever's set-backs end in pessimism, for, deluded by false optimism and its doctrine of inevitable progress, he had never visualized the disappointment he has met. H. G. Wells, who for years glorified the prospects of human progress through science with its test tubes and its evolution, ended his life saying: "In spite of all my dispositions to a brave looking optimism, I perceive that now the universe is bored with man, is turn-ing a hard face to him, and I see him being carried less and less intelligently and more and more rapidly . . . along the stream of fate to degradation, suffering, and death." (*The Fate of Homo Sapiens.*) But the Christian has never expected this earth to be his paradise; he has ever before him the words of the Saviour: "In the world, ye shall have tribulation." For this reason, Christianity alone can answer defeat, wherever it comes—for Christianity was born in defeat: in the world-shattering defeat of Good Friday. One lesson of the Cross is that although we cannot prevent some kinds of defeat, we can always prevent a wrong reaction to defeat. "Meanwhile, we are well assured that everything helps to secure the good of those who love God, those whom He has called in fulfill-ment of his design."

We can actually defeat defeat—use our failures as assets and our sins as steppingstones to sanctity. This Christian at-titude stands in sharp contrast to the methods of education. Education takes hold of what is best in a person, e.g., a talent for music, a gift for invention, or a taste for literature and develops that, to the exclusion of the arts and sciences for which we have no bent. And this is proper—we do not want our sculptors forced to specialize in law. A man's vocation is decided to a great extent by his capabilities.

But character training, on the contrary, takes as deep an interest in a person's greatest lacks as in his greatest gifts. It singles out his predominant failing and, by fighting against it, finally perfects the personality in the virtue contrary to the previous vice.

The first step in character training, then, is to discover what is worst in us. This is done by an examination of the sin to which we are most frequently tempted. It is very wrong to think that, because we are tempted, we are wicked. Sacred Scripture tells us: "Consider yourselves happy indeed, my brethren, when you encounter trials of every sort, as men who know well enough that the testing of your faith breeds endurance." (James 1:2.) The blessedness of temptation is twofold. It reveals the weak spot in our character, showing us where to be on guard; and the same temptation gives us an occasion for gaining merit by refusing to submit to it. Self-examination reveals the basic defect in each man's character, what is known as his predominant fault. The predominant fault is the one which prevails over all other faults and to some extent inspires our attitude, judgments, and sympathies; every individual temperament, despite its variegated expressions, generally follows one consistent line. *Natura determinatur ad unum.* Some persons are inclined principally to sensuality, others to laziness, others to anger; others have a tendency to allow gentleness to degenerate into effeminacy or force into cruelty. It makes little difference that the hidden evil may be in the most remote corner of the heart; it may have been covered from others' sight, but the mind cannot help being aware that it is there. No spiritual progress can be made until the master fault is dug up from its hiding place, brought into the light, and laid before God. For until the position of the enemy is known, he cannot be attacked.

The secret of character training is to strengthen this weak spot in our character in cooperation with God's Grace. The evil must be called by its right and ugly name when it is discovered; otherwise we shall excuse our lack of fortitude as an "inferiority complex" and our inordinate love of the flesh as a "release of the libido." Judas missed salvation because he never called his avarice by its right name—he disguised it as love of the poor.

Considerable probing is necessary to drag out the predominant fault; it always fights against being recognized. Sometimes the master sin can be detected by discovering what defect makes us most angry when we are accused of it: the traitor flies into a rage when he is first accused of being disloyal to his country. The sin we most loudly and vehemently condemn in others may be the sin to which our own heart is most addicted: Judas, again, accused Our Lord Himself of not loving the poor enough. As Aristotle wisely remarked: "Every man judges of what is good according to the goodness or badness of his interior disposition." If we confront the world with the idea that every man is dishonest, it is amazing how often that initial bias will be confirmed. It is a well-known fact that investigators of sex habits are sought out by those who are conspicuous for such sins and are avoided by the pure. This is because, just as water seeks its own level, so does the mind seek the level of its prejudice. Thieves consort with thieves; drunkards with drunkards; the prejudiced with the prejudiced.

The predominant fault is discoverable not only in the environment it keeps, or in the atmosphere it breathes, but also in the way that others act toward us. Nature acts as it is acted upon; be suspicious of a neighbor, and the neighbor acts suspiciously. Show love to others, and everyone seems lovable.

The law of physics that every action has a contrary and equal reaction has its psychological counterpart. If we sow the seed of distrust in society, society always returns the harvest of distrust. The emotional reprises of others can be used as the mirror of our own interior dispositions.

Once one has discovered the master sin through any of these methods, the next step is to combat the interior defect. This requires a daily, even hourly struggle; sanctification is not a *place* at which one arrives but a *way* one travels. There are generally four ways of overcoming the predominant fault: (1) By asking God in prayer to illumine the dark places of the soul and to give us strength to conquer the sin. As the Council of Trent says: "God never commands the impossible; but in giving us His precepts, He commands us to do what we can, and to ask for the Grace to accomplish what we cannot do." (2) By daily examination of conscience. Almost everyone counts the money in his pockets daily to determine whether the current expense of the day can be met; but how few of us ever balance the conscience to see if we are going into debt morally and spiritually? (3) By imposing on oneself a penance, every time we succumb to the predominant fault, e.g., by saying a prayer for the absent person against whom we bore false judgment, or by giving five times the amount of a cocktail to the poor every time we are tempted to intoxication by the first drink. (4) By making the predominant fault the occasion of a greater virtue.

This fourth method is one which is too often ignored, although strength of character cannot be had without a knowledge of our weakness and the ultimate mastery of it. "My strength finds its full scope in thy weakness." (II Cor. 12:9.) The storm reveals the weakness in the roof: but the part of it that was damaged and repaired is apt, later, to be the strongest. Scar tissue is the strongest skin of all. Kites and airplanes rise against the wind, not with it. Earth does not reveal its harvest without plowing, nor the minds their treasure without study, nor nature its secrets without investigation. The defect, overcome, may become the greatest strength.

Goodness is too often confused with passivity. There are a number of people who are considered to be good, when really they have not enough courage to do either a very good or a very evil act of any kind. But character does not depend on a want of energy to do wrong; it requires the use of great energy in doing right when wrong solicits us. The greatest sinners sometimes make the greatest saints: a Saul who hated became a Saul who loved—a sensuous Magdalene became a spiritual Magdalene. The convents and monasteries are full of potential devils—saintly souls who could have been very wicked men and women, in their vitality, if they had not corresponded to God's Grace. Little St. Thérèse said that if she had not been responsive to God's mercies she would have been one of the most evil women who ever lived. On the other hand, the prisons of our country house a population of potential saints; the energy the criminals used in sinning was not wrong—it was the use to which they put their energy that was wrong. Lenin was probably a saint in reverse; if he had used his energy in violence toward self and the cultivation of love, instead of in violence toward others and the cultivation of hate, he could have become the St. Francis of the nineteenth century.

Some years ago, a young boy was badly burned in an explosion at his country school and was told he would never walk again. Instead of becoming discouraged, he concentrated on his infirmity, rubbed his legs, exercised them, then walked, and finally became one of the greatest mile runners in the history of America. This boy's power was made perfect in infirmity. Demosthenes not only stuttered in his youth, but he had a weak voice; he would never have become one of the world's greatest orators had he not worked to correct this weakness, transforming it into his greatest strength. Abraham Lincoln was defeated in almost every office for which he ran—until he was elected President of the United States. When Ludwig von Beethoven became deaf, he said, "What a sorrowful life I must lead"; then, rising above the first defeat, he said, "I will seize facts by the throat," and wrote great music he could never hear. When Milton went blind, he used his blindness itself as the inspiration for one of his finest poems.

Apply this valiant spirit to the spiritual life; here, too, the handicaps can be a spur. It is a basic fact that no saint ever found it easy to be good; to believe differently is the great mistake most people make in judging them. The law running through heaven and earth is that "the athlete will win no crown, if he does not observe the rules of the contest." (II Tim. 2:5.) The Church never canonizes anyone unless he has shown a degree of holiness which is called heroic—and the virtues of the saints were the *opposites* of the natural weaknesses they had to overcome. The special quality of soul which might have made someone else a devil gave the saints their greatest opportunities for growth. The moral quality always associated with Moses is meekness—but Moses was not born meek; he was probably hotheaded, quick-tempered, and irascible. For Moses killed an Egyptian—and that is not the mark of a meek man. He was also the first one to "break" the Ten

Commandments; coming down from the Mount where he had conversed with God, he found his people adoring the Golden Calf and, in a fit of anger, smashed the Tablets of the Law. Anger is not meek; the weak spot in Moses was his hotheadedness. But this man turned the worst in him into the best, so that later on—in his conduct toward the fickleness of Pharaoh, in his attitude toward the ingratitude and waywardness of those whom he delivered, in his bearing toward his family, in his final disappointment at not entering the Promised Land—he maintained such an even temper that Sacred Scripture describes him as "a man exceedingly meek." (Num. 12:3.) Moses acquired meekness by fighting against an evil temper. He rooted out the worst in him; and then, with God's help, he became one of the best of men.

In the New Testament, the character most often praised for charity is John; toward the end of his life, he preached incessantly on the theme, "Love one another." John describes himself as the "beloved disciple," and to him was given the privilege of leaning on the breast of Our Divine Savior on the night of the Last Supper. But John was not always so loving. He once tried to play politics through his mother, getting her to ask Our Lord to give him and his brother the seats closest to Our Lord when He came into His Kingdom. Charity does not try to dominate or rule. On another occasion, when the city of the Samaritans rejected Our Lord, John and his brother, James, asked Our Lord to rain down fire from heaven to destroy the city. Charity is not vengeance. There must, in truth, have been a tendency toward hatred in John, for his Master called him a Son of Thunder. But at some time or other in John's life, he *seized* upon the weak spot in his character—upon his want of kindness to his fellow man—and

through cooperation with Grace he became the greatest
Apostle of Charity, the virtue he had lacked before.

Matthew, who wrote the first Gospel, is another example
of the way that character can be made strongest at its weakest
point. If there is any one quality that stands out predominantly
in this Gospel, it is Matthew's love of Israel; he was one of
the greatest patriots who ever lived. But do not think that he
came by patriotism easily; the weak spot in his nature was
his want of this very love of country. Matthew was the first
Quisling of Christian history: he sold out his own people to
the Romans, collected exorbitant taxes from his fellow citizens
for their overlords, becoming rich as a collaborator of an invader. One day when he was collecting the hated taxes, Our
Lord said to him, "Come, follow Me"—and Matthew left his
customs house, and followed the Lord, and became one of the
greatest of all patriots. In his Gospel, Matthew goes back
ninety-nine times to recall the glories of his people, quoting
from David, Isaias, Jeremias, Ezechiel, and at the end he
exults—"Israel! This is your glory! This is your crown! From
our own Law and our people has come the Lord and Savior
of the World." Matthew became a patriot when he found
his God. By overcoming his weak spot with the aid of God's
strength, he became strong; power is made perfect in infirmity.

The temptations of the saints were seen as opportunities for
self-discovery. They allowed temptations to show them the
breaches in the fortress of their souls which needed to be
fortified until they would become the strongest points. This
explains the curious fact about many saintly people—that they
often become the opposite of what they once seemed to be.
When we hear of the holiness of some souls, our first reaction
is: "I knew him when. . . . " Between the "then" and the
"now" has intervened a battle in which selfishness lost and

faith won out. They followed the advice of Paul: "Let us rid ourselves of all that weighs us down, of the sinful habit that clings closely." (Heb. 12:1.) They became what they were not.

Because the development of character requires constant vigilance, our occasional failures must not be mistaken for the desertion of God. Two attitudes are possible in sin—two attitudes can be taken toward our laspses into sin: we can fall down, and get up; or we can fall down, and stay there. The fact of having fallen once should not discourage us; because a child falls, it does not give up trying to walk. As sometimes the mother gives the most attention to the child who falls the most, so our failures can be used as a prayer that God be most attentive to *us*, because of our greater weaknesses. I always liked the incident of the life of St. Mary Magdalen de Pazzi. One day while dusting a small statute of Our Lord in the chapel, she dropped it on the floor. Picking it up unbroken, she kissed it, saying: "If you had not fallen, you would not have gotten that." Sometimes, in the case of a continued weakness, it is well to count not only the falls, but to count also the number of times a temptation to do wrong was overcome. The reverses we suffer in the heat of battle can lead us to strengthen our purposes.

The trials and temptations of life prove that in each individual there is an actual I-potential. The "actual ego" is what I am now, as a result of letting myself go. The "possible I" is what I can become through sacrifice and resistance to sin. Persons are like those ancient palimpsests or parchments, on which a second writing covered over the first; the original gloss of sin and selfishness has to be scraped off before we can be illuminated with the message of Divinity.

No character or temperament is fixed. To say "I am what I

am, and that I must always be," is to ignore freedom, Divine
Action in the soul, and the reversibility of our lives to make
them the opposite of what they are. In baptizing the Duke of
the Franks, the Bishop reminded him of how he could reverse
his past: "Bend your proud head, Sicambre; adore that which
thou hast burned and burn that which thou hast adored." No
character, regardless of the depths of its vice or its intemperance, is incapable of being transformed through the cooperation of Divine and human action into its opposite, of
being lifted to the I-level and then to the Divine level.
Drunkards, alcoholics, dope fiends, materialists, sceptics, sen-
sualists, gluttons, thieves—all can make that area of life in
which they are defeated, the area of their greatest victory.
The time element is not as important as it seems, for it does
not require much time to make us saints; it requires only much
Love. Jacopine da Todi was an unfaithful husband with a
saintly wife. One day while they were watching a tourna-
ment, the grandstand collapsed. He was unhurt, but opening
his wife's dress to give her air, he noticed that she wore a
hair shirt—and at that moment she died. Realizing that her
self-imposed penances were to expiate his sins, the famous
lawyer sold his possessions and from then on he was seen in
the Churches in rags, always at prayer, to the great amaze-
ment of those who "knew him when. . . . "

Character building, however, should not be based solely
on the eradication of evil, for it should stress, even more, the
cultivation of virtue. Mere asceticism without love of God
is pride; it is possible to concentrate so hard on humiliating
ourselves that we become proud of our humility, and to concentrate so intently on eradicating evil as to make our purity
nothing but a condemnation of others. The difference in the

two techniques—pulling up the weed or planting good seed—is illustrated in the ancient story of the Greeks: Ulysses, returning from the siege of Troy, wished to hear the Sirens who sang in the sea, tempting many a sailor to his doom. Ulysses put wax in the ears of his sailors and strapped himself to the mast of the ship—so that even if he wished to answer the appeal of the Sirens he would be saved from doing so. Some years later, Orpheus, the divine musician, passed through the same sea; but he refused to plug up his sailors' ears or bind himself to a mast. Instead, he played his harp so beautifully that the song of the Sirens was drowned out.

A positive and not a negative goodness is the Christian ideal. A character is great, not by the ferocity of its hatred or evil, but by the intensity of its love of God. Asceticism and mortification are not the ends of a Christian life; they are only the means. The end is charity. Penance merely makes an aperture in our ego into which the Light of God can pour. As we deflate ourselves, God enters. As we empty ourselves, God fills us. And it is God's arrival that is the important thing.

When a Christian character is motivated by love alone, it finds much more goodness in the world than before. As the impure find the world impure, so those who love God find everyone lovable, as being either actual or potential children of God. This transformation of outlook takes place not only because love moves in an environment of love, but principally because, in the face of the love diffused by the saint, love is created in others. As jealousy in A begets jealousy in B, so generosity in A begets generosity in B. Love begets love; if we are kind, we get kindness back. The lover gets much more out of the world than the man who is cool or indifferent: he has not only the happiness of receiving but the happiness of giving, as well. Even when his love is not reciprocated by the wicked, the barbed word or the insult never hurts him. A priest once told St. John Vianney that a priest as ignorant of theology as he was should never go into a confessional box. The Curé answered: "Oh, how I ought to love you, for you are one of the few who know me thoroughly. Help me to obtain the favor I have been seeking so long . . . to withdraw myself into a corner and to weep for my sins."

Love makes us loathe the faults that hold us back from love. But we are not disheartened over them—for our failings are never insurmountable, once they are discovered and recognized as such. It is excusing them or labeling them falsely— calling egotism an "inferiority complex" or self-indulgence "gracious living"—which prevents spiritual progress. Most important of the rules for attacking evil in ourselves is to avoid direct in favor of indirect assaults. Evil is not *driven* out—it is crowded out. Drunkenness and alcoholism are not mastered by saying, "I will not drink," but through the expulsive power of some contrary good. When the soul begins to love God, it no longer has such morbid fears that they must be drowned in drink. The joys of the spirit also crowd out the pleasures of the flesh; we must have happiness, but the man who has found in on the high road of the spirit will no longer need to pursue it on the low road of carnality. If I raise my fist against a man, he will throw up his arms in self-defense; and so it is with evil under a direct attack. "But I tell you that you should not offer resistance to injury." (Matt. 5:39.) The little, illicit loves of the egotist are driven out by the larger loves of things beyond the self. Basically, there is no cure for selfishness until one learns to love others more than the ego; there is no cure for sex until the soul is loved more than the body; no relief from avarice until the treasures which rust does not consume are loved more than those which thieves can break through and steal. Sustaining all these efforts to develop character, there is a memory of the Divine plea: "Come to me, all you that labour and are burdened; I will give you rest." (Matt. 11:28.) Not until a nobler, finer love is found can a man master his vices or overcome his mediocrity. In a complete conversion, souls which were formerly addicted to vice, like Augustine, no longer feel any desire for their old sins, but rather a disgust. As the eye blinks at dust, so the soul now blinks at evil. Sin is not fought; it is rather no longer wanted. Love casts out sin as well as fear; the great tragedy of life is that so many persons have no one to love. As a man in love with a noble woman will give up all that displeases her, so a soul in love with God gives up all that might wound that Love.

There is today far too much public discussion, analysis, and probing of evil, drunkenness, infidelity, sex. It is as if the investigators reveled in uncovering sordid details. But the Church, in her understanding, demands that the details of our sins be excluded even from Confession. Nothing so induces morbidity as concentration on the disease, while offering no cure except the patient's own homemade remedies, or those of an analyst, who silences suggestions when the fee stops. Relief from fundamental evil is never found on the human level, but on the Divine. When Charles Foucauld, a hero of France but still an evil man, entered a church one day, he knocked at the confessional of Father Huvelin and said: "Come out, I want to talk to you about a problem." Father Huvelin answered: "No, come in; I want to talk to you about your sins." Foucauld, struck by Divine Grace, obeyed; later on he became a solitary in the desert and one of the saintly men of our times.

A distinguished man once called on Father Vianney, better known as the Curé of Ars, and said: "I have not come to go to Confession, but to talk things over." The Curé said: "I am no good at discussion, but I am good at consolation." Once inside the confessional box, the penitent contacted Divine Grace, found a new energy and love to displace the old ego, and his personality was born.

He who is charged with character formation will do well if he lays hold of what is best in people, searching for the gold and not the dross. There is something good in everybody. After the death of a street cleaner who had a reputation for dissolute living and infidelity and cruelty to his wife and children, most of his fellow street cleaners recalled all the evil about him—except one companion who said: "Well, whatever you say about him, there was one thing he always did well. He swept clean around the corners." In dealing with ourselves, we should look for what is worst and make it, with God's Grace, the occasion of spiritual growth. But in dealing with others, we should look for what is best, in order that, as we show mercy to others, God may show the Grace of His Mercy to us.

The right and the wrong methods of character formation are revealed in Our Lord's story of the unclean spirit:

"The unclean spirit, which has possessed a man and then goes out of him, walks about the desert looking for a resting-place, and finds none; and it says, I will go back to my own dwelling, from which I came out. And it comes back, to find that dwelling empty, and swept out, and neatly set in order. Thereupon, it goes away, and brings in seven other spirits more wicked than itself to bear it company, and together they enter in and settle down there; so that the last state of the man is worse than the first. So it shall fare with this wicked generation." (Matt. 12:43,45.)

Our Lord is telling us here that it is never enough to be free from the powers of evil; we must also be subject to the power of the good. The elimination of an ego does not necessarily imply the happiness of the I, unless the I, in its turn, lives by a higher spirit of love. The ego in the story has been rid of its evil occupant—it looks orderly and decent—it is swept and garnished. But it is empty, and an empty house decays more quickly than one that is occupied. So, when there is no ruling principle or master enthusiasm to take over the soul vacated of its ego, the emptiness can be preempted by some other force that is also evil. There is a parallel to this in the political order, from which, a few centuries ago, men exiled ethics and morality and religion—only to find that, in the twentieth century, irreligion, atheism, and antimoral forces entered the political order to take their place. Casting out the unclean spirit is not enough, unless there is a new possession by a cleaner spirit. Nature abhors a vacuum. There is no such thing as a nonreligious man; he is either religious or antireligious. Consciously or unconsciously, as time goes on, his mind takes on some new allegiance; if God is lacking, he becomes more and more captive to some temporal mood or fancy. Unless the new spirit of love comes in to take possession of the atheist, one of three other spirits will take charge of him—that of pride, or lust, or avarice.

No man is ever safe against the tyranny of the ego except through the power and love of God. The only way of keeping evil out is to let God in. Character building does not consist in the elimination of vice, but in the cultivation of virtue; not in the casting out of sin, but in the deepening of love. The man who wishes to expel evil without praying for the presence of God is doomed to failure. Nothing is secure until He is there and until His Love is spread throughout our hearts.

Great patience is required to effect this transformation. If characters become impatient, it is because they fail to realize the great heights that have to be attained. When children watch a parent work, they generally complain about the slowness of the work. That is because they do not see the task as the parent does, nor understand how much detail has to be completed to attain the wished result. Even those who have some degree of sanctity find it hard, sometimes, to remain on the Cross until the end; the world is full of half-crucified souls, who have come down from the Cross at the challenge of the world after an hour, or two hours, or even after two hours and fifty-nine minutes. Few are like the Saviour, who will stay until the end that they, like Him, might utter the cry of triumph: "It is finished." Because the perfection at which we aim is lofty and difficult, human souls need and should gladly accept the calm, pure happiness the Infinite Designer sometimes sends them. We should not insist on constant strife against ourselves; there is a time for reaping in the spiritual life. Joylessness can hold us back from God.

A want of resoluteness, too, can spoil our efforts, for, as St. James says: "A man who is in two minds will find no rest wherever he goes." (James 1:8.) This halfhearted temper in character development sees prayer as something which may do good, and in any case can do no harm; it trusts in God, but it places a greater reliance on the economic solution for its ills. It first plans and prays, and then tries to perform the plan without the prayer. Character cannot develop under conditions of such disorder, confusion, and dividedness. Conflict of such a kind makes the mind tired, as it tries to blend two things that will not mix, fatigues itself in crossing from one road to the other.

Character is built by singleness of purpose, and nothing so unifies our goals as a temptation that is overcome, a conflict resolved by the love which not only shows the answer, but gives us the strength to reach for it. The search for spiritual unity is identical with the effort to perfect the character. And since there is no unity except in the Truth which is God, the quality of our search will depend on where we place the emphasis in the sentence: "I seek the Truth." If the stress is put on the *I*, the character is ego-centered still, and truths are merely values to be assimilated for our vainglorious growth. But if it is the *Truth* toward which we wish to grow, our souls are able, at last, to disregard the self and overflow its narrow boundaries. Then freedom is our climate, for "the Truth will make you free."

12

The Effect of Conduct on Belief

THE way we live has an influence on the way we think. This is not a denial of the intellectual factors in belief, but merely an attempt to emphasize a neglected element. Some people imagine that they can bring a person to Divine Love merely by answering a doubt he has expressed. They assume that men are irreligious only because they are ignorant; that if atheists read a few good books or listened to a few choice arguments in favor of Divinity, they would immediately embrace the Faith. Religion seems to them to be a thing to be *known*, rather than a Personality to be *embraced* and lived and loved. But our Divine Lord, Who is Truth itself, could not convince the Pharisees and certain sinners; they were intellectually confounded by His knowledge so that, after one encounter, no man dared question Him again—but still they did not believe. Christ told those who watched the resurrection of Lazarus that some of them would not believe, though one rose *daily* from the dead. Intellectual knowledge is not the "one thing necessary": not all the Ph.D.'s are saints, and the ignorant are not demons. Indeed, a certain type of education may simply turn a man from a stupid egotist into a clever egotist, and of the two the former has the better chance of salvation.

Many men today are ignorant, full of prejudice and mis-information about the Faith, and it is regrettable that they have had no opportunity for instruction, for acquiring knowl-edge of the Truth. But though God can be discovered by study, instruction, and reading, these alone will not bring one to God. There must also be a willingness to accept the Truth personally, that is, in *all* its implications. It is easy to find Truth; it is hard to face it, and harder still to follow it. Modern education is geared to what it calls "extending the frontiers of truth," and sometimes this ideal is prized and used to excuse men from acting on old truths already discovered. The dis-covery of the size of a distant star creates no moral obligation; but the old truths about the nature and destiny of man can be a reproach to the way one lives. Some psychologists and sociologists like to rap their knuckles at the door of truth about mankind, but they would run away if the door ever opened, showing man's contingency on God. The only people who ever arrive at a knowledge of God are those who, when the door is opened, accept that Truth and shoulder the re-sponsibilities it brings. It requires more courage than brains to learn to know God: God is the most obvious fact of human experience, but accepting Him is one of the most arduous.

The moral conditions for knowing Divine Truth are, next to Grace, the most important requisites for conversion. There are, indeed, some who do not come to the Truth because they do not know it; but there are many more who do not come because of their present behavior. It is not the way they think, but the way they live which constitutes the obstacle to union with the Spirit. It is not the Creed that keeps most people away from Christ and His Mystical Body; it is the Commandments. The intellectual factors of belief are generally known, as is the important factor of Divine illumination; but here we wish to concentrate upon three neglected factors influencing a man's assent to Divine Truth:

1. Good will.
2. Living up to the Truth he already knows.
3. Habits of living.

Why is it, when a strong intellectual argument for the Faith is given to person A and person B, that A will accept and B will not? Since the cause is the same, the effect ought to be the same—but it is not. There must be some other factor present which makes one man embrace, the other reject, the truth—something in the mind it touches. A light striking a wall appears different from a light striking a window. Similarly this x factor, which makes for the rejection of Divine Truth in one case and its embrace in the other, is the will. As St. Thomas put it in his finely chiseled way: "Divine things are known in different ways by men according to the diversity of their attitudes. Those who have good will perceive Divine things according to Truth; those who have not good will perceive them in a confused way which makes them doubt and feel that they are mistaken." What a man will intellectually accept depends to a great extent on what man is or what he wants to be. The will, instead of admitting a truth presented to the mind, can ward it off and bar it out. God's pursuit of a mind is bound to fail unless the mind is also in pursuit of goodness. The message of the angels on Christmas night told us that only men with good will would become God's friends. This good-will factor is so important that it seems probable there is no such thing as intellectual atheism. Reason is on God's side, not the Devil's; and to deny His absolute is to affirm a competing absolute. But if there is no intellectual atheism, there is a frequent atheism of the will, a deliberate rejection of God. That is why the Psalmist places atheism not in the mind but in the heart: "The fool has said in his *heart*, there is no God." This primary requirement of good will holds not only for those who are looking for Divine Truth but also for those who found It and who still make little progress spiritually. God's Grace is never wanting to those who long to cooperate with it. The will to be wealthy makes men rich; the will to be Christ's makes men Christians.

The second important prerequisite for coming to God in the domain of the will is living up to the demands of Divine Truth as we presently see it. A sculptor could have an idea for a statue in his head for years, but the idea would gradually fade and disappear if he did not finally work it out in stone; so a man could have a particular Christian truth in his head for a lifetime, but unless he put it into practice, he might never be given another, larger truth. Many of us know a great deal about God, but few of us realize that knowledge in our lives. Those who do, become all they ought to *be*. They know the Truth in their hearts—a different thing from knowing it as a blackboard demonstration. There is no longer a partition in them separating intellectual truth from action. Some professors and knowledgeable men know the proofs of the existence of God and the dogmas of the Church, yet never become men of God. The reason is that they have never acted on that knowledge. Since they never dynamized the degree of Truth they knew, they were given no more; the knowledge they refused to fertilize by action remained sterile. The corn that is kept in the cribs too long will rot. To such unproductive souls, the Saviour orders: "Take the talents away." (Matt. 25:28.) But the simple soul, living up to the moral implications of the knowledge he possesses, is given new knowledge, and finally his wisdom surpasses that of the intellectuals. Our Blessed Lord went so far as to thank His Heavenly Father that He hid His Truths from the intelligentsia of His day and revealed them to the little ones, who would live by them. A simple girl like Catherine of Alexandria confounded learned professors with the wisdom given her by God, because she had won to a practical understanding of Divine Truth. When we climb a hill, a new vista is opened, which was hidden from the valley below. If, then, we rest passively on that hill, no new perspective will ever be revealed; but if we act on the knowledge received, walk to the end of the vista, then we shall discover that still new horizons open to the eyes and mind.

Christianity is founded on the historical fact: "The Word became Flesh." Wisdom became incarnate; God became man. Thus, knowledge passes into act; ought-ness becomes is-ness, and theory becomes practice. Our Lord not only gave the Truth. "For if you will forgive men their offences" (Matt. 6:14), but from the Cross. *He acted* on it: "Father, forgive them, for they know not what they do." (Luke 23:34.) He pleaded with His followers to become like little children, but only after He Himself had become a child and been wrapped in swaddling clothes. He not only taught the theory that the greatest of all His followers should be the least, but He washed the feet of His own disciples in demonstration. His hearers, too, were asked to become doers, because He said: "I have given you an example." (John 13:15.) The order runs: first the Word, and then the Incarnation. This was reversed by Goethe, who gave the modern man an escape from all moral obligation by saying, "In the beginning was the Deed"—first, you live; and then you rationalize your life. First you act; then you think of a way to justify your action. First you seize property; then you write a law to sanction the theft. From this false primacy of the act over Truth comes all the moral disorder of the present day, as men no longer fit their lives to a creed, but choose a creed to suit the way they live.

The truths of the Church are not abstract truths like the truths of science, which are impersonal and a-ethical. Some escapist minds take refuge in the use of scientific truths as a basis for ordering their lives for precisely this reason. Psychological statements about man rarely demand moral amendment; they permit us to remain mere interested spectators of our own reality. Divine Truth, on the contrary, involves *me* uniquely, and with an urgency that is at first frightening; it even demands separation from the world. The full Truth permits no easy compromise on this point. There are a thousand other religious attitudes one can take without provoking the enmity of the spirit of the world, but that is because the spirit of the world recognizes that, following these sects, one is still identical with it. Our Lord gave the test of whether we were His: were we hated by the world? "I have taken you out of the world, therefore, the world will hate you." (John 17:14.)

It is, therefore, not enough for us to read and study about Christianity, for Divine Truth is not such abstract truth as a theorem in geometry. It will do us no good to know theology if all the while pride, sensuality, and selfishness are allowed their license and their anarchy in our lives. In that case, we may possess a knowledge of the love of God for us, but we have no love of Him. Love is meant to be reciprocal.

The moral preparation for the Faith or for making Divine Truth dynamic in us is as important as the intellectual; both kinds of readying should go together, as the Wisdom and the Love of God, the Son and the Holy Spirit are equal in the Trinity. If the reason is neglected, a different sort of error follows. Those in whom the moral development outstrips the intellectual generally end in a religion that is negative, critical, and pharisaical, or else in a vague, emotional piety without content—as those who have intellectual without moral growth become sceptics, cynics, and doubters. We can never love until we know; but once we love, then love can increase knowledge: "If any one love me, he will keep my word, and my Father will love him, and we will come to him, and will make our abode with him." (John 14:23.)

Many people like to discuss religion, to argue about it, but as if it were impersonal, as if they were discussing Indonesian ritual dances. They miss the many-splendored thing because they never relate what they know to their own lives. A perfect example of this escape is to be found in the Gospel story of the woman at the well. The woman came to draw water, and Our Lord asked her for a drink. But when He tried to spiritualize the idea of thirst, to make her yearn to satisfy the thirst of her soul with the waters of everlasting life, she thought the waters He offered were something to be enjoyed

and discussed, like poetry—that they carried no moral obligation. To jolt her out of such impersonality, the Saviour said:
"Go, call thy husband, and come hither." (John 4:16.) As
God, He knew the smallest detail of her life; and she saw,
now, that her moral failings were in question. To avoid ex-
posure, she answered: "I have no husband." (John 4:17.)
Jesus told her: "Thou hast said well: I have no husband: For
thou hast had five husbands: and he whom thou hast now is
not thy husband. This thou hast said truly." (John 4:17–18.)
This, to the woman conscious of her adultery, seemed an in-
trusion into her private life; she did have many marriages
and divorces, it is true, but why need He bring that up?
Couldn't religion be discussed "in a civilized way," without
allowing it to become personal? Like anyone caught in an
embarrassing situation, she changed the subject. She shifted
the conversation away from her guilty life back to the intellectual plane, changed it to the less embarrassing topic of
whether she should worship on the Samaritan hill near by or
in Jerusalem. That was her effort to escape the Saviour's plea
that she lay bare her sin—and it has been repeated a thousand
times since then. Bring the necessity of repentance to a sinner
and, nine times out of ten, he will shift the subject to the
impersonal, will pretend that it is his reason which keeps him
back, will choose a safe topic with, "But what about the
Decretals of Constantine?" or some such question.

The intellect *does* play its role—but it is not until one has
begun to live right that one is able to reason well in this field.
So long as self-will and egotism refuse to surrender, the mind
is used only to justify the effort at escape. Until the resistance
to reform is broken, nothing can get into the soul—neither
truth nor goodness. That is why, when Our Lord was approached to settle an inheritance claim between two brothers,

He refused to settle the dispute: "Man, who hath appointed Me Judge, or divider, over you?" (Luke 12:15.) He would not arbitrate between two selfish claims—but He *would* tell them how to avoid having any dispute at all: "Take heed, and beware of all covetousness; for a man's life doth not consist in the abundance of things which he possesseth." (Luke 12:15.) Here it was covetousness—in the case of the woman at the well, it was carnality—that kept the questioners of Our Lord back from Divine Truth. We do not know what happened to the brothers, but we do know that the woman at the well met the moral demands and later saluted the Lord as "Saviour of the World." (John 4:42.)

The final factor affecting assent to the Truth is our habit patterns. These are the *result* of our failure to act upon the moral truths we already recognize (the second obstacle to belief described above). Customs have won through, now, to a hegemony of their own. They are so strong they can defy the weakened will. They stand as armed and angry guards at the gates to the intelligence and will let no truth past which threatens them. When the Christian truth comes to any mind, it is known according to the manner of the knower; and some knowers have a vast army of acts and habit patterns, prejudices and desires ready to war upon the Divine purpose of life. What the mind receives is received against a background, which already forms a pattern of its own—and one it will reluctantly disarrange or change. In the face of Divine Truth, the habit patterns with their inferior motives arise to contest the high motive driving the mind toward the True. Then one may say: "I fear to believe because I will be ridiculed," or "Because my family will not like it," or "Because I will have to break with my companions and will make enemies."

A struggle ensues between the intellectual comprehension

of a Truth and the habit patterns of inferior motives inherited
from the pre-Christian way of life. When a man stands off
from religion and admires the Truth from afar, he is full of
praise of it and says: "If I ever became religious, I would
certainly join the Church." But the real crisis begins when the
Truth is seen as personal—when admiration gives way to obligation, and when the Word becomes Flesh. The Divine
Word, when He became Flesh, suffered crises such as suffering, hunger, thirst, contempt, the Cross—all as experienced
facts: something of the same kind faces the mind that sees the
Truth, and it shrinks back. Many souls fear to make Truth
personal, intimate, or incarnate, because they know it may involve a Golgotha.

This is often the explanation of those escapists who want
a religion without a Cross or who call themselves agnostics
in order to avoid the moral consequences of Truth. Agnosticism, scepticism, and cultivated doubt do not represent an
intellectual position—for wherever there is a shadow there
must be light, and negation would not exist if there were
nothing to deny. These attitudes are rather a moral position,
in which a person attempts to make himself invulnerable to
Divine Truth by denying Its existence and turning his back on
It, as Pilate did. It is not doubts that cause our loose behavior,
as often as such behavior causes doubts. Our Lord was extremely emphatic on this point: "Anyone who acts shame-
fully hates the light, will not come into the light, for fear that
his doings will be found out. Whereas the man whose life is
true comes to the light, so that his deeds may be seen for what
they are, deeds done in God." (John 3:20–21.) "You pore
over the scriptures, thinking to find eternal life in them (and
indeed, it is of these I speak as bearing witness to Me): but

you will not come to Me, to find life. I do not mean that I look for honour from men, but that I can see you have no love of God in your hearts." (John 5:39–42.) St. Paul reaffirms his Saviour: "They profess recognition of God, but their practice contradicts it; it is they who are abominable, who are disloyal, who are ill qualified for the practice of any true virtue." (Titus 1:16.)

What is important is not *what* people say against God, or His Divine Son, Our Beloved Saviour, or His Mystical Body, but *why* they say it. The "what" is often a rationalization of their habits of life. A fallen-away Catholic who says, "I can no longer believe in the Sacrament of Penance," really means, "I am leading an evil life, and I refuse to break my habits of sin to make my peace with God." Reason is used to create sham doubts and to weave cloaks with which to cover our real motives. No wonder God must judge us—we are so slow to judge ourselves! St. Augustine at one time, before his conversion, rejected Divine Truth solely because of his behavior. One day, Pontitianus told Augustine the story of how he had walked with a friend outside the gates of Trier, discussing the life of Anthony of the desert. To drive home the example, the holy man made Augustine consider his own life.

He writes:

"But Thou, O Lord, while he was speaking, didst turn me round towards myself, taking me from behind my back where I had placed me, unwilling to observe myself; and setting me before my face, that I might see how foul I was, how crooked and defiled, bespotted and ulcerous. And I beheld and stood aghast; and whither to flee from myself I found not. And if I sought to turn mine eye from off myself, he went on with his relation, and Thou didst set me over against myself, and thrustedst me before my eyes, that I might find out mine iniquity, and hate it. I had known it, but made as though I saw it not, winked at it, and forgot it.

"Thus was I gnawed within, and exceedingly confounded with a horrible shame, while Pontitianus was so speaking. And he having brought to a close his tale and the business he came for, went his way; and I into myself. What said I not against myself? with what scourges of condemnation lashed I not my soul, that it might follow me, striving to go after Thee? Yet it drew back; refused, but excused not itself. All arguments were spent and confuted; there remained a mute shrinking; and she feared, as she would death, to be restrained from the flux of that custom, whereby she was wasting to death.

"Then in this great contention of my inward dwelling, which I had strongly raised against my soul, in the chamber of my heart, troubled in mind and countenance, I turned upon Alypius. 'What ails us?' I exclaim: 'what is it? what heardest thou? The unlearned start up and take heaven by force, and we with our learning, and without heart, lo, where we wallow in flesh and blood! Are we ashamed to follow, because others are gone before, and not ashamed not even to follow?'

"The very toys of toys, and vanities of vanities, my ancient mistresses, still held me; they plucked my fleshy garment, and whispered softly, 'Dost thou cast us off? and from that moment shall we no more be with thee for ever? and from that moment shall not this or that be lawful for thee for ever?' And what was it which they suggested in that I said, 'this or that,' what did they suggest, O my God? Let Thy mercy turn it away from the soul of Thy servant. What defilements did they suggest! what shame! And now I much less than half heard them, and not openly showing themselves and contradicting me, but muttering as it were behind my back, and privily plucking me, as I was departing, but to look back on them. Yet they did retard me, so that I hesitated to burst and shake myself free from them, and to spring over whither I was called; a violent habit saying to me, 'Thinkest thou, thou canst live without them?' "

A little later, Augustine's will embraced God's Grace as he opened the Scriptures:

"I seized, opened, and in silence read that section on which my eyes first fell: 'Not in rioting and drunkenness, not in chambering and wantonness, not in strife and envying; but put ye on the Lord Jesus Christ, and make not provision for the flesh, in concupiscence.' No further would I read; nor heeded I: for instantly at the end of this sentence, by a light as it were of serenity infused into my heart, all the darkness of doubt vanished away."

What often holds an atheist back from being a believer in God, and a believer in God from accepting the Divinity of Christ, and a believer in the Divinity of Christ from embracing the Divinity of His Mystical Body, and a Catholic from shining forth the Truth and Charity of Christ in His life? It is not that these blessings challenge credulity, but that they challenge character. As Chesterton so well answered when it was objected that Christianity had been tried and found wanting: "Christianity has been found hard, but not tried." Those who say that Christianity is impractical mean that they refuse to put it into practice—because their habit patterns protest the change. God's sunlight is shining outside our windows—but what good will it do to debate about its beauty if we are not willing to clean the windows of our behavior and see it for ourselves? Few are ignorant of sunlight; many are afraid to let it enter their lives.

There are three kinds of dirt that can accumulate as habits, on the window of the soul, to keep God's Grace from coming in. These are carnal dirt, or inordinate love of fleshly pleasures; money dirt, or the lust of possessions; and ego-centric dirt, or selfishness and vanity. Cleaning the window of the soul even a little brings God much closer. "Blessed are the clean of heart for they shall see God."

Those, then, are the three main obstacles to belief which operate within the will: not wanting truth; not activating the truth we already have, so that more will come to us; resisting truth because it threatens the wrong habits we have come to love as portions of ourselves.

There are also three psychological changes essential for the removal of these barriers to Divine Truth: adoption of the thoroughgoing scientific attitude; acting on what we already know; and reformation of our conduct.

If we adopt the humility of the true scientist, we shall be prepared to welcome truth wherever we find it, whether it suits our accustomed ways or not. For the ego to start with itself as an absolute in religion is very unscientific—it would be just as silly to attempt an egotistic mathematics or a self-centered astronomy. It is becoming very popular in our modern world to affirm the subject and to deny the existence of the object—to make the ego the standard of all that is right and true—to set up our own biased minds as the determinate of everything outside of us. This denial of objective reality is one of the basic causes of the confusion of our day. It is an intellectual error made oftenest in religion and philosophy: no biologist ever sits down before the squirming amoeba and says, "This is my idea of life." He allows life itself to de-termine his views. No sound geologist imposes his own theory of the strata of the earth upon the facts which he collects; he studies the rocks, and whatever the rocks tell him about their nature, he accepts. The scientific attitude toward religion is precisely the same. It begins with an inquiry into God's idea of religion and not *my* idea of religion. What is discovered is not what I want to find, but what He wants me to know—not what I believe to be true, but what He says is true—not what I think would be good, but what He says is good. This requires a humble attitude, and it opens the way to a richer understanding of both reality and God.

Secondly, as we act on the truth that we know, more truth will be given to us. It is a law of nature that no one ever gets his second wind until he has used up his first wind. So it is with knowledge. Only when we practice the moral truths which we already know will a deeper understanding of those truths and a fuller revelation come to us. Each new height the mind reveals must be captured by the will before greater heights come into view. Religion, then, is not just a subject of *discussion;* it is a subject for *decision.* There is a progress here, as in all research. Our knowledge of Truth will be cumulative, if we really wish it to grow. "Ask, and the gift will come; seek, and you shall find; knock and the door shall be opened to you."

The final condition necessary is the reformation of our lives. Just as there are some people who dare not open a letter from a bank, because they are afraid their bank balance is overdrawn, so there are some people who will not investi-gate the truths of Divinity, lest the complacency of their false way of life be made manifest. Once the truth about the

overdrawn bank balance is known, it will create an obligation;
and while refusal to open the letter does not in any way increase the balance, it defers the judgment, puts off the unpleasant task. To face our faults is never easy—but to defer
the moment of judgment, through cowardice, is to prolong
our unhappiness and guilt. All souls receive actual graces—
letters of reminder from God. Many are afraid to let these
messages penetrate their conscious minds.

Abandonment of self to Truth is a prelude to entering into
the joy of the Lord. Before a lump of clay can be formed into
a shapely piece of pottery, it must first be abandoned to the
potter and must lie passive in his hands. If a human soul is
ever to be made a vessel for God's honor, it must itself detest
those evil rebellions which resist the Divine Artist.

In the lives of many individuals, there is a great desire to
bestow many blessings and affections on others—if the others
would only permit it. They wish to bring what is fine, and
good, and beautiful as gifts, pouring them out from lavish
hands, if only those they love did not resist. With His vastly
greater generosity, God, too, wants only an opportunity to
empty His treasures into our souls.

We may be fearful of the demands Divinity will make on
us—but our fears are foolish, for what we dread is the only
lasting happiness that men can know. A man let down in a
well by a rope may be filled with fear as to what might happen to him if he finally let go; in the darkness of the well, he
cannot see its depth, nor know that he would actually touch
bottom a very few inches from the top, while imagining he
was dropping to his death. So it can seem that in giving oneself
to God, one will be losing everything—and yet the fall is only
a few inches, and one soon hits solid rock. If one is in doubt

as to what he ought to do, or where Truth lies, then this should be his daily prayer: "Lord, illumine my mind to see the Truth and strengthen my will to follow it." He who lives up to that prayer will be surprised at how far he will travel, and at how happy he will be when he arrives.

13

Black Grace and White Grace

THERE are two great moments in the life of every soul as it advances to the Christ-centered level. The first is negative and passive; the second is active and Divine. The first crisis is an overwhelming sense of emptiness, which is actually "Black Grace"; the second is a sense of the Divine presence, or "White Grace." The first experience involves a discontent, a disgust, a fed-upness with life; the second awakening is the consciousness that God is making an impact on the soul. The first condition is a result of Godless living; it might be called the negative Presence of God in the soul, as God's actual Grace is His positive Presence.

The first feeling of tension is the product of man's desire for an Infinite, and all the ennui and boredom results from the realizations, sometimes very sharp, that he has not realized his desire. We may not know what it is that we are seeking,

but in all of us there is a longing for something unattained—
and a restlessness with everything else for lack of it. We feel
deprived of something that ought to be ours. We see ourselves moving through the world not so much as peasants, who
never had anything, but as royalty in exile, ever conscious of
our original dignity. We are searching and looking—not so
much because we hope to hit on a new treasure, but to recover one we have already had and lost.

What increases this sense of emptiness is the misplaced
Infinite. Instead of striving for the true Infinite which is God,
we erect a false Infinite of our own ego, or of wealth, of
power, of pleasure, looking for full satisfaction for our spirit's
hungers here. Since none of these can completely satisfy us,
we are thrown back upon ourselves, more miserable than
before. The mistake lay in imagining that the craving could
be quieted by earthly things. In the physical order everyone
wants health, though some people seek it by such unlikely
methods as living on a diet of gin and aspirin. Similarly, to
seek joy from any infinite except the true God of Love is a
disastrous mistake: our treasures multiply, but not our peace;
our pleasures increase, but not our satisfaction; we try to
solace ourselves by diminishing the outer causes for misery,
but the inner misery remains. As the Chinese say: "When the
wrong man uses the right means, the right means work the
wrong way." The spirit within us groans, and whispers, and
finally shouts for attention; if we are stubborn, still, in our
attachment to the misplaced infinite of pride or sensuality, we
shall end like Prometheus: "the vulture eats away our very
hearts and souls."

The reason for our misplacement of the Infinite is perverted self-love. As St. Thomas Aquinas said: "The fact that

a person desires a temporal good overmuch is due to the fact that he loves himself too much." But man's nature is too amply patterned for these temporal toys to content it for long. As Pascal has said:

"The greatness of man is so evident that it is even proven by his wretchedness, for what in animals is called nature we call wretchedness in man; for who is unhappy at not being a king except a deposed king? Who is unhappy at having one mouth and who is not unhappy at having only one eye? Probably no one ever ventured to mourn at not having three eyes, but anyone is inconsolable at having none."

Restlessness, even when we have won our worldly triumphs, is proof that we were made for something more than the world. Pain always means that something is amiss, that two warring purposes are involved, that there is a collision between two things each seeking its own separate end. Why does a hot coal placed on our hand burn it? Because the purpose of the coal contradicts that of the hand—the coal is a "not" to our hand, its negation and frustration; if the nature of our hand were the same as the nature of coal, there would be no pain, because there would be no contradiction. In like manner, if a man, made to the image and likeness of God, aspires by every word, deed, and prayer to make his end purpose identical with God's Will, he has no contradiction in his nature, and therefore he is at peace. But the man who contradicts his end on earth by antispiritual living, who allows his senses to seek their ends regardless of the larger end of his whole nature, will suffer the pain of anxieties, fears, and mental disorders. His ego aches with every thought and deed which thwarts the Divine purpose. The contradiction in our natures is both metaphysical and moral: metaphysical because we are composed of body and soul, and the immediate demands of the soul often contradict the cravings of the body; moral because, in our egotism, we once rebelled against our creatureliness and thereby intensified the tension. This frustration exists in all men, but it is vastly intensified in the egotist. For he must recognize the tremendous disproportion between his resources and the obstacles he has to overcome. He wishes to turn his ego into infinity, and yet he finds it crossed and negated by other egos; he wills a life of pleasure, and he finds that pleasure negated by a quick satiety; he craves unlimited freedom, and he finds that hope frustrated by a million limitations of time and space and power. If there is any one symbol that might be chosen to describe the modern soul, in its moment of misery, its crisis of Black Grace, it is that of a cross, with one bar in contradiction to another bar. Man at war with his nature, seeking the Infinite where it is not, is self-crucified.

But there is a second crisis of the soul. In this moment it becomes conscious of its relationship to Divinity, to what we call White Grace. This most important step takes place when the little cross on which we suffer catches sight, on the hill of Calvary, of the Great Cross of Christ. At the moment when a man realizes that these two crosses are related, a double truth dawns on his soul: First, he feels a sense of his guilt, such as one could never know until he felt himself in relationship to a Divine Person—for no one ever feels guilty toward the impersonal. He now understands what sin is: it is the killing of Goodness. As a poet put it: "I committed murder, I killed a man, I committed a sin."

But there is a second lesson which comes from the Cross, and it is more important than the recognition of guilt. That is a recognition of the healing powers of Him Who is upon the Cross. The human heart which grasps this reality will not concentrate upon its own disease, but on the curative powers of Him Who can cure it. He pardoned us with His "Father, forgive them for they know not what they do"; yet even that would not suffice to help us if He were only a man and not God; the human soul would feel eternal remorse for having taken a life that could not be restored again. But He Who is on that Cross *is* God as well as man, and by rising from the dead, He bestowed on us the very Life we would have taken away.

The Cross is the most inescapable reality of life. If we will not accept it outside of ourselves, to pardon us and to heal, then we will have it on the inside, as frustration and despair. There is an almost unbearable contradiction in human life. These cross-purposes of spirit and senses in our nature are resolved only if we blend our wills with the Divine Will on the Cross. There is no other course. They are mere escapists who hope to avoid the Cross on Calvary by seeking a streamlined cross freed of self-discipline and any need for God's Grace. In their own heart of hearts, such men know that they are demanding Christianity on their terms, and not God's terms, and that thus they increase the very egotism they must heal.

Feed man until he is fed-up; surround him with every material condition to satisfy every passion; give him license to do whatever he pleases; castle him; cajole him; satiate him; coddle him; amuse him—and invariably, after a short time, he will seek what he has not, grasp for something which is beyond his reach, and weep for the unworldly even in the heart of the world, as he stretches out his hands for that "unpossessed that makes all possession vain." Without the great reality of a Love Who suffered death because of the supreme contradiction of man's love, the human heart is isolated and in agony: it has more love to give than any earth-bound object can receive—it clamors to be loved more lastingly and comprehendingly than by any human lover. But both the longings—to love perfectly, to be loved perfectly—are mere vacuums in man; the most real part of his nature turns out to be a void. He is built around a hole—formed like a cup, whose existence gains its points from what it is made to receive. When a man faces reality, he finds the most important fact about himself to be his insufficiency. He says: "I am nothing." And only then does he dimly perceive the need of Him Who says: "I am Who am." In the face of his own incompleteness, man bears witness to the Divine Complement. At first he fears, "lest having Him he must have naught else beside"; but once his soul is stirred to its depths, so that it cries out for mercy and pardon—then God is perceived no longer as a vague power behind the universe, but in His real relationship to the soul and its needs. When once this impact has been felt, the soul is never the same again.

It is this very tremendousness of the Cross, the violence of its effect on human life, which makes some souls fight so hard against submission to its influence. They avoid books with a religious tone, keep away from people who might speak of Divine things, tune out any program on the air which would speak of God, and seek on every occasion to find fault with religion. Such fugitives from Christ often say that religious people are hypocritical, are imperfect; they forget that if the Church were as perfect as they demand it must be, then the Church would have no room in it for them, with their own faults and sins.

When men feel the first impulses of God's Grace summoning them from misery to peace, they are sometimes inclined to shrug their shoulders and to say: "This impulse to surrender does not come to me from any God; it is just a weakness of my human nature." Yet this explanation is patently untrue, because when God begins to affect the soul, it breaks with nature. A love of God inspires us to discipline and mortification, to give up the occasion of our sins. If the impulses were from nature alone, nature would not thus lift the knife against itself. Some opponents of religion say the experience of God is a projection of something we ourselves create in the subconscious mind. But there is nothing in the unconsciousness which was not once in consciousness; and here the soul is in the presence of a great Inexperience, a Divine Novelty, never known or even suspected before. Furthermore, when once the impulse of God strikes the soul, it moves us to behavior contrary to either our conscious or our unconscious previous plans. This could not be, if there were not present a force from without, stronger than ourselves, and yet One with which we could cooperate. There is no need to multiply the answers to these false objections men raise against God. For there will always be perverse souls in the world who persist in disbelief, no matter what evidence is offered them. Their determination to deny Love is very great, and they will go out of their way to find elaborate denials of the beautiful Obvious—as if a man should try to dissuade us from enjoying the fragrance of a rose by saying that it really originated in a distant perfume factory.

The invasion of Divinity is a valid and unmistakable reality. Its effects are a contentment with what we are and a yearning to be what we are not; it thus implies that a response is expected of us. No gift or favor ever has to be accepted; but once we consent to a favor, this creates an obligation. A refusal to respond to grace, at such a crisis, always leaves the soul more emptily bereft than ever. It is no slight thing to bar God from our doors when He has urgently asked us to let Him enter.

Though this impact of God on the soul, calling it to union with Him and away from sin, may come through human instruments, these are, of themselves, no more important than a pencil in the hand of a writer; God uses them to write His message on another soul. This is one of three obvious differences between all human, natural, psychological aids to human betterment and the action of God in the soul. For the effort of a teacher of Christianity to assist God's indirect action *on* the soul is also fortified at the same time by God's direct action *in* the soul. God's action *on* the soul takes place through the impression He makes on us in the beauties of nature, the majesty of the mountains, and the glory of the sunset; in the beautiful correlation that exists among the truths of human reason, such as the way in which the infinitesimal atom repeats, in miniature, the almost infinite solar system; in our human loves and friendships; in the impact of the life of Christ and His teachings on our minds. But God's action *in* the soul affects the spiritual faculties of the soul itself—it transforms the intellect and the will. Yet this interior event must not be confused with an emotional experience; the emotions belong to our bodies, our material and physical selves. When God acts on the soul, there may be a simultaneous rush of feeling, or a complete aridity, a lack of any emotional sense, at all, that something important has occurred. In either case, it is one of the several crises leading to reform, it is the action of Grace in the soul.

The first fundamental difference between human and

Divine teaching is this: all human appeals, arguments, and coaxings toward moral betterment—like all psychological appeals to a morally disordered soul—*are external to the person to be reformed*. Since the action comes from without, the reformer can only ring the bell—he cannot get inside of the house, and he has no ally within its doors. An alcoholic may admit that all the arguments a reformer or psychologist presents to him are true, but there is a world of difference between knowing what is right and doing what is right. It is conceivable that the alcoholic, knowing that he is doing wrong, knows also that his will power, unaided, is not capable of freeing him from his vice. Or he may resent the effort of any other human being to interfere with him: precisely because of their extrinsic character, many legal and humanistic reforms are regarded as an impertinence by those they seek to help.

Divine action on the soul, on the other hand, is internal and is so incommunicably personal that the man may sometimes feel that it is own creation. The impact of God on the soul is not that of a proselytist, for a proselytist works from without, and—in the language of philosophy—uses a "transitive activity," such as one billiard ball might exert upon another. But God, although working through His Apostles, allows their words to affect the soul from within by "immanent activity," which is the characteristic method by which living things grow. When this actual Grace of God gets into the soul, it acts something like light, shining through a Gothic window to suffuse it with a brilliance which the stained glass does not have of and by itself. It is not easy to describe this Divine action on the soul, for it is as invisible and as spiritual as a natural truth in the mind, although it is not merely natural.

The truth that two and two makes four takes up no space, no latitude or longitude in our minds—yet it is there, and it can influence our thinking and our actions. On the higher level, God acts in the intellect as truth, and in the will as love. He sometimes strikes the soul with a terrific mystical impact which demands a complete break with everything external.

The Divine action in our souls does not exclude external help such as we find in a sermon or a book; God may use these as carriers of His Grace. But few people realize what a difference there is between a soul's response to a Communist propagandizing Marx and to a Christian instructing on the Faith; the Communist operates without Divine help—even against it—but the Christian has the aid of God Himself, working within the soul, while he operates from the outside.

The soul itself may not be certain when the Divine invasion has occurred. One might almost say that God enters the soul like a thief in the night—we may choose whether to welcome Him or to reject Him, but we cannot *prevent* Him from invading the soul that He has made. As the sun rises without asking permission of the night, so Divine life invades us without consulting the darkness of our minds. God establishes His beachhead in our most unsuspecting moments, almost in secret, without our being consciously aware of Him. He comes as a sudden thought that springs into the mind, an intense desire that moves the will. His entrance is imperceptible; in the beginning, we do not know that it is He. We do not resist Him, for we have no sense of an alien interference. We may even think that the sudden upsurge of our spirit is our own, with no suspicion that it comes from God— just as we may think that our eyes do all the seeing, without being conscious of their reliance on the sun. It is only later that we understand, looking back, that the initiative was Divine and Eternal.

The occasion on which the Divine Thief chooses to steal away our unhappiness may be a moment of satiety with sin, as it was with Léon Bloy, or the sight of death, as it was with St. Francis, or the closeness of the stars and the desert, as it was with Ernest Psichari, or the reading of a book, as it was with Jacques Maritain, or the sound of church bells, as it was with Paul Claudel. Whatever the external circumstances, they are of no importance; they are the occasions on which one individual has met God—but God can be met anywhere. Though God has reserved to Himself the right and power of acting in the soul, of soliciting it to virtue and distracting it from evil, nevertheless He has left man a choice between welcoming the God he finds in his soul or ordering Him out. But enter it He does, stirring the soul, agitating it, shaking the grates of the heart to get rid of the clinkers and ashes of sin, so that the faint sparks of Grace may blaze and burn. One can dispute the plea for goodness if it is spoken by a voice outside ourselves—but this voice speaks within us, and it does not argue. Our choice is not between agreeing or disagreeing with God's revelation in our souls; the only alternatives are to embrace or to reject the appeal, whose verity we have to recognize.

The second difference between humanistic, psychological aids to ethical improvement and the action of the Grace of God is that the former are impersonal, while Grace is always personal. An external appeal seems never to be meant for *us*. The sinful, the selfish, or the intemperate man can say to the reformer: "Try it on someone else; *I'm* satisfied the way I am." The implication is that the homily is like the statistics of a life insurance company, which do not apply to anybody in particular. A mother who once tried to get her boy to eat spinach said, "There are a million boys in the United States who would love that spinach," to which he answered, "Name three of them." We reject the persuasion which is not custom-made; only when an appeal is personal is it effective. The individuality of the soul demands a specific remedy. The one sheep that is lost in the brambles cries out for its own unique salvation. We must return to the safety of the fold of our own will—as we left it of our own will. No individual is ever made better by having his guilt excused as the result of his external environment, of bad playgrounds, of Oedipus or Electra, of Grade B milk, bad politics, or want of social opportunity.

God solicits each of us by a dialogue no other soul can hear. His action on the soul is always for us alone. He sends no circular letters, uses no party lines. God never deals with crowds as crowds—they could give Him only earthly glory—but what He wants is each soul's singular and secret fealty. He calls His sheep by name; He leaves the ninety-nine that are safe to find the one that is lost. On the Cross He addresses the thief in the second person singular: "This day, *thou* shalt be with Me in Paradise." God never sells His bread of life wholesale. He tempers the wind to the individual sheep—heals the particular man. Once the soul becomes conscious of the Divine Presence, it feels itself under a Divine Imperative and whispers to itself: "This is a message sent to me and to no one else." This inner influence of God, which is so personal, arouses it to a knowledge of its own responsibility—we know, now, that it was God Whom we offended in the past. External things are no longer blamed for the soul's condition; we, rather, strike our breast and say: "*Mea* culpa, *mea* culpa, *mea* maxima culpa." At last, we are fully conscious of the two great realities of human life: the soul and God.

There is a third difference between psychological appeals to us to change and the influence of Divine Grace: the former have not the power to heal. They are external to the sick patient—and even though his mind might be convinced of their necessity, he is nevertheless too weak to apply the remedy himself. How often a mother will say of a delinquent daughter or son, "If I could only get *inside* her," or "If I could get *hold* of him"—the implication being that an outsider's pleading can never cause an inner regeneration. The false remedies for poor, weak humanity never work because they never recognize the necessity of a voluntary redemption in the soul of each individual, answerable man. Pleas for a little more tolerance, an increased indifference to right and wrong, a new love to replace the old one—all efforts to change the rules of conduct to give the sinner peace of mind—may make his last condition worse than the first. The lock that opens the door to healing is on the side of the wounded, not on the side of the reformer. Bringing in lax doctors, who deny that our sicknesses are serious, is not a help to health.

Divine Grace proves its transcendence over the human, here again, in its ability to heal the soul. If man is to be made better, there must be the introduction of a new life principle and a new source of energy from without himself—yet it must be made a part of himself. Cut off a furnace pipe, and the furnace will not grow another; but cut off the leg of a salamander, and it *will* grow another leg. Man, in the spiritual order, is like the salamander in the physical plane: thanks to Divine Grace, coming from without, he has the power to become a new man after he has spoiled the old man that he was.

There can now be healing where there was once disease, resurrection where there once was death, and joy where anxiety prevailed. God stirs within a man, giving him sufficient power to be all that he ought to be—and if man throws the Divine medicine out of the window of his soul, then he must blame himself, and not God, for his subsequent misery. The human reformer can influence a man up to a certain point—just as an orchestra leader can inspire the musicians under him; but he cannot give an untrained, untalented man the power to play. But God's Grace can do just that. God can infuse into the soul a capacity for virtuous living which was not there originally and which cannot be acquired naturally. When the healing power of Grace enters the soul, its four wounds are remedied; it acts upon the wound of ignorance which affects the intellect, the wound of malice which affects the human will, the wound of weakness which makes us reluctant to do the hard things necessary for salvation, and on the wound of concupiscence which impels us to carnal pleasures in preference to spiritual joys. New habits are created in the soul, new insights born, and a veritable revolution of the self occurs.

To give a concrete example of how God acts on the soul of a man, consider a married man contemplating divorce and remarriage because he loves another woman. He may have debated the subject back and forth inside of himself, have lined up all the arguments against divorcing his loving wife, have said: "I am a cad for doing this, I know I am. Also, I will have to pay alimony, and it will be bad for the children, and I made a promise to be this woman's husband until death parted us." Then, he lines up the counterarguments for breaking up the family, such as: "Everybody is doing it. You can no longer live according to the outmoded Christian code. The new wife will be prettier, and she and I have more in common intellectually." After deciding on divorce and consulting his lawyers, he finds himself increasingly easily irritated with his wife and children—without ever suspecting that he hates them because they are a reproach to his own conduct. He sleeps less well at night, and there is something about the darkness that makes him see things differently. Suddenly there emerges in his mind a new light on the problem: there looms before him a previously neglected factor. The idea comes with such a terrific certainty that he feels he has never understood it before. Perhaps it is the words of the Saviour, "What God hath joined together, let no man put asunder," which flash across his mind. Or the reflection: "I have only about twenty years of my life left, and then what?" Under the impact of that enormous Grace, he may reverse his direction, abandon the other woman, and reestablish his home. In early stages of his reformed living, such a husband might not guess that God caused this new light to flash. He might even attribute the decision to himself, saying: "Well, I thought the matter over more seriously, and I . . . " But later on, if he seeks a permanent, intimate union with God, he will know that it was God who put the saving thought in his mind.

What happens to this theoretical husband has happened to every one of us—Jew, Christian, pagan, idolater. God is always acting on the soul. As the sun never stops shining—though we cannot always see its rays—so God is always shedding His Graces and His healing powers on each of us. It would be difficult to give a mathematical calculation of the number of actual Graces that come from God, but certainly they would run into thousands for each soul every year. Many souls reject these Graces out of indifference, which for the moment saves them from having to make responsible decisions. But this very indifference is in itself a decision—the souls have decided to reject the Grace.

The willingness to accept an actual Grace and let it change us may come in a moment of fed-upness after sin, or in some moment of misery and disappointment, when a consciousness of emptiness and loneliness throws a soul back on God. It may come to some people when they see the happiness on the face of a nun and contrast it with their own despair—or when, in panic, they face the fact that life, so far, has been wasted. Many souls are like blind men walking through life, too proud to ask the way until tragedy threatens them. Then they are newly humble, and willing to accept a Guide— to take instructions, and to see with the cured eyes of Faith.

Because the Divine aspirations are often very subtle, gentle —and are sometimes carried by poor human instruments— God is not, at once, seen as their cause. For He often speaks to us through many messengers we do not count as His: a child, a parent, a radio, a satiety, a disgust, a yearning, a good deed, a symphony, a sunset sky. Because He is so well disguised in these, He goes unrecognized. St. Augustine tells us how he imagined it was only his mother warning him against his evil life, when actually she was the mouthpiece of God:

"And Whose but Thine were these words which by my mother, Thy faithful one, Thou sangest in my ears? . . . I remember she warned me in private with great anxiety: not to commit fornication and especially not to defile another man's wife. These seemed to me womanish advices which I should blush to obey. But they were Thine, O God, and I knew it not. I thought Thou wert silent and it was she who spoke. . . . So I rode headlong with such blindness, that among my equals I was ashamed of a less shamelessness, when I heard them boast of their wickedness . . . and I took pleasures, not only in the pleasure of the deed, but in the praise. What is worthy of dispraise but one? But I made myself worse than I was, that I might not be dispraised; and when in anything I had not sinned as the abandoned ones, I would say I had done what I had not done, that I might not seem contemptible in proportion as I was innocent or of less account because the more chaste."

Years later, looking back, St. Augustine saw the emptiness of his old life had also been God's negative way of calling him to himself: first came the Black Grace of boredom, then the White Grace of a summons from God, which He entrusted to the mother of Augustine to deliver for Him. Both experiences were gifts of God, for which the saint later gave thanks to him:

"What shall I render unto the Lord, while my memory recalls these things? I will love Thee, O Lord, and thank Thee, and confess Thy name. To Thy grace I ascribe it and to Thy mercy that Thou hast melted away my sins as it were with ice. To Thy grace, I ascribe also whatsoever I have not done of evil, for what might I not have done, who even loved sin for its own sake? . . . Let him who reads this not scorn me, who being sick was cured by the Divine Physician and for this let him love Thee as much as I, yea and more, since by Whom he sees me to have been recovered from such deep consumption by sin, by Him he sees himslf to have been from like consumption preserved."

Black Grace, or the inner sense of loneliness and fear, is commoner now than it was several generations ago when the moral atmosphere of the world was healthier. More people nowadays know the solicitation of God by sensing their own emptiness. But there is still an immense gap between the acceptance of Black Grace and White Grace. The first is only the thirst; the second is the water of life. The first is a sensing of one's need, without always knowing Who will supply it; the second is the beginning of an intimate fellowship through the Sacraments with Christ, Who is the Author of Grace.

From one point of view only, the modern ego may be closer to perfection and happiness than the I—for the ego knows himself to be a failure. The I, on the other hand, can conceivably underestimate his weakness, be content with moderate happiness and mediocre, merely decorous behavior. The I-personality is not led to God through the sharp suffering of Black Grace. Graces he *will* have to show him the inadequacy of his standards, the superlative values of the holiness which is possible on the Christ-level alone; but if he wishes to change, it must be on the same horizontal plane—for the only motion possible for him is to go faster in the same direction. He is already "good," and the good may be the enemy of the best. The poor disillusioned ego, however, with Black Grace to help him, is in no doubt about his worthlessness—he may be willing to pay any price at all to attain happiness.

14

Man's Capacity for Self-Transcendence

Our world, which has been living on its moral fat for the last few centuries, has now reached a point of moral and spiritual debility. It is at last forced to face the problem of how it may acquire the new spiritual energies needed to remake both itself and the individual soul. It is tempted to seek a way that will not hurt and will not demand a radical revision of its errors. It would like to find the answer by a human remedy, in preference to the more heroic methods Divinity employs.

All reforms on the human level can be reduced to four—they are education, ethics, reason, and the making of stronger resolutions.

Education once seemed to some men the gateway to Heaven-on-earth for everyone. Now we have tried it, and we know that schooling, alone, will not save our society.

Never before was there so much education, and never before so little arrival at the truth. The twentieth century is the century of the greatest attempt at universal education in the history of the world—and yet it is the century of the most terrible conflagrations, wars, and revolutions of history. We have stuffed our children's minds with facts, and neglected to teach them how to live. Any system of education which fails to discipline the will also fails to train the character. Such teaching may succeed in making men into walking encyclopedias; it does not make them responsible citizens for a democracy. Education can never make a man better unless it teaches him the true purpose of man—and the difficulties he must overcome to realize that purpose. Much education today is based on the Socratic error that ignorance of good is the cause of evil, and that all we need do to overcome evil is to give men information. If this were so, every educated man should be a good man; but we know this is not true.

A second panacea offered us is the adoption of new ethical systems—the tailoring of new standards of "morals" to suit our unmoral ways of living. This, on the face of it, is no remedy for our ailments: it is merely an attempt to change the definition of health to fit the prevalent disease—it is as if doctors should say, "Cardiovascular diseases affect so many modern men that hardening of the arteries and heart disease are now the standard of a healthy man," or "Common colds afflict almost everyone at some stage of his life. Let us agree that only the man who sneezes is normal in this century." But besides these reckless efforts to adjust the tape measure of true morality to fit our puny statures, there are other, clearer thinking attempts to teach true and solid virtues as a way of life to modern men. Those who attempt to teach goodness separated from religion soon find, however, that they have set themselves an impossible task. Ethical systems alone cannot save the world, because they are effective only in a religious environment. It is its air such systems breathe; it is its substance they reflect. When the religious spirit is lost, ethical systems quickly lose their force. Moreover, no ethical code is ever precise enough to cover every situation; that is why equity had to be added to codes to make the law. A spirit can embrace all situations, but not a rule, a code, a set of written injunctions. For that reason, those who live under codes always feel a conflict between duty and inclination, between what they ought to do and what they feel like doing. Responsibility, instead of being the free expression of their own personality, becomes a formula of obligation. A code implies duty and not love; therefore, personality resents it, unless the code is made acceptable by entering the area of love. And a mere code always appears to be a restraint upon our freedom; therefore, it is not long before the longing for liberty leads to license, and anarchy then becomes the rule.

But if neither education nor an ethical standard will save society, there seems still a chance that reason might prove a possible means of salvation. Right reason, indeed, could help us today; but the use of reason has undergone a degeneration in recent times, and men ask it to solve unreasonable riddles in our day. The purpose of reason is primarily to discover goals, aims, and destinies; this is what is known as *teleological* reason. About two centuries ago the mind of man was demoted, relegated to the side show of what might be called *technical* reason. Thinkers took their eyes off ends and purposes, as being either unworthy or unknowable, and began to concentrate on means, detached from consciously chosen goals. This error begot capitalism, or the amassing of wealth in economic life, and pragmatism, or the substitution of the useful for the true in philosophy. The chaos resulting from this degradation of reason cried for an ordering principle. Men introduced, finally, totalitarianism, or planning reason—which is the wrongly rigid and brutally compulsory organization of a chaos created by capitalism, pragmatism, and liberal thinking in all fields. Law, which was meant to be a dictate of reason, was now perverted into an instrument to justify deeds already done, and philosophy rotted into the rationalization and justification of evil. Reason today is like a knife so dulled by wrong uses that it will no longer cut cleanly through the problems of our life. A further objection to placing our hopes in modern man's ability to reason himself out of his moral dilemma is this: one result of a life of lust and carnality is that the reason becomes befogged, dull, and unreliable, particularly in judging practical questions of conduct. Even at its best, human reason alone could not grasp the fullness of natural truths and morals except with the greatest difficulty, and after a long period of time, and with some admixture of error still. The wise men of the ages, relying on reason, each has discovered only a fragmentary and isolated portion of the moral truth, and generally they came to that very late in life. Something more than reason is required to rescue man.

Some thinkers who admit this fact believe that reason might save us if backed up by a stronger will, deeper resolves, and more vigorous human efforts at betterment. But the human will is quite as incapable as reason of lifting us to the high plane of altruism necessary to save the world—for it is precisely in our wills that the sickness lies. If man might, under his own power, will to be saintly and heroic instead of sinful and cowardly, who of us would not long ago have made the change? But the will cannot wish itself well—just as the arm, if it is broken, cannot set itself. Too often it is assumed that the will is something outside of us, independent of us, to be summoned from without in an emergency. But the will is not a thing apart from us; it is our character, the sum of our choices and decisions, the heritage of our decisions. Because of the inherent gravity of past defections, it is very difficult for most wills to begin a new mode of life on the human level—and impossible for them to do so alone on the Divine level. But the difference between a "weak" will and a "strong" will lies not so much in the weakened will itself as in the lack of a strong, deeply loved master purpose or ideal to direct the will. When the master ideal is sublime—when it is the love of God—the will is strong; when the ideal is confused, or when there is no ideal, the will is weak. Because the will is frequently solicited by our passions and our prejudices, it needs more strength than it contains within itself to adhere to truth. A ball set in motion will continue in that line unless it is redirected by another force; similarly, for a radical shift from selfishness to altruism, the will often needs an added impulse from without to organize it around a new ideal, a loftier set of purposes.

All these four naturalistic and humanistic "solutions" assume that man can rise above the human level through lifting himself by the lobes of his own ears. When holders of this view are told that supernatural help is needed to conquer the ego and perfect the I, their rejoinder is: "A man must stand on his own feet." But man did not do so at birth— he did not prepare his coming, or cushion himself on his mother's breast. Even when he is grown, he does not weave his own clothes, or cook his own meals, or originate his own world news. His eyes do not see without light; his ears do not hear without the waves of sound; his lungs do not breathe without air. Man is not self-sufficient for any of his basic needs.

Man is, in truth, like a clock whose mainspring is broken; he has all the necessary parts, but they do not work. To repair the clock a mainspring must be supplied from without by a watchmaker, but it has to be applied *within* the clock itself; so man, too, needs a new energy within himself, but it has to be supplied from the outside by his Lord and Saviour. The introduction of a higher source of strength to help our weak human nature does no violence to it, for every man has a yearning for self-transcendence, a desire to get beyond himself and above himself. His restlessness is born of an inability to find complete satisfaction within the limitations of space and time.

Man's power to generate ideas shows that he is already at home in a spiritual world; infinity is implicated in such ideas as Charity, Hope, Beauty, and Goodness. No one ever saw Charity or weighed Hope, set down the color of Beauty or described the latitude or longitude of Goodness. Being spiritual, such values solicit us beyond any concrete realization of their meaning in a charitable deed or a hopeful outlook, a beautiful rose or a good man. To think of these abstract ideas, man has to move above the world of the senses, and this implies that his mind is open at the top, able to gaze upward to the heavens while still enjoying the sights of earth. Because man is summoned by the infinite, yet never able to find it here, he is frustrated—a thing which animals cannot be, because they do not have this urge toward infinity. An elephant must always be an elephant, a primrose must be a primrose, but man has a potentiality to become something he is not; if he refuses to try to realize that strange capacity, he hurts his mind and his heart. When the plant and animal cease to develop in their natures, they decay; so man, if he refuses to develop *beyond* his nature, becomes less than he was before. The man who will not be supernatural becomes unnatural; the one who refuses to be more than human descends to the subhuman. Instead of tending toward Perfect Life, Truth, and Love, which is God and is his happiness, he may seek a substitute god in the form of more and more pleasure, more and more money, more and more self-will. Because man's emotions, desires, hopes, and ambitions are never fully satisfied with any particular thing, he may mistakenly seek compensation for his emptiness by amassing more of the same in an infinite, wearying series. Because one wife fails to satisfy his craving for the infinite, he may delude himself into believing that five wives will do what one will not. He may imagine that although five thousand dollars would not make him happy, five million dollars could. In the end such a seeker discovers that all he has been adding are zeros —mere quantity does not make the wrong remedy right. If one gulp of salt water does not satisfy, a barrel of it will not. Man's desire for self-transcendence cannot be fobbed off by losing himself in an infinity of trifles. The prodigal son was right in being hungry—that is the nature of man. He was wrong in living on husks.

Man could not build up such false infinities to worship if he were not made for the true Infinite. Only a being made for God can make himself a god. But this deification of the self is the saddest mistake of all—the self-worshipper soon cries: "I would like to get away from myself." Whenever he tries to get out of himself, however, he gets hit with the very boomerang of pride that he threw. The ego which hoped to lose itself in anything sub-Divine—from egotism, to inordinate pleasure, to dope—is thrown back on itself, because of the unsatisfying character of the object it is trying to fix its love upon. Misdirected worship of creatures reacts, as a golf ball rebounds when it hits against a tree.

It is well to recall here what was said in the beginning— that it is possible for man to live on three levels of existence: the level of the ego, of the I, and of the Divine. The ego is properly subordinated to the I by self-knowledge and self-discipline and the development of character. But when personality, or the I, has emerged, we are still on the level of the purely human; this is the level of a keen and sensitive natural love, which manifests itself in the mutual surrender of husband and wife, in parental and filial affection, and in fraternal love, as well. But all this is still a form of love that can live independent of the conscious love of God. Its expression becomes ennobled in the beautiful bonds of friendship, in the congeniality of minds which share the same struggles; it unfolds itself in sacrificial love of country, and of art, and of science; it provokes and draws forth from the breast the noblest feelings of consecration and sacrifice; but it is still a natural love and can be found in the most contrary causes on a battlefield. It still leaves our natures brimful of unrealized capacities for something more.

Even in the best and highest stages of love on the I-level, there are always definite limitations and boundaries, beyond which the I alone may not pass. Laggards who refuse to rise

higher than this can understand why one sacrifices for a
human love, but not why anyone should make a sacrifice for
the Divine. On the I-level, there is often a half-conscious
rejection of the summons to a higher life, but the hold of the
natural and the human is so powerful that, despite its capacity
for self-transcendence, the personality is reluctant to receive
what God has to give. Our heads have become so full of our
own ideas and our hands so full of our own business that there
is little room for *His* thoughts or for *His* deeds. Those whose
lives are confined to the I-lowlands are often willing to con-
cede that Jesus of Nazareth presents the most perfect speci-
men of human life that ever lived; they would be willing to
grant Him a certain moral superiority over Buddha, or to
say that he had perhaps a greater consciousness of God than
Socrates, but they are not prepared to accept Him for what
He is and what His Resurrection proved Him to be—uniquely
Divine. Such men admit Christ's moral attraction and speak
admiringly of the Beatitudes—without seeing that anyone
who preached the Beatitudes to a world such as ours must
necessarily be condemned to death. His sympathy and gentleness, His self-control and kindness to the poor, His readiness to
break down all class barriers are admitted as an evidence that
He is one of the greatest examples and inspirations that ever
walked this earth. All these, the I can accept, for they made no
demands upon it for self-transcendence. Thus, when Our
Divine Lord was crucified, His enemies were willing to admit
that He opened blind eyes to the light of God's sunshine
and unstopped deaf ears to the music of the human voice—but
they bade Him come down from the Cross, abandon the work
of redeeming sin. That was too supreme an example of love,
and one which offered too violent a reproach to them.

While the ego never wishes to admire anyone but itself, the I, then, is willing to admire Christ. But the problem involved in I-transcendence is not one of aesthetic approval—the question is whether a man is willing to follow Him; and to follow Him means to be united with Him in the sacrifice of self, the taking up of a Cross for the complete perfection of personality through pain. The I draws back from this demand. It may sincerely believe that it is impossible for a change to take place in human nature to the point where it can become a living manifestation of Divine Love among men. This is because the I concentrates upon its own powers and capacities, which could not, certainly, effect the change. But Divine Power, which is a gift, can operate within a man to elevate him to a higher level; it does not give him a change in direction on the same horizontal plane, for it performs an elevation. The change is not the product of a development, but the fruit of a generation. Inertia makes a body in physics continue in a state of rest or move in uniform motion in a straight line unless it is compelled to change its condition by an outside force. Man, too, remains on the I-level through inertia, unless he is moved from the outside: men of and by themselves do not become children of God.

When the possibility of self-transcendence through this infusion of Divine Power is acknowledged by the I, it may still rationalize its refusal to make those sacrifices which are essential for its ultimate perfection. The commonest rationalization is the statement that the Divine Life (or the supernatural) contradicts reason and therefore is opposed to the natural. This is the very opposite of the true state of affairs: as our reason is the perfection of our sense, so Divine Light and Power are the perfection of our reason. A second objection to the Divine lies in the misplacement of ambition—men fear Divinity because He would interrupt their desire to satisfy their own egos or to keep things the way *they* like them; they are not ambitious to have things the way *God* likes them. In the economic order such people cry for higher standards of living, but in the field of religion, when better housing conditions are offered for the mind and soul, it is difficult to convince them of the desirability of the change. And as for the second part of the objection, there is, indeed, a *difference* between the I-level and the Divine-level, but there is no *opposition* between the two. As St. Thomas said: "Grace is the perfection of nature." By nature we are made creatures of God; by Grace we become the sons of God. It is odd that a world that talks much of "emergent evolution" refuses to accept true evolution when it implies surpassing the human. For the supernatural is not an incongruous superstructure built upon reason, like a hut built on a tree, nor is it an accidental aid, like a magnifying glass to the eye and a loud-speaker to the ear; it is an enrichment, through the love of God, of the personal relationship which already exists, even in the natural order, between man and God. Man cannot bring about this ennoblement of his character; he can merely receive it as a gift; he has only a passive potency for it—as a dry stick has a potency for burning which a wet stick lacks. And although God desires that every man shall respond to this gift of self-transcendence, He nevertheless leaves each one free to reject His infusion of love—for gifts cease to be gifts if they are forced on us. God respects man's freedom of will; He did not even enter into this human order of ours without consulting a woman. So, neither, does He elevate us to partake of His Divine Nature without our free consent.

But suppose the rationalizations were to be swept aside, and

Grace accepted? This would not only enable the ego to over-come all of its frustration and thereby become more genuinely human—but it would also lead the I to actions of which previously it had thought itself incapable. Wonderful things Grace will do to a soul— but we retain the decision, even now, to rebel against it, and to slip back to a worse condition than before. This is man's ultimate power against God, which he can retain even to eternity. For hell is one of the negative guaranties of freedom—as heaven is its positive guaranty; a man can have his own will and make it infinite, for love or hatred, beyond all time and space. The passions of the ego enslave its votary; the freedom of the I enables it to discover or reject truths on the natural order; but God's gift of Grace shows it a freedom stronger than the bare power of choice, namely, the freedom of identifying itself with Love Divine.

The God-life which realizes our passive capacity for the infinite is, then, a gift. Because it is *gratis,* or free, it is called a *Grace.* Precisely because it is a gift, we play a part in its acceptance. Our dignity before the Eternal is something like the dignity of bride and groom at the altar, where love answers professed love with the words: "I will." Sunlight is all about the house, but to get in we must open the blinds. The Physician of souls can cure, but we must know that we are sick and must want to be cured. God calls! We can pretend we do not hear, or we can accept Him, or we can reject His voice. It is each man's inalienable right to decide: over 140 times Sacred Scripture emphasized the free acceptance of God's Grace. "Return, you rebellious children, and I will heal your rebellions." "Be mindful therefore from whence thou art fallen; and do penance, and do the first works." "Therefore will I judge every man according to his ways, O house of

Israel, saith the Lord God. Be converted, and do penance for all your iniquities; and iniquity shall not be your ruin."

But suppose the soul cooperates and lets God in; what happens? Once there is cooperation between Divine life and the will, those things which before seemed insufficient by themselves become endowed with new power and light. Education ceases to be a mere mechanical substitute of one theory or set of statistics for another or an amassing of uncorrelated data and begins to be the deepening of mystery, the unfolding of ever deeper insights into truth and the purpose of life. Reason becomes stronger, for faith helps it, as sunlight aids the eyes. Ethics ceases to be commandments and begins to be an act of love; and morality becomes a by-product of intimacy. The will is now transformed, so that our deeds cease to be the duty this day requires of us, but are a responsive echo to God's love. A good action is no longer prompted by external circumstances—such as the sight of a sick man on the street—but by the spirit of Christ within. The ego has given way to the I, and the I has begun to live in Christ.

The Divine Invader Who thus establishes a beachhead in the soul does not do so to give us an emotional sense of well-being or a warm feeling of "devotion" in the pit of the stomach. The Divine Presence may not affect our ganglia and our nerves at all. But it most certainly affects our intellects and our wills, and it implies a hard, deliberate reorientation of our lives in a God-ward direction. The Divine Power is not an inner glow; it is Christ Himself now present in His Spirit.

This suprahuman Divine Energy is poles apart from all human ideals which our minds can conceive, and which are themselves powerless to aid us; mere notions of virtue cannot strengthen us with an energy we do not have of and by ourselves. Ideals which are of our making have only *our* strength, and therefore they are weak. But the Divine Dynamo is our efficient cause, as well as our goal, our final cause. Since the Heavenly Power is outside us, it brings us strength from the outside, gives us the power of God as a ready help. A stick can be set on fire only by fire itself; man who wants to become more than he is can do so only if he is kindled by the Divine Fire from Heaven. All human ideals, human codes, and human systems—whether Aristotelian, Confucian, Platonic —treat man as a self-contained being whose highest potentialities exist within his own nature. But the pressure of the Eternal on his soul incites the Christian to become something he is not—entices him to permit himself to be lifted to a higher level than the human alone can ever possibly attain. That is why the initiative must come from God, as He works within us. Our moral endeavors still remain our own, but they are now far more than they used to be—they are transformed into responses to summons, they are contacts with God Himself, as He agitates our minds and wills. Thanks to this influx of Divine Energy, the change that now takes place in our character derives its principle not from our temperament, our education, our environment, our ethics, our unaided reason, or our human will, but from God. We can fall by ourselves, but we can be lifted up only by Him Who can raise also men from the dead. "Not that we are sufficient to think anything of ourselves, as of ourselves; but our sufficiency is from God."

Without this Divine Action on the soul of a sinner, he would never be able to turn from his evil ways. It is as unthinkable for a man living a deliberately wicked life to reverse his course under his own power and to become a child of God, as it

would be for him to stop himself in mid-air after he had
thrown himself off a bridge. God's action within the soul is
also necessary to help those, not deliberately evil, who have
lost their moral sense or who have plunged unthinkingly into
sensuality, drunkenness, and avarice. If God did not interfere
with them, their passions might one day leave them, but they
would never leave their passions; left to themselves the bigoted
merely become more bigoted, the sinful more sinful, the
greedy more avaricious, the hateful more cruel. But thanks to
the Divine Energy acting on the soul and in it, these people
can be turned completely around and can begin life all over
again—even though evil habits have become ingrained, and
the love of the good has been lost, and melancholy now sits in
their soul as on a throne. Augustines become saints, Magda-
lenes are turned to penitents. Peters change from traitors into
martyrs, Pauls abandon hate; but these things come about only
because God is there, urging the sinner toward a new path,
and directing him toward an unseen city on the everlasting
hills. Once the seed is planted, the earth becomes fruitful; but
the dirt may not boast that it alone brought forth the white-
ness of the rose. It is easy for a man to think that he did it
all—that *he* has made himself wise and well behaved, for the
Divine Action is imperceptible, subtle, and silent. As sometimes our best friends hide the kindly things they do for us,
so God in His Love throws minted gold into our souls and
lets us believe we mined it and refined it by ourselves.

God does not come in the thunder, but in the April breeze.
Because He does not shout but only whispers, the soul must
be careful not to neglect the visitation. "The kingdom of God
comes unwatched by men's eyes; there will be no saying, See,
it is here, or See, it is there; the kingdom of God is here,

within you." When this Divine Awareness transforms the personality, a new service of charity to fellow man is born. One sees then that men are distinguished from one another not by their education, wealth, charm, beauty, or cleverness, but rather by their responsiveness to the Divine Action in the soul. To the eyes of Faith only two classes of people exist: those who say "yes" to God and those who say "no" to Him.

There would be no hope for perverted souls were there no Heavenly Grace to touch and heal them. A thief could not at one moment curse a Man on a nearby Cross and the next ask Him for forgiveness and Paradise, unless he were transformed by the Divine, Who said to him: "This day thou shalt be with Me in Paradise." Only when men begin to be infinitely wicked, and God ceases to be infinitely good, may any man rightfully despair—and that will never be. But the despair that is Black Grace is a blessing sent to show the proud or misguided man that only suffering can ensue if he seeks his end in any lesser love than the God he has ignored.

Black Grace may be a potent treasure even to those who are moved to ask God's help as a last resort—a longshot risk. More than half sceptical of His power, they call on Him, and He answers them. So long as man is strong in his pride, God seems weak; so long as man believes himself to be a god, God seems scarcely to exist. But let a man doubt his own deity for a moment—let him become humble—then God begins to show Himself as strong. God in His Mercy thus makes some souls weak; at first they cry out: "Why did God do this to me?" But if they reflect, they will discover that unless the skin is rotted from the seed, it can never spring forth to life— we, too, have to shed our skins of pride through suffering. Such blessings, masked as misfortunes, strike all levels of men.

No one is ever happy in his ego; a man can be relatively happy in his I-personality, but it will fail him in great crises, in sorrows, sickness, trials, and the imminence of death—and that is when God reaches souls like these. Humanism is a brotherhood without tears; but when the tears flow, there is need of something more than it supplies. Even the best of human ethics centers a man's world around himself, and this results in spiritual pride (when the I obeys its ethical system and exults) or in despair (when the ego rules.) The path of true human perfection is the one through which a man so overshadows both his ego and his I as to see both his neighbor and his I through the eye of God. Our Lord said that a man cannot add one cubit to his stature by thinking; neither can the I attain that profound love of God and neighbor which the saints enjoy without the Divine Dynamic from above. Self-centeredness, even in the morally good, is a snare; God-centeredness is the only solution to our life's enigma.

15

Prayer and Meditation

THIS is probably the most talkative age in the history of the world—not only because we have more mechanical devices to diffuse our talking, but also because we have little inside our minds which did not come there from the world outside our minds, so that human communication seems to us a great necessity. As a result, talk is deified as a means of solving all problems. Even the young—who have not yet studied the philosophy of human rights—are called upon to solve the problems of the world in their "progressive" classrooms. There are few listeners, although St. Paul tells us that "faith comes from hearing." If the bodies of most of us were fed as little as the mind, they would soon starve to death. Hyperactivity and love of noise and chatter characterize our age, as a compensation for the modern man's profound distrust of himself. Not knowing clearly what he *is*, the American of today tries to become important by what he *does*—for the more anxious a man is, the more active he becomes. Expectant fathers walk like caged beasts in the waiting rooms of maternity hospitals. The rocking chair, it has been said, is a typical American invention; it enables man to rest as he is restless, to sit in one place and still be on the go. In the days of a truly Chrisitan civilization, man was active because of his body—he worked to eat. In the post-Christian era, man is active because of his mind—he works to stop thinking. The external necessity of labor is less exigent and cruel than the inner compulsion to "work off" anxiety. Man keeps in futile motion partly to escape having to ask himself two questions: "Why am I here?" and "Where am I going?"

Because of his inner chaos and division, man cannot endure chaos around him—he longs for uniformity in everything. Having lost his internal unity through union with God, he tries to compensate by seeking an *external* unity with other human beings in the collective. Life becomes standardized. Today nearly all newspapers have the same standards of what is news. Mass opinion is created by the few magazines which are most widely sold. Our proper internal likeness to others through Divine Grace has given way to an external likeness brought about by slavish imitation. Mechanized opinion, imitation of our cheap "celebrities," dependence on "they say" or "they are wearing" for our guidance dwarf the modern man's individuality. The one who lives close to God cares not if he is unlike everybody else; but as one loses unity with Divinity, he develops a fear of being alone. He hopes (falsely) to derive some sense of protection from similarity to others.

Another result of our loss of inner peace is the replacement of quality by quantity. Having lost Grace, a qaulity of the soul that makes us God-like, a compensation is sought in the worship of quantity. Thus we boast of the "biggest," the "highest," the "greatest." The biggest university becomes the best university. Educators cease to be interested in the discovery of truth that unifies and strive only for a colossal accumulation of unrelated facts. As Pliny said: "Not being able to make our values beautiful, we make them huge." The greatness of our civilization is sometimes reckoned in terms of New York's Babels towering against the sky; we forget that Egypt built her greatest pyramids on the eve of her decline.

Finally, as the soul becomes impoverished through want of God-likeness, the body seeks compensation in excessive luxury and show of all sorts. Inner nakedness is atoned for by a new ornateness of dress. A rich boy can dress poorly and still be known as rich; a poor boy who wants to be known as rich must wear the semblance of wealth. A truly learned man does not have to talk about all the books he has read to be known as educated; but the sophomore who wants to be a member of the intelligentsia must intersperse his conversation with: "What! You never read *that?*" It is so with spirituality, too—the soul that has put on Christ does not need to pray publicly in the market places, to draw attention to its piety, as the Pharisees do. The show-off in any area is the man who lacks the quality he so carefully pretends to have. Those who love publicity are always people who do not want their real selves to be known to anyone; they have to advertise a legendary self. When these starved souls are told that they cannot take their various masks and pretences with them, we seem to hear them say: "Well then, we will not go." The "act" which they put on has come to them to seem more precious than any truth or any reality.

No human being is happy when he is as externalized as

most men are today. Everyone wants peace of soul, knowing that he cannot be happy on the outside unless he is happy on the inside. As a Chinese said: "Americans are not happy; they laugh too much." He may have seen the million photographs we show of people laughing, with nothing to laugh at but with a grim desire to create the illusion that they are having fun.

More important than an analysis of our excessive "outwardness" is its cure; for no one is happy in such extrinsic posturings. As one looks back to the Gospel, one finds Our Divine Lord warning us against such forms of ersatz peace, against standardization and conformity to the world. He said: "If the world hates you, be sure that it hated Me before it learned to hate you. If you belonged to the world, the world would know you for its own and love you; it is because you do not belong to the world, because I have singled you out from the midst of the world, that the world hates you." (John 15:18,19.) Against Colossalism, He warned in the parable of the man who built bigger and bigger barns, only to have an angel tell him that that very night his soul would be required of him. Our Lord cautioned against hyperactivity when He told Martha that she was busy about too many things. The night He suffered His Agony, He rebuked Peter for substituting action for prayer, when, instead of watching a silent hour, he drew his sword. We have been amply warned—yet it is possible that those who today claim to be God's servants are sometimes so busy in their projects for the Kingdom of God that they forget the Kingdom of God itself.

All these externalizations are signs that we are trying to escape God and the cultivation of the soul. The very fact that anyone becomes disquieted when noise and excitement cease proves that he is in flight from his true self. Gregariousness, the passionate need to lose oneself in a crowd, the urge to identify oneself with the tempo of New York and Hollywood, is a strong proof that one is seeking distraction from the inner self, where true joy alone is found.

One of the most powerful means of overcoming the externalization of life is to find support in prayer and meditation. But as soon as prayer is suggested, there are those who will immediately retort: "Praying does no good." This statement has an element of truth in certain cases: not theological truth, but psychological. When it is said by those who are unwilling to curb their promiscuous habits or to tame their carnality, then the statement, "It does no good to pray," is true—but only of themselves. Their prayers are ineffective, not because God refuses to hear them, but because they refuse to fulfill the first condition of prayer, namely, a longing to revise their natures to accordance with God's laws. To have any effectiveness, a prayer for help must express an honest desire to be changed, and that desire must be without reservation or conditions on our part. If we pray to be delivered from alcoholism, and yet refuse to stop drinking, that fact is an acknowledgment that we did not really pray. In like manner, the man who prays to be delivered from sexual perversions and excesses— and that very day deliberately exposes himself to such pleasures—has destroyed the efficacy of the prayer by a reservation. All prayer implies an act of the will, a desire for growth, a willingness to sacrifice on our own part; for prayer is not passive, but is a very active collaboration between the soul and God. If the will is inoperative, our prayers are merely a list of the things we would like God to give us, without ever asking us to pay the price they cost in effort and a willing-

ness to change. Prayer is dynamic, but only when we cooperate with God through surrender. The man who decides
to pray for release from the slavery of carnal pleasures must
be prepared, in every part of his being, to utilize the strength
which God will give him and to work unreservedly for a
complete freedom from the sin. In dealing with other men it
is possible to have one's cake and eat it, but with God that
is impossible.

Sometimes—even when the will is operative—a prayer seems
worthless because we approach God with a divided will. We
want him, but we want something else incompatible with Him.
We are demanding that the laws of the universe be lifted, so
that He will give us the reward of perfect trust in Him, while
we continue to place half our trust in other things. In such a
case, we keep one hand behind our back; we hold on to something that would compensate us if God should fail. We prepare a substitute satisfaction to fall back on if He does not
come through—such as a comfortable bank account, when one
is praying for guidance from Divine Providence. Human
friendships are often broken for want of a complete and total
confidence; and Divine Friendship does not bestow all of its
gifts, either, when complete trust in Him is wanting. Faith
precedes the answered prayer.

It is not difficult to understand why many people do not
pray, at all. As a workman can become so interested in what
he is doing as not to hear the noonday whistle, so the egotist
can become so self-infatuated as to be unconscious of anything
outside of himself. The suggestion that there is a reality beyond him, a power and an energy that can transform and
elevate him, strikes him as absurd. Just as there are tone-deaf
men who are dead to music and color-blind men who are

dead to art, so the egotists are Deity-blind, that is, dead to the vision of God. They say they cannot pray, and they are right, *they* cannot. Their self-centeredness has paralyzed them. There is also some truth in their statement that they "do not need prayer," because they do not want to be any better than they are—their purpose is to remain unchanged, and this stultification can be accomplished by themselves alone. Animals do not need prayer, either, for none of them has a capacity for self-transcendence, which man has. A man is the only creature in the world who can *become* more than he is, if he freely wills to grow. The man who boasts that he is his own creator need never acknowledge dependence on God; he who affirms that he has never done anything wrong has no need of a Saviour. Before such egotists can pray, their selfishness must be corrected. Many refuse to correct it—not because they fear what they will become if they do, but because they cannot face the surrenders they would have to make before they could be elevated to a higher level of peace and joy.

There must always be a relationship between the gift and the recipient—there is no point in giving anyone a treasure he cannot use. A father would not give a boy with no talent for music a Stradivarius violin. Neither will God give to egocentrics those gifts and powers and energies which they never propose to put to work in the transformation of their lives and souls.

Some object that, inasmuch as God's Will will always be done, it can make no difference whether we pray; this is like saying: "My friend will either get better or worse; what good will it do to send for a doctor and give him medicine?" In the physical order medical power takes into account the physical factors within a sick body; in the spiritual order God's Will makes allowance for our desire to do better. It is true that in answering a prayer, God will not do what He did not will, merely because we asked Him; but He will do that which without our prayer He would not do. God will not make the sun shine through a dirty window—but the sun will shine through the window if it is clean. God will not do what we can very well do for ourselves; He will not make a harvest grow without our planting the seed. It is a conditional universe in which man lives—to bring about an effect we wish, we must proceed along the road to it through its cause. If a boy studies, he will know; if he strikes a match, it will ignite. In the spiritual order we have the words of Our Lord: "Ask, and the gift will come; seek, and you shall find; knock and the door shall be opened to you." (Matt. 7:7.) But there must be the preparation for God's help through the asking, and the seeking, and the knocking. Millions of favors are hanging from Heaven on silken cords—prayer is the sword that will cut them. "See where I stand at the door, knocking; if anyone listens to my voice and opens the door, I will come in to visit him, and take my supper with him, and he shall sup with me." (Apoc. 3:20.)

This text reverses the order that many people think to be the law of prayer. They assume that when we pray we ring God's doorbell and ask for a favor. Actually, it is He Who rings our bell. "I stand at the door, knocking." God could do much more for any soul if its will were more conformable— the weakness is always on the receiving end. Broadcasting stations wish to send programs into the home, but the programs do not become available unless a listener tunes in to them.

Many blessings and favors come to those individuals and

families which put themselves wholeheartedly in the area of God's love—their lives are in sharp contrast to those who exclude themselves from that area of love. In the raising of a family, if the economic is made a primary concern and the Providence of God secondary, it is not to be expected that there will be the same showering of gifts and care on God's part as in a family where Providence comes first. The parents who trust God can tap a source of power and happiness which the other family does not make available. As human friends give us more in proportion as we trust them, and less in proportion to our mistrust, so it is with the Divine Friend. Those who make it possible for God to give more through their trust in Him receive more. In those families where the economic is a primary goal and where prayers are still said, it is very likely that the prayer will be like that of the prodigal: "Give me . . . " In the other family, where Providence is primary, the prayer is more likely to be that of the prodigal after his conversion, when he said to the father: "Make me. . . . " In proportion as we pray to be more faithful and loving sons of God, there will be a corresponding bestowal of those gifts which a Heavenly Father can give to His children—whom He loved so much He died for them.

The essence of prayer is not the effort to make God give us something—as this is not the basis of sound human friendships—but there is a legitimate prayer of petition. God has two kinds of gifts: first, there are those which He sends us whether we pray for them or not; and the second kind are those which are given on condition that we pray. The first gifts resemble those things which a child receives in a family—food, clothing, shelter, care, and watchfulness. These gifts come to every child, whether the child asks for them or not. But there are other gifts, which are conditioned upon the desire of the child. A father may be eager to have a son go to college, but if the boy refuses to study or becomes a delinquent, the gift which the father intended for him can never be bestowed. It is not because the father has retracted his gift, but rather because the son has made the gift impossible. Of the first kind of gifts Our Blessed Lord spoke when He said: "His rain falls on the just and equally on the unjust." (Matt. 5:45.) He spoke of the second kind of gifts when He said: "Ask, and the gift will come."

Prayer, then, is not just the informing of God of our needs, for He already knows them. "You have a Father in Heaven who knows that you need them all." (Matt. 6:32.) Rather, the purpose of prayer is to give Him the opportunity to bestow the gifts He will give us when we are ready to accept them. It is not the eye which makes the light of the sun surround us; it is not the lung which makes the air envelop us. The light of the sun is there if we do not close our eyes to it, and the air is there for our lungs if we do not hold our breath. God's blessings are there—if we do not rebel against His Will to give.

God does not show Himself equally to all creatures. This does not mean that He has favorites, that He decides to help some and to abandon others, but the difference occurs because it is impossible for Him to manifest Himself to certain hearts under the conditions they set up. The sunlight plays no favorites, but its reflection is very different on a lake and on a swamp.

A person's prayer often keeps step with his moral life. The closer our behavior corresponds with the Divine Will, the easier it is to pray; the more our conduct is out of joint with

Divinity, the harder it is to pray. Just as it is hard to look in the face of someone whom we have grievously wronged, so it is hard to lift our minds and hearts to God if we are in rebellion against Him. This is not because God is unwilling to hear sinners. He does hear them, and He has a special predilection for them, for as He said: "I have come to call sinners, not the just." (Mark 2:17.) "There will be more rejoicing over one sinner who repents, than over ninety-nine souls that are justified and have no need of repentance." (Luke 15:7.) But *these* sinners were the ones who corresponded with His Will and abandoned their rebellion against it. Where the sinner has no desire to be lifted from his evil habits, then the essential condition for prayer is wanting.

Everyone knows enough about God to pray to Him, even those who say that they doubt His existence. If they were lost in the woods, they would have no assurance whatever of anyone nearby who might help them find their way—but they would shout, nevertheless, in the hope that someone would hear. In like manner, the sceptic finds, in catastrophe and in crisis, that though he thought himself incapable of prayer, he nonetheless prays. But those who use prayer only as a last resort do not know God very well—they hold Him at arm's length most of the time, refusing Him the intimacy of every day. The little knowledge of God that such people possess does not become fruitful or functional, because they never act upon that knowledge: the Lord ordered that the unproductive talent be taken away. Unless a musician acts upon the knowledge that he already has of music, he will not grow either in knowledge or in love of it. In this sense, our conduct, behavior, and moral life become the determinants of our relations with God. When our behavior is Godless, licentious, selfish, egotistic, and cruel, then prayer is an extraneous thing —a mere attempt at magic, an attempt to make God serve our wishes in contradiction to the moral laws He has laid down.

The man who thinks only of himself says only prayers of petition; he who thinks of his neighbor says prayers of intercession; he who thinks only of loving and serving God, says prayers of abandonment to God's Will, and this is the prayer of the saints. The price of this prayer is too high for most people, for it demands the displacement of our ego. Many souls want God to do *their* will; they bring their completed plans and ask Him to rubber-stamp them without a change. The petition of the "Our Father" is changed by them to read: "*My* will be done on earth." It is very difficult for the Eternal to give Himself to those who are interested only in the temporal. The soul who lives on the ego-level or the I-level and refuses to be brought to the Divine-level is like an egg which is kept forever in a place too cool for incubation, so that it is never called upon to live a life outside of the shell of its own incomplete development. Every I is still an embryo of what a man is meant to be.

Where there is love, there is thought about the one we love. "Where your treasure-house is, there your heart is too." (Matt. 6:21.) The degree of our devotion and love depend upon the value that we put upon a thing: St. Augustine says, *Amor pondus meum;* love is the law of gravitation. All things have their center. The schoolboy finds it hard to study, because he does not love knowledge as much as athletics. The businessman finds it hard to think of heavenly pleasures because he is dedicated to the filling of his "barn." The carnal-minded find it difficult to love the spirit because their treasure lies in the flesh. Everyone becomes like that which he loves: if

he loves the material, he becomes like the material; if he loves
the spiritual, he is converted into it in his outlook, his ideals,
and his aspirations. Given this relationship between love and
prayer, it is easy to understand why some souls say: "I have no
time to pray." They really have not, because to them other
duties are more pressing; other treasures more precious; other
interests more exhilarating. As watches that are brought too
close to a dynamo cease to keep time, so, too, hearts that
become too much absorbed in external things soon lose their
capacity to pray. But as a jeweler with a magnet can draw
the magnetism out of the watch and reset it by the sky, so, too,
it is possible to become de-egotized by prayer, and be reset to
the Eternal and to Love Divine. Though prayer is a duty, it
is not well done unless the greatest motivation for it is love.
The lover always has an overwhelming desire to fulfill the
will of the beloved; human hearts find prayer unrewarding
if they have too many other desires and wishes besides that of
fulfilling God's Will, which is always our perfection. Some
would like to please themselves without displeasing God:
they do not want to be on "outs" with God, as a clerk
does not want to be on "outs" with his boss. When there
is such little love as this, religion and prayer are regarded as
mere correctives, as something negative and restraining to our
wishes. Such people ask of prayer and religion only that they
keep them out of mortal sins—restrain them to moderate
avarice, to moderate selfishness, and to moderate intemperance.
If the heart and mind are lifted to God in such moods of
mediocre hopes from Him, it is not to find out what God
wants, but to tell Him what we want Him to do—so much,
no more.

We pray as much as we desire to, and we desire to in ratio

with our love. But the capacity for prayer belongs to every soul, and even those who do not acknowledge any love of God pray under stress. Our Divine Lord told two parables, sometimes badly interpreted as saying that God is reluctant to grant favors but may be persuaded by our repeated pleading; actually, the stories do not have that meaning.

"Suppose one of you has a friend, to whom he goes at dead of night, and asks him, Lend me three loaves of bread, neighbor; a friend of mine has turned in to me after a journey, and I have nothing to offer him. And suppose the other answers, from within doors, Do not put me to such trouble; the door is locked, my children and I are in bed; I cannot bestir myself to grant thy request. I tell you, even if he will not bestir himself to grant it out of friendship, shameless asking will make him rise and give his friend all that he needs." (Luke 11:5,9.)

"And he told them a parable, showing them that they ought to pray continually, and never be discouraged. There was a city once, he said, in which lived a judge who had no fear of God, no regard for man; and there was a widow in this city who used to come before him and say, Give me redress against one who wrongs me. For a time he refused; but then he said to himself, Fear of God I have none, nor regard for man, but this widow wearies me; I will give her redress, or she will wear me down at last with her visits. Listen, the Lord said, to the words of the unjust judge, and tell me, will not God give redress to his elect, when they are crying out to him, day and night? Will he not be impatient with their wrongs? I tell you, he will give them redress with all speed. But ah, when the Son of Man comes, will he find faith left on the earth?" (Luke 18:1,8.)

The real meaning of the parables is this: if a grumpy man, selfishly interested in his rest—or a scoundrelly judge—will grant favors to those who solicit them, then how much more will God do good things for us if we ask? Prayer is not the overcoming of a reluctant God, but an identification of our needs with the highest kind of Willingness to help. In the parables the tardy selfishness of one man is set against the prompt liberality of God, and the unrighteousness of another man is contrasted with the righteousness of God. A second meaning lies in the stories: they tell us that prayer is natural in time of crisis, for one of them deals with a physical and the other with a social catastrophe. The suggestion is clearly made that if the neighbor were not in need of bread and the widow were not in need of justice, they would not have pled. He who says that he cannot pray or will never pray is stating only an opinion, held in times when no grave crisis troubles him. He is not revealing his basic impulses. An atomic bomb dropped on any city would make millions pray who had denied such a possibility. George Herbert said: "He that will learn to pray, let him go to sea." And Abraham Lincoln said: "I have been driven many times to my knees by the overwhelming conviction that I had nowhere else to go; my own wisdom and that of all around me seemed insufficient for that day."

If God sometimes seems slow to answer our petitions, there are several possible reasons. One is that the delay is for the purpose of deepening our love and increasing our faith; the other is that God is urging us. God may defer for some time the granting of His gifts, that we might the more ardently pursue, not the gift, but the Giver. Or we may be asking Him for something He wants us to learn we do not need.

Jacob once asked God to bring him home safely, promising that he would give ten per cent of his income for an altar as a thanksgiving. Later on, after Jacob had wrestled with the angel, he forgot what favor he had wanted to get from God; he merely said, in the joy of communion with Deity: "I have seen God face to face." The greatest gift of God is not the things we think we would like to have, but Himself. And as all love grows, it asks less and less, seeking only to give and give. God, likewise, does not always give us what we *want*, but He always gives us what we need. Often this is a gift so great and generous that we should never have asked for it because, until it came, we did not know of it.

Our Lord never promised safety to His Apostles; He promised persecution: "You will be hated by all men because you bear My name." He did not promise them health or comfort; He promised strength to bear their trials. St. Paul prayed that the thorn in his flesh—some kind of illness— should be taken from him. This request was made three times and never granted; yet his prayer was answered. He received the answer: "My grace is enough for thee." And so, although the illness continued, St. Paul did not rebel against the God Who did not cure him, but rather said :"More than ever, then, I delight to boast of the weaknesses that humiliate me, so that the strength of Christ may enshrine itself in me. I am well content with these humiliations of mine, with the insults, the hardships, the persecutions, the times of difficulty I undergo for Christ; when I am weakest, then I am strongest of all." (II Cor. 12:9,10.)

A little girl at Christmas once prayed for a thousand dolls. Her unbelieving father on Christmas Day said: "Well, God did not answer your prayers, did He?" And she answered:

"Yes, He did. God said *no*." This was the humble acceptance of His will of the truly faithful. The three youths in the fiery furnace, who were condemned to death because they would not fall down before the false image which Nabuchodonosor had erected, prayed that God would deliver them—but they were also prepared to accept whatever His Will might be. Their prayer ended: "For behold our God, Whom we worship, is able to save us from the furnace of burning fire, and to deliver us out of thy hands, O king. But if He will not, be it known to thee, O king, that we will not worship thy gods, nor adore the golden statue which thou hast set up." (Dan. 3:17,18.)

A higher form of prayer than petition—and a potent remedy against the externalization of life—is meditation. Meditation is a little like a daydream or a reverie, but with two important differences: in meditation we do not think about the world or ourselves, but about God. And instead of using the imagination to build idle castles in Spain, we use the will to make resolutions that will draw us nearer to one of the Father's mansions. Meditation is a more advanced spiritual act than "saying prayers"; it may be likened to the attitude of a child who breaks into the presence of a mother saying: "I'll not say a word, if you will just let me stay here and watch you." Or, as a soldier once told the Curé of Ars: "I just stand here before the tabernacle; He looks at me and I look at Him." Meditation allows one to suspend the conscious fight against external diversions by an internal realization of the presence of God. It shuts out the world to let in the Spirit. It surrenders our own will to the impetus of the Divine Will. It turns the searchlight of Divine Truth on the way we think, act, and speak, penetrating beneath the layers of our self-deceit and egotism. It summons us before the Bar of Divine Justice, so that we may see ourselves as we really are, and not as we like to think we are. It silences the ego with its clamorous demands, in order that it may hear the wishes of the Divine Heart. It uses our faculties, not to speculate on matters remote from God, but to stir up the will to conform more perfectly with His Will. It cultivates a truly scientific attitude toward God as Truth, freeing us from our prepossessions and our biases so that we may eliminate all wishful thinking from our minds. It eliminates from our lives the things that would hinder union with God and strengthens our desire that all the good things we do shall be done for His Honor and Glory. It takes our eyes off the flux and change of life and reminds us of our *being*, the creatureliness, the dependence of all things on God for creation, moment-to-moment existence, and salvation. Meditation is not a petition, a way of using God, or asking things from Him, but rather a surrender, a plea to God that He use us.

Meditation has two stages—withdrawal from worldly consideration, and concentration on the Nature of God and His Incarnate Son, Jesus Christ. Meditation uses three powers of the soul: the memory, the intellect, and the will. By memory we recall His Goodness and our blessings; with the intellect we recall what is known of His Life, Truth, and Love; by the will we strive to love Him above all else. When we study, we know about God; when we meditate, we know God's Presence in ourselves, and we capture the very heart of our existence. So long as the ego or the I stands aloof from God, we are unhappy. But when our personality becomes lost in God's, so that His Mind is our mind, His desires are our desires, His loves are our loves—then the I realizes itself in self-forgetfulness. In the words of St. Paul: "And yet I am alive; or rather, not I; it is Christ that lives in Me." (Gal. 2:20.)

For meditation the ear of the soul is more important than the tongue: St. Paul tells us that faith comes from listening. Most people commit the same mistake with God that they do with their friends: they do all the talking. Our Lord warned against those who "use many phrases, like the heathens, who think to make themselves heard by their eloquence." (Matt. 6:7.) One can be impolite to God, too, by absorbing all the conversation, and by changing the words of Scripture from "Speak Lord, Thy servant hears" to "Listen Lord, Thy servant speaks." God has things to tell us which will enlighten us—we must wait for Him to speak. No one would rush into a physician's office, rattle off all the symptoms, and then dash away without waiting for a diagnosis; no one would tune in the radio and immediately leave the room. It is every bit as stupid to ring God's doorbell and then run away. The Lord hears us more readily than we suspect; it is our listening to Him that needs to be improved. When people complain that their prayers are not heard by God, what often has happened is that they did not wait to hear His answer.

Prayer, then, is not a monologue, but a dialogue. It is not a one-way street, but a boulevard. The child hears a word before he ever speaks it—his tongue is trained through the ear; so our soul, too, is trained through its ear. As Isaias the Prophet said: "He wakeneth in the morning, in the morning he wakeneth my ear, that I may hear him as a master." St. Paul tells us that the Spirit will tell us for what things we ought to pray; as the Spirit brooded once over the formless waters, so now it brings spiritual expression to the voiceless void of our hearts. If our tongues are crude in their petitions, it is because our ears have been dull in their hearing of the faith. One of the important details of the Sacrament of Baptism is the opening of the ear: the priest touches it and says, as Our Lord did to the deaf man, "Ephepheta; be thou opened." The words imply that once a soul is brought into the state of Grace, the ears which were closed are open to the World of God. There is a more sublime philosophy than we suspect in our saying that we learned our prayers from our mothers' *lips*. Prayer is arduous when it is only a monologue, but it is a joy when our self-absorption gives way to the act of humbly listening.

The best exposition of the steps in meditation is found in the account of Easter Sunday in the Gospel. The disciples on that day were most forlorn. In their sadness they fell into talk about Our Lord with a traveler whom they had met by chance on the Emmaus road. This marks the first stage of meditation: they spoke *about* Our Lord, not realizing He was present. This is followed by Our Lord's disclosure of His presence—we listen, then, as the disciples did when He began to unfold to them the meaning of His Passion and Death. Finally, there comes a stage of communion—signified by the breaking of bread at supper in the Gospel; at this point the soul is united to God, and God to the soul. It is a moment one reluctantly abandons, even when the day is far spent and fatigue is great.

Besides the joy it brings in itself, meditation has practical effects on our spiritual lives. First, it cures us of the habit of self-deception. Man is the only creature on earth capable of self-reflection; this possibility exists because he has a rational soul. Since the soul is also spiritual, it has a longing for the infinite; we sometimes seek to slake our infinite thirst in the waters of the world—which have a glamour for us that is

lacking in the things of God—and when this effort tem-
porarily provides us with pleasure, we deceive ourselves.
Meditation enables us to hold the mirror up to our souls,
to perceive the fatal disease of self-love in the blinding light
of the Radiant Christ. Because talk is a principal cause of
self-deception, our friends dupe us with their flattery, and
much of our inward conversation with ourselves is apt to
be pitched on a note of self-justification. The silence which
meditation demands is the best cure for this; in silence the
workmen of the soul clear away its rubbish, as trash collectors
clean our cities in the quiet night. Anyone awake at night
sees his sins more clearly than in daylight; this is because the
soul is now beyond the distraction of all noise. Sleeplessness
is thus more of a burden to those with a sense of guilt than
to the innocent, who, like the Psalmist, can raise their night
thoughts to God in prayer. Meditation provides an artificial
quiet by shutting out the din of day. It replaces the criticism
of others, which is probably our mental habit, by a self-
criticism which will make us less critical of others. The one
who sees the most faults in his neighbor is the one who has
never looked inside his own soul. Unjustified criticism of
others is self-flattery—for by finding others worse than ourselves, we become comparatively virtuous; but in meditation,
by finding ourselves worse than others, we discover that most
of our neighbors are better than ourselves. The poorer a man
is, the greater the fortune of which he dreams; so, the humbler
we are in our meditation, the higher the ideal to which we
aspire. As there is no egotist who is not also a self-deceiver,
so no one accustomed to meditate has any illusions as to his
own grandeur. The clearer we see our souls in relation to
God, the less ego-centric we become.

There is a definite correlation between knowing God and

knowing oneself: God cannot be known unless we know ourselves as we really are. The less a man thinks of himself, the more he thinks of God. God's greatness does not depend objectively on our littleness; but it becomes a subjective reality to us only if we are humble. As we make ourselves "gods," we perceive God less and less. The consciousness of our need for help in being good is the condition of knowing Goodness Itself.

Meditation also improves our behavior. It is often stated that it makes no difference what we believe, that all depends on how we act; but this is meaningless, for we act upon our beliefs. Hitler acted on the theory of Nazism and produced a war; Stalin acts on the ideology of Marx and Lenin and begets slavery. If our thoughts are bad, our actions will also be bad. The problem of impure actions is basically the problem of impure thoughts; the way to keep a man from robbing a bank is to distract him from thinking about robbing a bank. Political, social, and economic injustices are, first, psychic evils—they originate in the mind. They become social evils because of the intensity of the thought that begot them.

Nothing ever happens in the world that does not first happen inside a mind. Hygiene is no cure for immorality, but if the wellsprings of thought were kept clean, there would be no need to care for the effects of evil thinking on the body. When one meditates and fills his mind for an hour a day with thoughts and resolutions bearing on the love of God and neighbor above all things, there is a gradual seepage of love down to the level of what is called the *subconscious*, and finally these good thoughts emerge, of themselves, in the form of effortless good actions. Everyone has verified in his own life a thousand times the ideomotor character of thought. Watching a football game, the spectator sees a player running with

the ball; if there is a beautiful opening around right end, he
may twist and turn his own body more than the runner does,
to try to take advantage of the chance. The idea is so strong
that it influences his bodily movements—as ideas often do.
Thoughts of fear produce "goose-pimples" and sometimes
make the blood rush to the hands and feet. God has made us
so that, when we are afraid, we should either fight or run.

Our thoughts make our desires, and our desires are the
sculptors of our days. The dominant desire is the predominant
destiny. Desires are formed in our thoughts and meditations;
and since action follows the lead of desires, the soul, as it becomes flooded with Divine Promptings, becomes less and less
a prey to the suggestions of the world. This increases happiness; external wants are never completely satisfied, and their
elimination thus makes for less anxiety. If a man meditates
consistently on God, a complete revolution takes place in his
behavior. If in a morning meditation he remembers how God
became a humble Servant of man, he will not lord it over
others during the day. If there were a meditation of His Redemption of all men, he would cease to be a snob. Since Our
Lord took the world's sins upon Himself, the man who has
dwelt on this truth will seek to take up the burdens of his
neighbor, even though they were not of his making—for the
sins the Lord bore were not of His making, either. If the
meditation stressed the Merciful Saviour Who forgave those
who crucified Him, so a man will forgive those who injure
him, that he may be worthy of forgiveness. These thoughts do
not come from ourselves—for we are incapable of them—nor
from the world—for they are unworldly thoughts. They come
from God alone.

Meditation effects far more profound changes in us than
resolutions to "do better"; we cannot keep evil thoughts out

of our minds unless we put good ones in their place. Super-nature, too, abhors a vacuum. In meditation one does not *drive* sin out of his life; he *crowds* it out with love of God and neighbor. Our lives do not then depend on the principle of avoiding sin, which is a tiresome job, but on living constantly in the climate of Divine Love. Meditation, in a word, prevents defeat where defeat is final: in the mind. In that silence where God is, false desires steal away. If we meditate before we go to bed, our last thought at night will be our first thought in the morning. There will be none of that dark brown feeling with which some men face a meaningless day; and in its place will be the joy of beginning another morning of work in Christ's Name.

As a third largesse, meditation gives us contact with new sources of power and energy. "Come to me, all you that labour and are burdened; I will give you rest." (Matt. 11:28.) No one has sufficient knowledge and power to carry him through all the difficulties and trials of living. We think we have sufficient wisdom when we give advice to others; but we learn we do not have it, when we have to live on our own intellectual fat. The more an orchestra plays, the more it has to be tuned up; the farther an airplane flies, the more it needs to be serviced. When our spiritual batteries run down, we cannot charge them by ourselves; and the more active the life is, the greater the need to vitalize its acts by meditation. But each meditation must be personalized—brought from the realm of thought and reduced to a lesson we ourselves are able to apply. No man is better because he knows the five proofs for the existence of God; but he becomes better when that knowledge is permitted to transform his will. Purity of heart is therefore the condition of prayer; we cannot be intimate with God so long as we cling to unlawful attach-

ments. The needed purity must be fourfold: purity of conscience, so that we will never offend God; purity of heart,
so that we keep all our affections for God; purity of mind so
that we preserve a continual consciousness of God; and purity
of action so that we keep our intentions selfless and abandon
our self-will.

Once our helplessness is rendered up to the Power of God,
life changes, and we become less and less the victims of our
moods. Instead of letting the world determine our state of
mind, we determine the state of soul with which the world
is to be faced. The earth carries its own atmosphere with it as
it revolves about the sun; so the soul can carry the atmosphere
of God with it, in disregard of turbulent events in the world
outside. There is a moment in every good meditation when
the God-life enters our life, and another moment when our
life enters the God-life. These events transform us utterly.
Sick, nervous, fearful men are made well by this communion
of creature with Creator, this letting of God into the soul. A
distinguished psychiatrist, J. D. Hadfield, has said: "I attempted to cure a nervous patient with suggestions of quiet
and confidence, but without success, until I had linked these
suggestions on to that faith in the power of God which is the
substance of the Christian's confidence and hope. Then the
patient became strong."

It is never true to say that we have no time to meditate;
the less one thinks of God, the less time there will always be
for Him. The time one has for anything depends on how
much he values it. Thinking determines the uses of time;
time does not rule over thinking. The problem of spirituality
is never, then, a question of time; it is a problem of thought.
For it does not require much time to make us saints; it requires
only much love.

16

Sanctifying the Moment

MILLIONS of men and women today lead what has been called "lives of quiet desperation." They are panicky, worried, neurotic, fearful, and, above all, frustrated souls. And frustration results from failure—either a failure that has already occurred or a failure in prospect. Man may become frustrated by comparing the immensity of the problems facing him with the feebleness of his resources for solving them; in such a case, he is too discouraged, too apprehensive of failure, even to try for a solution. Or he may become frustrated from a lack of someone to love, someone who will love him sufficiently in return. The first type of frustration puts a soul in the harried position of a householder who becomes more and more depressed as the bills mount up, and money fails to materialize: he dreads a future reckoning. The second kind of frustration involves the feeling that life is passing quickly and that the chances for emotional fufillment are growing less with every year. Both forms of misery are connected, then, with an unhappy individual's consciousness of the passage of time. The frustrated soul is the one most apt to shiver if he sees the old sundial warning: "It is later than you think."

All our anxieties relate to time. Man is the only time-conscious creature. He alone can bring the past to his mind, so that it weighs on the present moment with its accumulated heritage; and he can also bring the future into the present, so as to imagine its occurrences as happening now. No animal ever says: "I have suffered this pain for six years, and it will last until I die." But because man can unite the past to the present by memory, and the future to the present by imagination, it is often necessary to distract him in his sufferings— to break up the continuity of misery. All unhappiness (when there is no immediate cause for sorrow) comes from excessive concentration on the past or from extreme preoccupation with the future. The major problems of psychiatry revolve around an analysis of the despair, pessimism, melancholy, and complexes which are the inheritances of what has been or with the fears, anxieties, worries which are the imaginings of what will be.

In addition to cases of true insanity and mental aberration— when scientific psychiatry is essential—there are many others, in which this unhappy preoccupation with the past and future has a moral basis. A conscience, burdened with the guilt of past sins, is fearful of Divine Judgment. But God in His Mercy has given us two remedies for such an unhappiness: one is the Sacrament of Penance, which blots out the past by remission of our sins and lightens the future by our hope for Divine Mercy through continued repentance and amendment of our lives. Nothing in human experience is as efficacious in curing the memory and imagination as Confession; it cleanses us of guilt, and if we follow the admonitions of Our Lord, we shall put completely out of mind our confessed sins: "No one who looks behind him, when he has once put his hand to the plough, is fitted for the kingdom of God." (Luke 9:62.) Confession also heals the imagination, eliminating its anxiety for the future; for now, with Paul, the soul cries out: "Nothing is beyond my powers, thanks to the strength God gives me." (Phil. 4:13.)

The second remedy for the ills that come to us from thinking about time is what might be called the sanctification of the moment—or the Now. Our Lord laid down the rule for us in these words: "Do not fret, then, over tomorrow; leave tomorrow to fret over its own needs; for today, today's troubles are enough." (Matt. 6:34.) This means that each day has its own trials; we are not to borrow troubles from tomorrow, because that day, too, will have its cross. We are to leave the past to Divine Mercy and to trust the future, whatever its trials, to His Loving Providence. Each minute of life has its peculiar duty—regardless of the appearance that minute may take. The Now-moment is the moment of salvation. Each complaint against it is a defeat; each act of resignation to it is a victory.

The moment is always an indication to us of God's will. The ways of pleasing Him are made clear to us in several ways: through His Commandments, by the events of His Incarnate Life in Jesus Christ Our Lord, in the Voice of His Mystical Body, the Church, in the duties of our state of life. And, in a more particular way, God's will is manifested for us in the Now with all of its attendant circumstances, duties, and trials.

The present moment includes some things over which we have control, but it also carries with it difficulties we cannot avoid—such things as a business failure, a bad cold, rain on picnic days, an unwelcome visitor, a fallen cake, a buzzer that doesn't work, a fly in the milk, and a boil on the nose the night of the dance. We do not always know why such things as sickness and setbacks happen to us, for our minds are far too puny to grasp God's plan. Man is a little like a mouse in a piano, which cannot understand why it must be disturbed by someone playing Chopin and forcing it to move off the piano wires. When Job suffered, he posed questions to God: why was he born, and why was he suffering? God appeared to him, but instead of answering Job's questions, He began to ask Job to answer some of the larger questions about the universe. When the Creator had finished pouring queries into the head of the creature, Job realized that the questions of God were wiser than the answers of men. Because God's ways are not our ways—because the salvation of a soul is more important than all material values—because Divine Wisdom can draw good out of evil—the human mind must develop acceptance of the Now, no matter how hard it may be for us to understand its freight of pain. We do not walk out of a theater because the hero is shot in the first act; we give the dramatist credit for having a plot in his mind; so the soul does not walk out on the first act of God's drama of salvation—it is the last act that is to crown the play. The things that happen to us are not always susceptible to our minds' comprehension or wills' conquering; but they are always within the capacity of our Faith to accept and of our wills' submission.

One question is never asked by Love, and that is "Why?" That word is used only by the three D's of Doubt, Deceit, and the Devil. The happiness of the Garden of Paradise, founded on trusting love, cracked under the Satanic query: "Why has God commanded you?" To true love, each wish of the beloved is a dread command—the lover even wishes that the requests were multiplied, that there might be more frequent opportunities of service. Those who love God do not protest, whatever He may ask of them, nor doubt His kindness when He sends them difficult hours. A sick man takes medicine without asking the physician to justify its bitter taste, because he trusts the doctor's knowledge; so the soul which has sufficient faith accepts all the events of life as gifts from God, in the serene assurance that He knows best.

Every moment brings us more treasures than we can gather. The great value of the Now, spiritually viewed, is that it carries a message God has directed personally to us. Books, sermons, and broadcasts on a religious theme have the appearance of being circular letters, meant for everyone. Sometimes, when such general appeals do appear to have a personal application, the soul gets angry and writes vicious letters to allay its uneasy conscience: excuses can always be found for ignoring the Divine Law. But though moral and spiritual appeals carry God's identical message to all who listen, this is not true of the Now-moment; no one else but *I* am in exactly these circumstances; no one else has to carry the same burden, whether it be sickness, the death of a loved one, or some other adversity. Nothing is more individually tailored to our spiritual needs than the Now-moment; for that reason it is an occasion of knowledge which can come to no one else. This moment is my school, my textbook, my lesson. Not even Our Lord disdained to learn from His specific Now; being God, He knew all, but there was still one kind of knowledge He could experience as a man. St. Paul describes it: "Son of God though He was, He learned obedience in the school of suffering." (Heb. 5:8.)

The University of the Moment has been built uniquely for each of us, and in comparison with the revelation God gives each in it, all other methods of learning are shallow and slow. This wisdom is distilled from intimate experience, is never forgotten; it becomes part of our character, our merit, our eternity. Those who sanctify the moment and offer it up in union with God's will never become frustrated—never grumble or complain. They overcome all obstacles by making them occasions of prayer and channels of merit. What were constrictions are thus made opportunities for growth. It is the modern pagan who is the victim of circumstance, and not its master. Such a man, having no practical knowledge of God, no trust in His Providence, no assurance of His Love, lacks the shock absorber of Faith and Hope and Love when difficult days come to him. His mind is caught within the pincers of a past he regrets or resents and a future he is afraid he cannot control. Being thus squeezed, his nature is in pain.

The one who accepts God's will in all things escapes such frustration by piercing the disguise of outward events to penetrate to their real character as messengers of the God he loves. It is strange how differently we accept a misfortune— or even an insult—when we know who gave it to us. A bobby-soxer would normally resent it very much if a well-dressed young woman accidentally stepped on her toes in a streetcar; but if that same bobby-soxer recognized that the one who hurt her was her favorite movie star, she would probably boast of it to her friends. Demands that might seem outrageous from an acquaintance are met with happy compliance if it is a friend who asks our help. In like manner, we are able to adapt with a good grace to the demands of every Now when we recognize God's will and purpose behind the illness and the shocks and disappointments of life.

The swaddling clothes of an Infant hid the Son of God in Bethlehem, and the appearance of bread and wine hides the Reality of Christ dying again on Calvary, in the Mass. This concealment of Himself that God effects with us is operative in His use of the Now to hide His Will beneath the aspect of very simple, everyday things. We live our lives in dependence on such casual, common benefits as air and water; so Our Lord is pleased to receive from us in return the thousands of unimportant actions and the trifling details that make up our lives—provided that we see, even in our sorrows, "The shade of His Hand outstretched caressingly." Here is the whole secret of sanctity; the method is available to everyone and deserves particular notice from those who ask: "What can *I* do?" For many good souls are hungry to do great things for God. They complain that they have no opportunities for heroic virtue, no chance at the apostolate. They would be martyrs; but when a meal is late, or a bus is crowded, when the theater is filled, or the dance postponed, or the bacon overdone, they are upset for a whole day. They miss their opportunities for loving God in the little things He asks of them. Our Lord said: "He who is trustworthy over a little sum is trustworthy over a greater." (Luke 16:10.) The Divine Beloved speaks to the soul in a whisper, but because the soul is waiting for a trumpet, it loses His Command. All of us would like to make our own crosses—tailor-made trials. But not many of us welcome the crosses God sends. Yet it is in doing perfectly the little chores He gives that saints find holiness. The big, world-shattering things many of us imagine we would like to do for God might, in the end, feed only our egotism. On the other hand, to accept the crosses of our state of life because they come from an all-loving God is to have taken the most important step in the reformation of the world, namely, the reformation of the *self*. Sanctity can be built out of patient endurance of the incessant grumbling of a husband—the almost intolerable nagging of a wife—the boss's habit of smoking a pipe while he dictates—the noise the children make with their soup—the unexpected illness—the failure to find a husband—the inability to get rich. All these can become occasions of merit and be made into prayers if they are borne patiently for love of One Who bears so patiently with us, despite our shortcomings, our failures, and our sins.

It is not hard to put up with others' foibles when one realizes how much God has to put up with from us. There is a legend that one day Abraham was visited in the desert by an Arab, who set up loud complaints of the food, the lodging, the bed, and the wine which his generous host had offered him. Finally, Abraham became exasperated and was about to put him out. God appeared to Abraham at that moment and said: "Abraham, I have stood this man for forty years; can't you put up with him for one day?"

To accept the duty of this moment for God is to touch Eternity, to escape from time. This habit of embracing the Now and glorifying God through its demands is an act of the loving will. We do not need an intellectual knowledge of God's plan in order to accept it. When St. Paul was converted he asked merely: "Lord, what wilt Thou have me to *do?*" We can be warmed by a fire without knowing the chemistry of combustion, and we can be cured by a medicine without knowing its prescription. The Divine Will, pouring into the soul of a simple cripple resigned to suffering, will give him a far greater understanding of theology than a professor will get from a lifetime of theoretical curiosity about religion which he does not practice. The good and the bad thief on the cross had the same crisis of fear and suffering—one of them complained and lost his chance for Heaven that day; the other spiritualized the brief moment of suffering. Some souls win peace and sanctity from the same trials which make others rebels and nervous wrecks.

God cannot seize our wills or force us to use our trials advantageously, but neither can the Devil. We are absolute dictators in deciding whether we wish to offer our will to God. And if we turn it over to Him without reservation, He will do great things in us. As a chisel in the hands of Michael Angelo can produce a better statue than a chisel in the hands of a child, so the human will becomes more effective when it has become a liege of God than if we try to rule alone. Our wills operating under our own power may be busy about many things, but in the end they come to nothing. Under Divine Power, the nothingness of our wills becomes effective beyond our fondest dreams.

The phrase which sanctifies any moment is "Thy Will be done." It was that *fiat* of our Saviour in Gethsemane which initiated our Redemption; it was the *fiat* of Our Lady which opened the way to the Incarnation. The word cuts all the guy ropes that attach us to the familiar, narrow things we know; it unfurls all our sails to the possibilities of the moment, and it carries one along to whatever port God wills. To say and mean "Thy Will be done" is to put an end to all complaining; for whatever the moment brings to us now bears the imprint of the Divine Will.

There are great subjective advantages to such an act of resignation to God's Will. The first is this: we escape from the power which the "accidents" of life had over us. The accidents of life are those things which interrupt our ordered existence and cancel our plans—mishaps such as a sickness which forces us to defer a trip, or the summons of the telephone when we are tuned in to our favorite program on the radio. It is a medical fact that tense and worried people have more accidents resulting in fractures than those who have a clear conscience and a Divine Goal in life. Some men and women complain that they "never get a break," that the world is their enemy, that they have "bad luck." A person resigned to God's Holy Will utters no such complaint; whatever comes along, he welcomes it. The disorganized, self-centered soul tries to impose his own will on the universe—and always fails. He is in constant pain for the same reason that a stomach is in pain if it tries a diet of ground glass—it is living contrary to the Divine purpose. Such a soul cannot see how the thing bothering him at this moment can be justified, for he judges all that occurs by the narrow, unrealistic standard: "Is this what *I* had planned?" But life is a larger business than the egotist assumes. It will not be reduced to so small a thing that it can fit into any human brain. A man cannot even devise a "system" at roulette which will provide for all the possible contingencies of one small, spinning wheel. How can he possibly have the *hubris* to expect the immensely various world about him—its human beings with their own souls, its willful changes of climate, its complex possibilities of every sort—to accommodate itself to his infinitesimal capacity for making plans?

The difference between people who never get the breaks and those who make every Now an occasion for thanking God is this: the latter live in an area of love greater than their desire to "have their way." As a waif on the streets suffers misfortunes which the child in a loving family does not know, so the man who has not learned to place full trust in God suffers reverses and disasters which would not appear as troubles to loving souls. God does not show Himself equally to all creatures. He does show all men how to turn everything to joy. This does not mean God is unfair, but only that it is impossible for even Him to show Himself to certain hearts under some conditions. The sunlight has no favorites, but it cannot shine as well on a dusty mirror as on a polished one. In the order of Divinity, there is nothing accidental; there is never a collision of blind forces, hurting us, at random. There is, instead, the meeting of a Divine Will and a human will which has a perfect trust that ultimate good is meant for it, although it may not understand *how* until eternity. Every human being is, in point of fact, like a baby in the arms of its loving mother, who sometimes administers medicine. God sends us all the happenings of everyday life as so many invitations to self-perfection in His service. The baby cries, the egotist protests, but the saint in the arms of God is content, because he knows God knows exactly what is best for him. Thus the bitter and the sweet, the joys and sorrows of each moment are viewed as the raw material of sanctity. "Meanwhile, we are well assured that everything helps to secure the good of those who love God, those whom He has called in fulfillment of His design." (Rom. 8:28.)

Every commonplace event now becomes a mystery because it is the bearer of the Divine Will. Nothing is insignificant or dull—everything can be sanctified, just as goats and sheep, fish and wheat, grapes and eyes of needles were given dignity as parables of the Kingdom of God. Things the worldly-wise would trample under foot become as precious to saints as pearls, for they see "sermons in stones and good in everything." Even the bitterest of life's punishments are known to be joys in the making, rare spiritual treasures underneath their harsh and ugly appearances. At the beginning one loves God only for His gifts, for the emotions He sends us. He treats us, then, like a young woman who is being courted. If gifts are no longer given in such abundance after a true marriage has occurred, it is not because the husband's love is less but because it is greater. For now he gives himself. It is not the husband's gift that his wife loves, nor his compliments, nor even the thrill of pleasure she gets from his company. She loves *him*. The moment the Lover is loved for himself, then the nature of the gift ceases to matter. Similarly, if God withdraws all sensible gifts, all natural happiness, it is only because He wants the union between the soul and Himself to be more personal and less dependent on His generosity. But God never takes away a natural gift without giving a supernatural gift in exchange. Souls do not always understand it, for in the beginning all values are material. It is only later that they see that the void they suffered when they lost some prized form of happiness was filled by a more spiritual insight.

It will seem strange to the worldling, but even our enemies—even those who cheat, malign us—can become occasions for advancement toward union with God. All contradictions can be turned to good by those who have put their trust in God. Seeing the trial as issuing from the Divine Hand, one never has to wonder how to meet it, nor question why it came, nor seek defense against it. Each trial is an occasion for faith and an opportunity for virtue. Having put oneself in the deeper dimension of Divine Love, one knows as a child in a loving family knows, that even what is not understood is done kindly and for the best. There finally comes a period of union with God when everything seems unreal except Divine Love. The soul in the midst of trials and aches becomes like an airplane flying—it follows the beam of God's Will through the fog and mist.

It is for each of us to decide what he is working for—what reward he wishes. For everyone is trying for some prize: if he is not interested in eternal merit, in gaining ultimate union with God, then he is interested in winning the applause of men, or the approbation of a single person, at the very least. The comedian tries to increase his Hooper rating for the sake of mass popularity; the banker works hard to increase his assets so that the business community will think well of him; the student intensifies his pursuit of knowledge to win an A; the social butterfly makes conquests to be known as a "successful debutante." Our Divine Lord knew that most souls were interested only in temporal applause, when He said: "Be sure you do not perform your acts of piety before men, for them to watch; if you do that, you have no title to a reward from your Father Who is in Heaven." (Matt. 6:1.) If we do good deeds to others because we love them on the human level, we receive a human recompense in their affection —but not a Divine Supernatural recompense.

"What credit is it to you, if you love those who love you? Even sinners love those who love them. What credit is it to you, if you do good to those who do good to you? Even sinners do as much. What credit is it to you, if you lend to those from whom you expect payment? Even sinners lend to sinners, to receive as much in exchange. No, it is your enemies you must love, and do them good, and lend to them, without any hope of return; then your reward will be a rich one, and you will be true sons of the Most High, generous like Him towards the thankless and unjust." (Luke 6:32–35.)

Our Lord lists trivial little acts of goodness—such as giving a drink of cold water to a stranger—and assures us that a supernatural reward awaits us if we do them *for His sake*, for love of Him. But if we wish to seek these supernatural prizes, we will have to satisfy their conditions: these are not unlike the conditions set down for gaining competence on the natural plane. Suppose a man has the ideal of being a good runner. Three conditions are essential: (1) He must be a born runner. There are certain capacities and talents, certain structures of bones and muscles, certain powers of breathing which are never acquired. They are given. They constitute the capacity to run. Track scouts can look at a schoolboy before he has received any training and can tell whether he will ever be a runner. (2) He must be free to decide for himself. There are some boys who have a talent for running but who refuse to go out for the team. If a boy competes only because he is forced to, the chances are that he will never do it well. (3) Given the talent for running, and the desire for it, the actions a boy performs must all bear on his goal. Excessive smoking or drinking, laziness or disregard for the proper technique could ruin every realization of his talent. All he does must be directed toward the goal of championship.

Apply this to the soul which wishes to run in the race of eternal salvation, to win the incorruptible crown. Three conditions are again required: (1) He must be born to the supernatural order by baptism; he must enter into the state of Grace, which gives him the capacity, the gift, the talent for the supernatural. To gain a human reward we operate on the human level; to gain a reward from God we must become children of God—the branches must be united to the Vine. All the good acts of a person in the state of Grace merit salvation through God's mercy—for God is the principal cause of merit. "Only by God's grace I am what I am, and the grace he has shewn me has not been without fruit; I have worked harder than all of them, or rather, it was not I, but the grace of God working with me." (I Cor. 15:10.) (2) The soul must be free. There is no merit in virtue if one is forced to practice it or it is followed through necessity. When our human wills respond to the Divine action, they are only secondary to God's Grace as a cause of merit—but although secondary, our contribution is a very real one. God and man cooperate. (3) Whatever the soul does ought to be a morally good act, one destined by its nature to recompense in supernatural coin. There are no indifferent acts when one is in the state of Grace; an act is either meritorious or it is not. (Here, incidentally, sex reaches its sublimest conception, for in Christian marriage its use is a means of Grace; through sex a husband and wife can increase merit for Heaven and eternal union with God.)

Assume that the acts we do are morally good in themselves. Then each task or duty is like a blank check; the value it possesses depends on whose name is signed to it, on whether it is done for the I's sake or for God's sake. Motive is what makes the saint: sanctification does not depend on our geography, nor on our work or circumstances. Some people imagine that if they were in another place, or married to a different spouse, or had a different job, or had more money, they could do God's work so much better. The truth is that it makes no difference where they are; it all depends on whether what they are doing is God's Will and done for love of Him. We would all like to make our own crosses; but since Our Lord did not make His own, neither do we make ours. We can take whatever He gives us, and we can make the supernatural best of it. The typist at her desk working on routine letters, the street cleaner with his broom, the farmer tilling the field with his horses, the doctor bending over a patient, the lawyer trying his case, the student with his books, the sick in their isolation and pain, the teacher drilling her pupils, the mother dressing the children—every such task, every such duty can be ennobled and spiritualized if it is done in God's Name.

17

Beyond the Merely Human

A Christ-centered life does not mean a life in which one sings hymns, reads Scripture, and edifies his neighbors by hanging texts on the walls. One does not become a Christian by doing a good deed a day, nor by go-getting for religion, nor by engaging in economic and political reform movements, even though these things are done from the noblest of human motives. A Christian is one who, believing that Christ is the Son of God, has that Christ-life in his soul.

The difference between a truly Christian life and a good human life is like the difference between a rose and a crystal—a difference in levels of living. "He who refuses to believe in the Son will never see life." (John 3:36.) *Omne vivum ex vivo.* Life must always come from life—it cannot emerge from the inanimate. Human life must come from human parents, and Divine Life must be fathered by the Divine. The pos-

244

sibility of supernatural life was brought to fallen man through the Incarnation, when we were redeemed. For justice to be done, the Redeemer of man had to be both God and man: He had to be a man, for otherwise He could not have acted in our name as representing us; He had also to be God, for otherwise He could not have paid the infinite debt owed to God by human sin. God did not forcibly take this human nature from mankind; He accepted it as the free gift of a woman, Mary, whose free answer to the angel messenger was: "Be it done unto me according to Thy Word."

Once in possession of His human nature, He offered it as a sacrifice for all the guilt due from human sin. Just as a kind father may pay the debts of a wayward offspring, so the Heavenly Father had sent His Divine Son to pay our moral debts and so restore us into the loving relationship with the Father which we had broken in the Fall. Though Our Lord's human nature was sinless, it was, in the strong language of St. Paul, "made sin." Assuming our bankruptcy, He began the work of mankind's spiritual rehabilitation. To understand how this could be, we may consider the analogy of a chalice; suppose that a chalice which has been used daily in the Holy Sacrifice of the Mass is stolen and beaten into a beer mug and delivered over to profane uses. Before it can be used again on the altar, it must be put into the fire and have its debased form burned away. Then it must be re-formed into the shape of a chalice. Finally, when it has been blessed and consecrated, it can be restored to the service of God. That chalice is like our human nature; it was once well ordered, with its senses subjected to reason, its reason to faith, its body to soul, and the whole personality oriented to God. Then by a free act, human nature turned away from God to self-love. To undo this cosmic damage the Son of God took a sinless human nature from Mary and onto its purity grafted all the sins of the world, so that it was as if He Himself were guilty of them. It was this guilt and sin, frustration and fear which Our Lord felt as His own and which produced His bloody sweat in the Garden. To save us all, He plunged that human nature into the fires of Calvary so that all the evil shape of sin might be burned and destroyed. Beaten and hammered, made to suffer the greatest ignominy which sin could inflict—the crucifixion of the Son of God—Our Lord rose again on the third day with a perfected human nature. Mankind is now restored to its supernatural destiny—but only if it keeps in contact with Our Redeemer, uses His Glorified Humanity as the die or the pattern upon which we are to be cast.

This involves what is known as *incorporation;* for we do not become one with Christ by reading about Him, or by thinking about Him, or by admiring His Sermon on the Mount, or by studying biographies of His times. Union with Him is a vital process, a participation in Him: "What is born by natural birth is a thing of nature, what is born by spiritual birth is a thing of the spirit." (John 3:6.) The spiritual life is the gift of the Living Spirit of Christ, Who prolongs Himself in His Mystical Body and diffuses His life through its seven life-giving channels. This new life starts with a birth: "A man cannot see the kingdom of God without being born anew." (John 3:3.) For the economy of salvation is such that God descended to us in order that we might ascend to Him. He has presented us with an opportunity to become something higher than we are in nature—to become participants in His own Divine Life. He became the new head of the human race, as Adam was the old head; as we were descended from Adam by physical birth, so we can become incorporated to Christ by a spiritual birth. One of the effects of this incorporation—which St. Paul mentions—is that our bodies become the Temples of God; on this fact, St. Paul bases his appeal for purity, because the Temple of God should never be profaned.

The aim of Christian living is to make our own, to the fullest possible degree, the objective salvation that was given us by Christ. He brought salvation to us objectively, in all fullness and perfection; but the individual's free cooperation is still necessary for its fuller application and final perfection in his own soul. It is as if each of us had a fortune placed to our account in the bank; if we did not write checks on it, it would not help us very much to have it there. Subjective salvation is our free acceptance of the chance to become something we are not by nature—adopted sons of God. This is the beginning of a constant assimilation of His Grace and vital strength; it brings forth fruit in the Christian's daily life and an ever-increasing vital fellowship with Him, through which the Mystical Body of Christ grows and develops.

Man is distinguished from the animals by the possession of a rational soul which gives him his special human dignity. It is fitting that the principal effects of the infusion of Divine energy should be manifested in the two main faculties of the soul—the intellect and the will. Once the Divine Power penetrates the intellect, it becomes Faith; once It infuses the will, it becomes Hope and Charity. Thus are born the three great supernatural virtues, by which we can believe in God, and know Him, and love Him.

It is the intellect which first feels the impact of the Christ-life. Sanctifying Grace perfects the reason by the infusion of a new light. Just as the sun illumines our senses and the light of reason enlightens our human nature, so the light of Faith illumines our ways in relationship to God. Faith is as necessary for complete human living as light is for sight: we have the same eyes at night as during the day, but we are not able to see at night because we lack the light of the sun. Two individuals with the same intellectual gifts see differently if one has Faith and the other lacks it: gazing on a Divine reality, such as Our Lord in the Holy Eucharist, one sees Emanuel, or God with us, and the other sees only bread. It is because one of them has a light which the other lacks.

This new light is to our reason what the telescope is to the eye. The telescope does not destroy the eye, nor does it create new worlds, but it enables the eye to see realities which, although they were there before, the naked eye could never reach. To a person who does not "believe in" telescopes, it would seem that the astronomer is merely imagining the things he says he sees—that in describing distant stars and planets he is the victim of a superstition. It is not uncommon for those who lack the gift of Faith to attribute all belief in the supernatural world to imagination or to fantasy.

Faith is also like a microscope, in that it enables us to perceive a deeper meaning in truths which we already know; it gives a new dimension of depth to our natural knowledge. Knowledge without Faith is often made up of bits of information, jumbled in a heap, like steel filings in a random pile; Faith, like a magnet, marshals them in order. Faith takes our uncorrelated facts and relates them to a single unity. Thanks to its illumination, the intellect now has a new solid frame for judging and estimating all the various segments of reality. The world is now seen from the Divine point of view, and through the Christ-mind.

There is, thus, a completely different outlook between those with and without Faith, on such subjects as education, sickness, marriage, death, and the atomic bomb. The Christ-mind, looking at the field of education, insists not only on training for the intellect, but also demands training of the will. It adds to the purely worldly end of education (training for citizenship and service) the Divine goal (training in love of God and love of neighbor, for Christ's sake and for the salvation of souls). Sickness is seen by Faith as coming from the hand of God, either to detach us from the spirit of the world, or to give us the chance to offer our sufferings in union with Christ's for the salvation of the world. Marriage is no longer seen as a temporary union of two sexes, but as a mystical symbol of the union of Christ in the Church, and is therefore a lifelong privilege. Death is not viewed as a mere biological phenomenon, but as the moment of judgment when we must render to God an account of our stewardship. The atomic bomb is not an evidence of the progress of science, but rather a reminder of the perversity of men; for when James and John asked Our Lord to rain down fire upon the Samaritans, He turned on them and said: "You know not of what spirit you are." (Luke 9:55.)

Those who think that the supernatural Faith destroys reason assume that Faith is something exterior to reason, as a roof is exterior to one's eyes and prevents them from seeing the sky. The truth of the matter is that Faith is not exterior to the reason, but interior to it, as the light by which the eyes see the sky: it comes from the sun, and yet it acts within the eyes and lets *them* see the sky. The Divine enlightenment through Faith is not on the same level as reason; it is on a different and superior level. Faith caps reason, but it never contradicts it—any more than the reason of a wise man of sixty contradicts the reason that he had when he was seven. Yet to those who have not been enlightened by Faith it often appears that they would have to give up everything, would have to renounce common sense and clarity of thought, in order to accept it. This is due, in part, to the fact that such a man knows only what is in his mind now; he is without any experience of the larger truths that he would grasp if once he had the Faith. Reason is always stronger *with* Faith than without it: just as reason is the perfection of the senses, so Faith is the perfection of the reason. A drunkard who has lost his reason still has his senses, but his senses do not function properly; he stumbles, falls, sees double images, talks thickly, does not feel heat or cold. These things occur because his senses need reason to function well. In like manner, man's reason needs Faith to function well. The highest development in philosophical wisdom ever attained by man was in the age of Faith of the thirteenth century; our own Godless age, which has abandoned Faith, is correspondingly a time of great irrationality.

Faith lights up all the faculties of a man, as light inside reveals the pattern of a stained-glass window. For Faith is far more than the passive acquiescence to a proof; it is a dynamic thing, accompanied by an intense desire for the possession of God as the Author and Finisher of our life. The certitude that Faith gives is out of all proportion to the stated reasons which led one to become incorporated to Christ; it somewhat resembles the certitude of a child that the head of his home is, in truth, his father, a conviction far greater than any reason he could give to prove his sonship.

Religious faith is not alien to fear—but this is not the servile fear a citizen would have for a dictator in a Communist state; it is the filial fear a child feels for its loving father. The man of faith *fears* God in the sense that his reverence makes him shrink from doing anything that might wound his father. In such a fear there is no I-centeredness, but only God-centeredness. This fear in its turn begets purity of the intellect, so that we seek to avoid all errors that might damage the living relationship of the soul and Christ. Truth is more precious to us than ever before, now that we see the True as one aspect of God. Heresy and error become to Faith what mud is to the body. "Blessed are the clean of heart; for they shall see God."

The God Who is Truth is also called "the Light of the World," for Light and Truth are twin concepts. Seeing is, indeed, believing; and when the catechism speaks of the "darkened intellect," it means a mind into which the daylight truth is not able easily to penetrate. The whole universe is intelligible in terms of light. Sir James Jeans has said that the most scientific description of the universe that was ever given is contained in the book of Genesis: "God said, Let there be light, and the light began." He referred to the fact—scientifically established—that atoms are composed of light. Physicists speak of two kinds of light—bottled light, which includes all material things, and unbottled light, which is illumination. The sound intuition of the ages has described reality in terms of light. There is the light of the sun for the senses, and the light of reason, which can grasp universal truth; and above both of these and completing them, is the light of Faith, which illumines reason more perceptibly than reason illumines the senses. All forms of light are a reflection of God, "Who dwells in accessible light." But only recently have we come to know that God, as Light, has left His signature on the invisible, light-composed atom of material things.

But light rises in a hierarchy within the created universe—from the atom to the human intellect, and higher still. For in the realm of Faith, the intellect no longer throws its searchlight along the earth, to enlighten itself on natural things; rather, its power and energy are directed toward the Divine. And thanks to the illumination which God gives the believing intellect, it has new powers and capacities, of which the first is a new serenity, a sense of having finally "arrived." Its adherence is so certain, its certitude so absolute, that it can be explained only as coming from one source, the First and Supreme Truth. If it can be argued that those who have faith in false religions have an equal certitude, it must be pointed out that their certainty is protected either by ignorance (as is the case with many good and simple men) or by the refusal to direct a searching rational inquiry toward the religious field. For as soon as reason begins to work on myths, the myths lose their ability to convince; but as reason works on Faith, the certitude of their truth grows stronger. Only those minds which have never perused the great *Ratio Theologica* of Christianity can ignore the power of reason sparked by the flame of Divine belief.

Faith pertains to the intellect of man. The other great virtues of Hope and Charity lie in the will. When grace incorporates us to the Christ-life, it gives us a measure of both of them in our souls. Hope is the supernatural equivalent of security; as some men are hopeful about the immediate future because of a fat bank account, the Christian has hope of the remote future because he possesses a share in the Divine wealth. Supernatural Hope is dependent upon Faith, for one cannot hope for a thing unless he believes it to exist. Although Hope comes from Faith and leads to Love, the first step of all must always be rational knowledge. Before we can love anyone, we must know him; then we may begin to hope that he will turn into a good friend. Finally hope is realized in love. It is never true to say that "the wish is father to the thought," for this would mean that the emotion precedes the knowledge, which is an absurdity: one does not receive a telegram announcing the death of a friend because one weeps—one weeps after receiving knowledge of his death. Hope can never be the foundation of sound knowledge or of sound religion. The object of Hope in the Christ-centered life is eternal happiness with God—Whose existence was first discovered by our reason and later ratified by Faith.

One of the beautiful effects of Hope is that it relieves us of the morbid fear of failure. The obsession with failure, as a danger to be avoided, is a direct result of egotism. As pride grows less in us, there is an accompanying relief from our old terror of humiliation through failure. Once God and obedience to His Will have become our all-encompassing desire, fear of the hostility of others completely evaporates; we are ready to be "fools for Christ." The Apostles reached a point where they were able to rejoice because of others' scorn, for thus they might bear greater testimony to their Lord. Oneness with Christ does not guarantee that we will be immune from crosses, trials, and difficulties; but it does mean that we need never be overcome by such setbacks. Our Lord said: "In the world, you will only find tribulation; but take courage, I have overcome the world." (John 16:33.) St. Paul, in the face of death, wrote: "Where then, death, is thy victory; where, death, is thy sting?" (I Cor. 15:55.) A true

Christian is aware of the transitory and relative character of all suffering, and in the midst of it he still feels himself sheltered by the all-powerful love of God. Despite the contumely he may encounter, the soul clings to God with a serene confidence, realizing that all attacks on him are powerless to damage him, since it was by the Cross that Christ redeemed the world.

Hope also releases us from other forms of anxiety: most of man's tense worry comes when he senses a disproportion between the resources of the I and the obstacles he must have to overcome to reach a temporal goal. If the I has only itself to trust and lean upon, in the face of a heartless world, then there is reason for some anxiety. But when the soul's resources are energized and supplemented by the infinite resources of Divinity, anxiety disappears. As Our Blessed Lord said: "For you have a Father in heaven Who knows that you need them all." (Matt. 6:32.) Despair also vanishes as Hope is born of faith in God—for the cause of despair is pride. Whenever the I was melancholy in the past, it was because it had failed to realize some ambition under its own power. Now, thanks to the influence of Divine Grace, the soul no longer trusts in itself, for its sufficiency is drawn from God. Now, the very thing which would once have seemed the greatest obstacle to peace and happiness—our weakness—becomes a source of joy. St. Paul says: "When I am weakest, then I am strongest of all." (II Cor. 12:10.) When we no longer trust in our own powers, then we are made strong with the power of God, for he who is joined to the Lord is one spirit with Him. We cannot despair over the future now, for it is in infinitely powerful and loving hands. Not even the abundance of our past sins will cause despair of God's mercy, for a contrite and humble heart will never be despised.

Hope gives us new buoyancy and boldness to attempt things we should never have felt able to undertake alone. Thanks to supernatural help, we can say with St. Paul: "Nothing is beyond my powers, thanks to the strength God gives me." (Phil. 4:13.) Timidity and procrastination of tasks that seemed too big for us give way to increased effectiveness, for the dynamism that we needed from God is now available. We cease to be the fearful hand and we begin to be the tool, confident and steady in its knowledge that He is guiding it. This is not a surrender of self, but a dedication of self to His larger purposes, which we are able to fulfill to the degree that we use all our powers, at white heat, in His service.

Hope becomes confidence, and confidence tranquilizes the heart and the soul. We no longer respond to this event as "discouraging" or to that one as "heartening": everything that happens, happens in a frame of trust and hope. Something similar occurs in human friendship; at first we appraise the newly introduced, taking this statement and that action as a clue to what we may expect such an individual to do. Later, when we come to know and love the person better, we have trust in him—we do not judge him any longer by each particular thing which he may do. A complete change in our outlook has taken place. Judging character by action has ended; now we judge our friend's acts by his known character. If there is one particular action which we do not understand, we attribute it to our ignorance of his intention, rather than assuming his perversity. So it is with confidence in God. When we are spiritually imperfect, we are inclined to judge God by the particular trial or blessing He has given us or sent to a neighbor. But later, when we understand the nature of God as Love and Mercy, we judge the particular event in the light of His Goodness, and we may even reach a point of perfect confidence where, like Job, we say: "Though He slay me, yet will I trust in Him." Particularly—in the light of His Crucifixion—we find it impossible ever to complain, "Why has God done this to me?" or to ask, "What did I do to deserve this?" Looking at the Cross on the Hill of Calvary, we know He did not ask: "What have I done to deserve this?" Through His example, we attain to patience and resignation in the momentary trial, knowing that the last act of life is the one that matters.

The second important Fruit of Faith in the domain of the will is Charity. There are various ways of loving people. We can love someone because he is generous, because his parties and his gifts give us pleasure; we can love a person because he is lovable and pleasant to be with; or we can love someone for God's sake, seeing him as either a potential or an actual child of God. Love proceeding from either of the first two motives is not supernatural Charity; for Charity always has as its motive: *Propter Deum* (for the sake of God).

"Beloved, let us love one another; love springs from God; no one can love without being born of God, and knowing God. How can the man who has no love have any knowledge of God, since God is love? . . . Beloved, if God has shown such love to us, we too must love one another. No man has ever seen God; but if we love one another, then we have God dwelling in us, and the love of God has reached its full growth in our lives. . . . If a man boasts of loving God, while he hates his own brother, he is a liar. He has seen his brother, and has no love for him; what love can he have for the God he has never seen? No, this is the divine command that has been given us; the man who loves God must be one who loves his brother as well." (I John 4).

By the supernatural virtue of Charity, Divine Love dwells in the soul and in a very personal, intimate relationship, for there are several different ways in which God can be present. First of all, God is present everywhere in the world, because He is the Power that made the world, the Wisdom that planned it, and the Love that executed it. God is also present— but personally—in the Eucharist, and in our souls so long as the Sacramental presence lasts. But there is still another Divine presence which is more abiding, and that is the presence of God in the soul through Charity. To be in the state of Grace through Charity does not mean that we *have* something, but that we *are* something. For one of the consequences of the Faith is that an extraordinary event happens to us: we receive a Gift. Many baptized souls are ignorant of this mystery, and remain ignorant of it throughout their lives; for just as it is possible for some families to live under the same roof and never communicate, so it is also possible for a man to have God in his soul and yet hold little intimate exchange with Him. The more holy souls become, and the more detached from the world, the greater their consciousness of God's presence. One might indicate the various steps in accomplishing this intimacy as four:

I am.
I ought.
I can.
I will.

In the first stage, there is consciousness only of our own existence, and this is egotism. On the second level, the soul is aware of conscience, which it feels to be an "ought": here the I, or personality, has begun to develop. In the third stage, there is the recognition that, thanks to God's Grace, the I can become something far greater than itself. This is the soul's first inkling of the possibility of self-transcendence. The fourth and final stage is an identification of the I-will with the will of God Who has taken up residence in the soul. Because of this special presence of God in the soul, the body now becomes a Temple of the Holy Ghost, not to be defiled by sins against purity or temperance. The Church, which always sees man's body as a tabernacle, is opposed to any violent destruction of it, such as mayhem or cremation. We would not destroy with fire a church which has passed its usefulness or a home we had loved—such abuse is contrary to our sentiments of reverence. And since the body is one day to become a more holy Temple of God after the resurrection, it is especially compelling that we treat it with respect and not deliver it to forces of destruction.

God's presence within us is a truth which has inspired many minds. We read how the father of Origen, one of the early Christian writers, used to bend over the child's cradle and say to those who stood around: "I adore God present in the heart of this little baptized Christian." Later, when Origen himself began to write on Grace, he said: "My soul is a dwelling place of Him: of God, of Christ, and of the Holy Spirit." A French Catholic who was unable to receive Communion once asked that a poor man be brought into the sickroom so that he might commune with Christ, living in the poor. St. Elizabeth of Trinity once wrote to her sister, saying: "Heaven is in the inmost recesses of our soul. Is not this a simple and consoling thought? Come what may, in the midst of all your cares as the mother of a family." She wrote further: "You can always withdraw to the solitude, when you are distracted by your numerous duties; you can, if you will, refresh yourself at any moment, by descending to the depths of your soul where the Divine Guest has His dwelling." It may well be that our body is only a veil that prevents us from seeing God; between Grace in this life and the glory of Heaven, there is nothing but a thin curtain of the flesh. At the moment of death, this veil will be withdrawn; and then we shall see Him Whom we unseeingly possessed on earth whenever we were in the state of Grace.

One day St. Catherine of Siena was attacked by very violent temptations against the virtue of purity. When finally the storm had passed, Our Lord appeared to her. She said to Him: "Lord, where were you when my heart was filled with such impure thoughts?" The Lord answered: "I was in your heart." St. Catherine said: "Yes, Lord, You are truth itself, and I bow before You, but how can I believe this, when my heart was filled with such detestable thoughts?" But God answered: "These thoughts, these temptations—did they cause you joy, sorrow, pleasure, or pain?" And she responded: "Terrible sorrow, terrible pain." Our Lord then told her: "Know then, my daughter, that you suffered because I was hidden in the midst of your heart. Had I been absent, the thoughts that penetrated there would have given you pleasure. It was My presence which rendered them insupportable to you. I was acting in you. I defended your heart against the enemy. Never have I been closer to you."

This would indicate that the resistance of saintly souls to evil is partly due to their consciousness of the Divine Goodness within. It may well be that souls devoid of a sense of Divine Love fall more readily into sin because they have less knowledge of what they will lose by that sin.

A struggle between nature and Grace goes on in the souls of the just throughout their lives—they do not deny that sin would give them a pleasure they refuse themselves because of their greater love of God. It is at this point that those who live sensate lives—enmeshed in habits of drunkenness and carnality—sometimes boast that they have pleasures which the saintly do not have. It is true; if sins included no pleasure, they would attract nobody. But there is this difference between the lives of those in the state of Grace and of those who are given over to sin: the sinner always gets the brief pleasure first, and the aftermath of pain, bitterness, emptiness, and disgust follows. The Christian endures the pain first (it is of a rather transitory character), but his aftermath is joy, peace, and happiness. The pagan celebrates the orgy, followed by the hang-over; the order of the Church reverses this, celebrating first the fast and then the feast. But it is an illusion to think that the worldly suffer no malaise worse than a morning-after headache; as Nietzsche wrote to his sister: "Remember, my dear sister, that unbelief, too, has its tragedies." Much of the melancholy, frustration, and boredom of the modern world is the psychological consequences of a life of sin. Sanctifying Grace, or White Grace, with its happiness, is the result of an infusion of Divine Life.

In the spiritual life, we make the down payment on our joys in advance of savoring them. The greater our trust in God, the more we shall be willing to do for Him, on credit; and if we turn our whole wills over to His control, He will reciprocate our love with ever greater gifts of His.

Divine Charity can be so all-pervasive in the soul that it views as traitorous any enjoyment apart from the beloved. As a dog will often refuse food from anyone but his master, so the soul in the state of Grace may deny any experience it cannot sanctify. God is everything. This soul turns from all worldly or indifferent pleasures in which God would not have a part. Charity thus detaches one from the spirit of the world without his conscious effort to be free of its attractions. It has another effect: it inspires great charity toward those not in the state of Grace, and particularly toward those who have fallen. Knowing something of the sweetness of God, it sees those who have departed from Him as being already punished —and applies this attitude particularly to those who have had the Faith and have abandoned it. An unfaithful soul, when it withdraws from God, is already tortured; because it once has loved the best, nothing less can satisfy it. The saintly in the state of Grace would not try to increase the suffering of such a fallen soul but would try to diminish it with a greater love. Just as it is wrong to push someone on the edge of a fire into the heart of the flames or to push a drowning man under water, so it is wrong to gloat over those who feel within their hearts the tragedy of the loss of God.

But those who have known the Faith and lost it are vastly outnumbered by those others who remain unfinished, undeveloped, incomplete because they have not yet received the Grace of God. "Many are called, but few are chosen." As in the material universe, there is here a possibility for rising above the natural level, but not everyone avails himself of it. There are many chemcials and minerals in the world which do not pass into the higher life of the plant. There are many plants which never are raised up to the lives of animals, and there are many animals which never find their way into the diet of a man. So there are many men who do not die to themselves by an act of their own will in order to live with Christ

His higher form of existence. They ignore the upward thrust of the universe and suffer correspondingly.

Love, which is Charity's other name, is our shortest stepladder to the supernatural. Love is always, at the beginning, a descent from above: God loved us first, and we Christians should also be the first in loving others. This love shines forth even where it is our enemy who is in question. "Love your enemies, do good to those that hate you, pray for those who persecute and insult you, so that you may be true sons of your Father in Heaven, Who makes His sun shine on the evil and equally on the good, His rain fall on the just and equally on the unjust." (Matt. 5:44–46.) Even when the enemy inflicts pain on us, even though we may have, in war, to take away his life, there is no taking away of love from him. Christian love bears evil, but it does not tolerate it. It does penance for the sins of others, but it is not broad-minded about sin. The cry for tolerance never induces it to quench its hatred of the evil philosophies which have entered into contest with the truth. It forgives the sinner, and it hates the sin; it is merciful to the person, it is unmerciful to the error in his mind. The sinner it will always take back into the bosom of the Mystical Body; but his lie will never be taken into the treasury of Her Wisdom. Real love involves real hatred: he who has lost the power of moral indignation and the urge to drive the buyers and sellers from the temples has also lost a living, fervent love of Truth.

Charity, then, is not a mild philosophy of "live and let live"; it is not a species of sloppy sentiment. Charity is the infusion of a Divine Spirit of Love. It is an integration of personality under the Spirit of God, which makes us love the beautiful and hate the morally ugly. Human love on its own is apt to be weak and to tire easily; human love supported by Divine Grace is as unshakable and strong as steel. As Divine Love becomes less common among men, marriage bonds become less firm; lovers cease to love persons and selfishly love, instead, the thrill the other person gives. Such love lasts only as long as passion lasts. In a truly Christian marriage, love of husband and wife is the reflection of the love of Christ for His Spouse, which is the Church. Our Lord will never be unfaithful to His Spouse, nor will He have many Spouses. Therefore sacramental marriage, a symbol of the spiritual, must be as strong and as enduring. Charity in the souls of husband and wife enables them to bring about this great reality.

Love on the Divine level is very different from love on the purely human level, and sometimes there is conflict between the two. Our Divine Lord warned us that those who loved Him would be hated by the worldlings. " . . . It is because you do not belong to the world, because I have singled you out from the midst of the world, that the world hates you." (John 15:19.) He also said that He came to bring not peace, but the sword, and that He would "set a man at variance with his father, and the daughter with her mother." (Matt. 10:35.) There will always be those who can understand why love of a man or woman may be strong enough to make a lover cut all other ties but who consider it folly for anyone to fall in love with God and count the world well lost for Him.

Divine Love when it enters a soul (or, better, when we permit it to enter) takes possession of it, refreshes it, penetrates it utterly. But it is as invisible as the wind, as mysterious as the falling of a meteor. It energizes what is slow to act; it strengthens what is feeble; it warms what is cold in us and makes even the bearing of our cross a joy. It removes all the

boundaries which had been set by human love: it brings the
Samaritan into the confines of the family. There is now neither
Greek nor Pole, Russian nor Jew, German nor Frenchman,
Japanese nor Chinese; they are all enfranchised to the realm of
Divine Charity. It eliminates all limits on forgiveness, for when
Our Lord said: "I tell thee to forgive, not seven wrongs, but
seventy times seven" (Matt. 18:22), He did not mean four
hundred and ninety, but a number beyond all mathematical
count. Love travels far beyond mere forebearance, mere
"goodness within reason." If a man forces us to walk one mile
with him to punish us, Our Lord suggests that we walk with
him yet another, to punish ourselves and thus come closer to
the sinlessness God wants in us. Love is always ready to exceed common sense—Magdalene poured out all the ointment,
for love knows no limits. Divine Love makes us want to give
all—and even if our all is very small, that fact will not detract
from the greatness of the Charity: the Lord valued the
widow's mite above the offerings of the rich. Charity is not
measured by what we give, but by the intensity of love with
which we give it.

Though such love of God is sometimes stern, it is also
paradoxically childlike. Saints are never blasé: "Unless you go
back, and become like little children, you shall not enter the
kingdom of heaven." (Matt. 18:3.) Our Lord did not wish
us to be childish, but childlike, simple enough to learn, näive
enough to wonder and enjoy. When Our Saviour found the
Apostles disputing among themselves as to who was the
greatest, He put a little child in the midst of the dispute to re-
buke them. The Saviour Himself had come into the world as a
child, and growth in love of Him from that day on has demanded that we be humble enough to enter the low-slung cave
where He was born. Proud men will not stoop; thus they miss

the drama of the cave where a child is discovered to be Lord of the universe.

Finally, where there is Charity or Divine Love, there is no more sense of duty. Obligation as a motive gives way to the motive of love. We cease to act because of a compulsion, either from society or from a conscience nagging at us that we should do this or that. We cease to be slaves, for it is impossible for anyone in love to feel in servitude. When our motivation in life becomes the love of Christ in the soul, there is no longer a tension between what we want to do and what we ought to do: the two have become synonymous. So long as the ego was the center of life, there was a narcissism, a self-love which sometimes ran counter to God, for he who loves the ego as his absolute hates the Divine as a "rival." Where the basis of our morality is merely law, commandment, and ethics —as on the I-level—there is always an opposition between our desires and our conscience, between the law of the flesh and the law of reason. But when the ego has been tamed and the I, by a free act of will, has surrendered itself to the Divine Will, then there is perfect freedom born of perfect love. To see pleasure in contrast to the laws of God means that the soul is at enmity with God; the identity of our joy and of obedience to God, on the other hand, is a sign that love has now replaced law—and where there is love, there is no need for law. No law tells a man to give a ring to the young woman whom he asks to marry him—but law does tell a man to pay his taxes. Where love fails, there justice begins.

True love is at once hard to satisfy and easy to please. It is hard to satisfy because it is dissatisfied with anything but the infinite ecstacy; it is easy to please because whatever the beloved gives is always what the lover wants.

"I may speak with every tongue that men and angels use;

if I lack charity, I am no better than echoing bronze, or the clash of cymbals. I may have powers of prophecy, no secret hidden from me, no knowledge too deep for me; I may have utter faith, so that I can move mountains; yet if I lack charity, I count for nothing. I may give away all that I have, to feed the poor; I may give myself to be burnt at the stake; if I lack charity, it goes for nothing. Charity is patient, is kind; charity feels no envy; charity is never perverse or proud, never insolent; has no selfish aims, cannot be provoked, does not brood over an injury; takes no pleasure in wrongdoing, but rejoices at the victory of truth; sustains, believes, hopes, endures, to the last. The time will come when we shall outgrow prophecy, when speaking with tongues will come to an end, when knowledge will be swept away; we shall never have finished with charity. Our knowledge, our prophecy, are only glimpses of the truth; and these glimpses will be swept away when the time of fulfillment comes. (Just so, when I was a child, I talked like a child, I had the intelligence, the thoughts of a child; since I became a man, I have outgrown childish ways.) At present, we are looking at a confused reflection in a mirror; then, we shall see face to face; now, I have only glimpses of knowledge; then, I shall recognize God as He has recognized me. Meanwhile, faith, hope and charity persist, all three; but the greatest of them all is charity." (I Cor. 13:1-13.)

Faith and Hope will disappear in Heaven—for there is no need of Faith when we see, no need of Hope when we possess. But Love endures forever.

18

Zeal for Others

THOSE who have found the Truth and the Peace of God may be puzzled as to the attitude required of them toward those others who still live on the ego-level, or the unsanctified level of personality, of I. The answer is a variant of Our Lord's injunction to hate the sin and love the sinner: we are to be intolerant of false doctrine but sweetly tolerant toward those who hold it. The modern world is less inclined to dispute the second portion of the sentence than the first: nowadays there is a temper abroad which wishes us to give evil equal rights with good. It pleads with us that wrong ideas should have as great a circulation as right ones and that one point of view in religion is as apt to be true as another. This excessive broad-mindedness, however, is not extended to the fields outside of religion or mortality: the most tolerant agnostic becomes dogmatic and a stickler for the truth if his grocer's bill adds

up to twice the sum it should. Nor do the city fathers encourage engineers to tamper with the laws of gravity, design-
ing bridges to suit their personal prejudices without respect to
the weight of steel. Reality—subject to laws we cannot repeal
—is recognized in every physical-science classroom. Reality—
subject to laws we cannot repeal—also prevails in the moral
world in which man dwells. Truth is not of our making; it is
God's own. We do not have rights over it; it has rights over
us. Dogma is truth as certainly as water is H_2O; as only one
chemical formula for water can be the right one, so only one
dogma concerning the Incarnation or the Sacrament of
Marriage or Transubstantiation can be correct. It is not a
universe in which half a dozen contradictory things are ever
true.

Our Lord said that not a single iota of His Teaching should
be changed; St. Paul told us that an angel who taught otherwise than this should be cursed. As a teacher of geography
is intolerant about any city except Washington being the
capital of the United States, so, too, there are absolutes in
Divine Truth which are not subject to our unmaking. Our
Blessed Lord did not tell us to free ourselves from law in our
search for truth; His promise reverses this modern order:
"And the truth will set you free." (John 8:32.)

But once having acknowledged the absoluteness of Divine
Truth we are faced by a need for charity toward those who
do not believe. Six precepts will help us to retain the kindliest
attitude. First, we should realize that all religions, all sects, all
ethical systems have a small or large arc of the circle of truth.
Buddhism, Confucianism, Zoroastrianism each expresses one or
another of the yearnings of the human race toward the infinite;
each sounds at least one true note on the keyboard of Divine

religion. Manuals of religion, in proving the transcendence of Divinity, too often dwell entirely on the flaws and defects in such systems, instead of seeking for the modicum of good in them. Those who know the full truth and reject it are in a special category; we do not discuss the intellectual aspects of the truth with them, for that is not where their difficulty lies. But those who are ignorant of the truth or are misinformed about it may well be shown how the whole truth completes the portion of it they already have and love. We can always accept the known good as a starting point for the completion of the circle. It is not meet to prove that members of the sects are wrong—for they are partly right—but rather to suggest that they find truth in all its fullness. When a man is hungry, we do not need to prove to him that he is better off without poisons; we need only give him bread, and he will relish it and gain strength from it. When souls are starving, too, it is unnecessary to discuss wrong notions of Divinity; we need only, by kindness and mercy, bring them the Bread of Truth. Divine Grace will do the rest. In a future day, some wise man of the Church may use Confucius as a natural steppingstone to Christ, as Augustine used Plato and St. Thomas used Aristotle.

There is some fine raw material in world religions which can be used, in cooperation with Grace, for building the fullness of Christ which is His Church. The sense of family solidarity possessed by the Chinese is a good natural foundation for the doctrine of the Mystical Body of Christ; the Hindus' emphasis on asceticism will make it easier, in the fullness of time, for them to accept Redemption through the Cross. Even the man-God cult of the Japanese is only a perversion of the yearning of all hearts for a God-man. St. Paul told the Corinthians:

"What we make known is the wisdom of God, His secret, kept hidden till now." (I Cor. 2:7.) Nothing human is foreign to Christ. "It was his loving design, centred in Christ, to give history its fulfillment by resuming everything in Him, all that is in heaven, all that is on earth, summed up in Him." (Eph. 1:10.) Those outside the Church are in error, not because they have only a sect or a section of truth, but rather because that section has been taken, in isolation, from the context, with a resulting disproportion of emphasis. It is wrong to condemn anyone for having a passionate interest in the fragment he already owns; it is Christ-like to add to his possessions, to enrich his savings by incorporating them into a higher synthesis.

A second great error is sometimes made by those of us who have been illumined by the Faith; to think that others are stupid or perverse because they do not see the Truth we have been taught. We may even flatter ourselves that we know because we are cleverer than they. This is to forget the enormous fact that we did not arrive at belief by our own human efforts alone—that it is largely thanks to God's Grace that we came to an understanding of the Truth. We did not create the sun which enables our eyes to see; and those who are blind did not deliberately put out their eyes to hide from the light of the sun. The attribution of ignorance to the unbeliever is never a mark of intelligence, but of contemptible pride. If we see what they do not see, it is because of a gift of God beyond our best deserts. The believer, then, has a special occasion for humility. We should all recognize our own unworthiness, realizing that, without that undeserved gift, we would be ignorant, indeed.

There is incumbent on everyone a duty of special benevolence and kindness toward those bigots who believe every lie they hear about the Church. On hearing their fantastic charges, one should say to himself: "If I believed the same lies *they* believe, and had the same antireligious training *they* have had, and had been as isolated as they from opportunities to learn the Truth, would I not hate the Church a thousand times more than they do?" For the bigot is often hating what he honestly believes to be an evil thing. Such men do not really hate the Church; they hate what they mistakenly believe to be the Chuch. Our Lord was once struck on the cheek—His answer was: "If there was harm in what I said, tell us what was harmful in it; if not, why dost thou strike Me?" (John 18:23.) By being sympathetic to the prejudiced, we disprove, in act, the theory in their minds. Moreover, the very hatred of the bigoted proves that they are thinking about Our Lord and His Mystical Body; the intensity of their prejudice is often caused by a secret suspicion that we may be right. All hatred is a proof of passionate interest. Our Lord chose the greatest bigot of his time to be His Apostle for the Gentiles, knowing that the energy which Saul had spent in hate would be violently effective if it were turned in the opposite direction of love. When the time comes to rebuild a modern Christian world, the greatest apostles of Christ may be recruited from the land that is now ruled by antiChrist. God is glorified even in His enemies.

Another point to be remembered is that everyone need not come to the Faith along the way that is outlined in the books. Theological students sometimes think that one brings souls to Our Lord by a simple program: master the arguments for the existence of God; memorize the proofs for the Divinity of Christ from prophecy, miracles, and consonance of Christ's doctrine with the aspirations of the human heart; and then shoot them all like bullets at the opposition. The expectation is that souls will fall before the machine guns of our syllogisms. But Cardinal Newman rightly said that "syllogisms make but sorry rhetoric with the multitudes." Many manuals are written from the point of view of one who has always had the Faith; they outline the logical steps by which one might approach it. But those who come to the Faith do not always begin with the logical steps; these proofs are necessary, later, for instructions and full understanding, but they do not mark the beginning of a conversion. A person drinks water for a long time before he knows that it is H_2O. Souls can come to Christ and His Church through many doors. If there was ever a philosopher whom one would expect never to arrive at a belief in the Divinity of Christ and the Church it was Henri Bergson. Here was a thinker who had repudiated the intellect, who scorned its first principles, and who made the God of Being into a God of becoming. Yet, at the end of his life, he asked that a priest be called before he died. A soul can come to God even from a hatred of reason, as Bergson did—even through a series of disgusts, as was the case with Léon Bloy. It is not difficult to understand how this can come about, for the cause of every conversion is the Grace of God. At first the Grace is actual, then sanctifying. There are myriad ways in which God's Grace can penetrate a soul; there is only one fold and One Shepherd, but there are a million roads to Him. The sheep can come from the valleys of despair, from the heights of knowledge, from the pools of aspiration, or even from the thorns and bramble patches of sin. Peter and Andrew came by way of the nets, Matthew from the counting table, Paul on his way to persecute the Christ, and Magdalene at a banquet.

The believer would make more progress in bringing peace of soul to others if he started all his conversations with a further assumption—that everyone is looking for God. It is amazing how different all souls look when one starts, as a first principle, with this truth. There is no doubt of its soundness—as the eye needs light and the stomach food, so does the soul need God. There is not a single person in the world, regardless of the enormity of his sins, who has not in his soul a craving for the Infinite. As St. Thomas says: "The whole is loved before the part, and the part is loved only because of the whole." All the tumult of human love is a secret pursuit of the Divine. Pascal has said: "There are two kinds of reasonable people, those who love God with their whole hearts because they have found Him, and those who search for God with their whole hearts because they have not found him." When the apostle goes out, knowing that everyone he meets is seeking God, he will have a kindlier approach than if he assumes that some are not interested, that others are rebellious. It is true that a man can be hungry, and still live on the wrong kind of food; and that a man can yearn for the infinite, and yet mistake the place it can be found. But it is the business of the apostle to declare the Unknown God to those who seek among the idols.

The apostle need never feel discouragement about any soul, regardless of its present state of either sinfulness or animosity. The man who boasts that he is in the service of anti-Christ must, to do so, breathe the name of Christ. As the creative power of God was shown by His drawing the created world from nothingness, so His Redemptive Power is shown in His drawing of souls from sin. The disciple who despairs of the conversion of any soul is judging the case in terms of human power and omitting the greater factor of God's Grace. To approach a sick man in the belief that he will never get out of his bed will probably do much to keep him there; to approach a sinner with a sense of hopelessness of his case is to drive him deeper into his despair. The very fact that the sower in the Gospel sowed his seed among thorns and rocks indicated that he held *some* hope of reaping a harvest even there. These unhappy souls without the Grace of God are really more anxious to receive it than is suspected, and disciples who act on the assumption of success make greater progress in bringing them to God than others do. There are, of course, some perverse souls with an evil will, of whom Our Lord said: "Do not cast your pearls before swine, or the swine may trample them under foot, and then turn on you and tear you to pieces." (Matt. 7:6.) The perverse, however, are easily recognizable, and they are few in comparison with the rest who are sincerely seeking, groping, searching, catching at any straw that they may find. Spiritually blind persons are not happy, and they know it. They want to see, for hearts made restless by their preoccupation with time and the flesh long for the peace the Spirit would bring.

Too often an apostle laments that he cannot bring a soul to Our Lord because he is "too ignorant." But it does not take knowledge to save a soul; it takes love—love of God, and love of neighbor. Knowledge is needed for instruction, but it is not needed for inspiration. Eloquence is not only unnecessary, but it can even prove a handicap. As St. Paul said: "And what we have received is no spirit of worldy wisdom; it is the spirit that comes from God, to make us understand God's gifts to us; gifts which we make known, not in such words as human wisdom teaches, but in words taught us by the Spirit, matching

what is spiritual with what is spiritual." (I Cor. 2:12,13.) To
bring a soul to God is not to proselytize, to dazzle him or
sweep him off his feet. There is a vast difference between a
proselytizer and an apostle, as the very derivation of the
words implies. The first is taken from two Greek words:
pros, meaning *toward*, and *elythein*, meaning *to come*; it
suggests an approach from the outside. But the word apostle is
taken from the Greek word, *apostellein*, which means to *send
away*, as a messenger, and it hints at the truth that we are carriers of a message and a mandate from Another. To win a man
to joining the Communist party, one has to be a proselytizer
—he must work upon the mind from the outside by means of
propaganda. To bring a man to God one needs to be an
apostle—he must allow Truth itself to work inside the mind
which was made to receive it, and shaped for it, as the nest
is shaped for the egg. When one man tries to win another to
a political program, he gets no help from the Grace of God.
But whenever an apostle tries to bring a man to Christ, God
is illumining that man's mind from within, preparing it to welcome and understand his words. The proselytizer converts to
a party; the apostle converts to a Person, to the living Christ.
Those who have the Faith and who despair of bringing peace
to others are relying solely on their own efforts, forgetting
that it is God Who gives the increase. In the early Church,
most of the faithful were recruited from paganism by labor-
ers, slaves, children, and the outcasts. When it is seen how our
Lord chose the commonest men for His world apostolate, it
is apparent that there are other factors at work besides the intellectual. If the believer is on fire with God, he will shoot
sparks and the Holy Ghost will fan their flame.

The Divine work is best done away from the periphery

and close to the center. We do not need an activism which, like Peter's, neglects the quiet task of watching and praying in favor of swinging swords because our enemies swing them. We do need a witnessing of Christ by the spiritualization of our lives. The remaking of the world must always begin with the remaking of one ego. The largest share of the burden of saving the world weighs on those who boast that their bread is the Bread of Life and their wine is the Wine of Christ. The gigantic task must be done in one soul at a time—each single response to Grace is a step taken toward peace and joy for all. For we are to bear one another's burdens—to teach all nations—to see in the Faith an export product with which the hungry shall be fed. Whoever saves a single sinner from the error of his ways, saves his own soul. "My brethren, if one of you strays from the truth, and a man succeeds in bringing him back, let him be sure of this: to bring back erring feet into the right path means saving a soul from death, means throwing a veil over a multitude of sins." (James 5:20.)

19

Making Up for the Past

In an earlier chapter the necessity of living in the Now was stressed: the moment and its opportunities were shown to be our only proper subject for concern. But this assumed that the past had, indeed, been rectified, robbed of its right to haunt our minds by penance done for its offenses. Until this is accomplished, the problem of what to do about our past misdeeds is a serious one, since we do not, like animals, live in the present. The past stays with us in our habits, in our consciousness of remembered guilt, in our proclivity to repeat the same sin. Our past experiences are in our blood, our brains, and even in the very expression that we wear. The future Judgment is also with us; it haunts us, causing our anxieties and fears, our dreads and preoccupations, giving us insecurity and uncertainty. A cow or a horse lives for the present moment, without remorse or anxiety; but man not only drags his past with him, but he is also burdened with worries about his eternal future.

Because the past is with him in the form of remorse or guilt, because the future is with him in his anxiety, it follows that the only way man can escape either burden is by reparation—making up for the wrong done in the past—and by a firm resolution to avoid such sin in the future. Disposing of the past is the first step to take, and in taking it, the important distinction between forgiveness and reparation for sin should be remembered. Some who have done wrong mistakenly think that they should only forget it, now that it is past and "done with"; others believe, falsely, that once a wrong deed has been forgiven, nothing further need be done. But both of these attitudes are incomplete, lacking in love. As soon as a soul comes in contact with Our Lord and realizes he has wounded such Love, his first response after being forgiven is apt to be that of Zachary: "I will repay all." Our Lord, in instituting the Sacrament of Penance, made it clear that there is a difference between forgiveness and the undoing of the past. That is why Confession is followed by Absolution, or forgiveness, and why, when Absolution has been given, the confessor says: "For your penance . . . . " Then he tells the penitent what prayers to say or which good actions to perform to make atonement for his sins.

The high reasonableness of this is apparent if we translate the offense against God into purely human terms. Suppose that I have stolen your watch. When my conscience finally pricks me, I admit it all to you and say: "Will you forgive me?" No doubt you will, but I am sure that you will also say: "Give me back the watch." Returning the watch is the best proof of the sincerity of my regret. Even children know there must be a restoration of the balance, or equilibrium, disturbed by sin: a boy who breaks a window playing ball often volunteers, "I'll pay for it." Forgiveness alone does not wipe out the offense. It is as if a man, after every sin, were told to drive a nail into a board and, every time he was forgiven, a nail were pulled out. He would soon discover that the board was full of holes which had not been there in the beginning. Similarly, we cannot go back to the innocence that our sins have destroyed. When we turned our backs upon God by sinning against Him, we burned our bridges behind us; now they have to be rebuilt with patient labor. A businessman who has contracted heavy debts will find his credit cut off; until he has begun to settle the old obligations, he cannot carry on his business. Our old sins must be paid for before we can continue with the business of living.

Reparation is the act of paying for our sins. When *that* is done, God's pardon is available to us. His pardon means a restoration of the relationship of love—just as, if we offend a friend, we do not consider that we are forgiven until the friend loves us again. God's mercy is always present. His forgiveness is forever ready, but it does not become operative until we show Him that we really value it. The father of the prodigal son had forgiveness always waiting in his heart; but the prodigal son could not avail himself of it until he had such a change of disposition that he asked to be forgiven and offered to do penance as a servant in his father's house. So long as we continue our attachment to evil, forgiveness is impossible; it is as simple as the law which says that living in the deep recesses of a cave makes sunlight unavailable to us. Pardon is not automatic—to receive it, we have to make ourselves pardonable. The proof of our sorrow over having offended is our readiness to root out the vice that caused the offense. The man who holds a violent grudge against his neighbor and who confesses it in the Sacrament of Penance cannot be forgiven unless he forgives his enemy. "If you do not forgive, your Father Who is in Heaven will not forgive your transgressions either." (Mark 11:26.)

The humiliation involved in confessing sins does much to make us avoid them in the future. But we must offer more than our humiliation: satisfaction is also required of us. If it is not given in this life, it will have to be made up in the next. "Saying penances"—"satisfying" for sins—would be a pitifully inadequate compensation for the damage we have done if it were not that Christ Himself offers satisfaction through our petty penances, giving them a value far beyond their own. If we look only at *our* part in satisfying for our sins, we should expect penances to be very arduous, as they were in the early Church; if we stress the Divine contribution to their efficacy, then we can understand why they are as light as they are today. But in neither case is it possible to fix any realistic scale of payment, for the satisfaction comes from our Lord. "So, on the cross, His own body took the weight of our sins; we were to become dead to our sins, and live for holiness; it was His wounds that healed you." (I Pet. 2:24.)

Associated with the Christian's amendment for the past is his resolution for the future. This must be more than a wish to avoid evil— it must be a will to do so. For there is a vast difference betwen *velleity*, or the mere desire to be better, and *volition*, or a firm determination to be better. Pilate *wished* to save Our Lord, but he did not *will* to save Him. Remorse for the past involves a wish to avoid the same sin, but in the vague hope that this can be accomplished without giving up anything; repentance uses no "ifs" and "buts" but sets to work on the unpleasant task of rooting up the evil. We cannot be like the dying woman who, when she was asked to renounce the Devil, said: "But I do not like to make enemies unnecessarily!"

The knowledge that a sin has been committed often in the past does not exclude a firm purpose against sinning the same way in the future, provided that it is accompanied by a strong trust in the Mercy of God, Who will not suffer us to be tempted beyond our strength. Those who have never gone to Confession or tried to amend their lives must not be too hard on the souls who are trying; people who give in to every temptation have no idea how hard it is for us to resist the sins which have been committed before. If anyone wants to find out how bad he is, let him try to be good. One tests the current of a river, not by flowing with it, but by fighting against it. Bad people know nothing about goodness, because they are always floating downstream with the current of badness. They should not be supercilious about those defeated swimmers whom Our Lord forgives "seventy times seven" or about His Mystical Body, which prolongs that Mercy to all sinners who really care and try. Moreover, anyone who refuses to avoid the proximate occasions of a grievous sin into which he has repeatedly fallen is considered as wanting in resolution to avoid that sin and is denied absolution in the Sacrament.

Unrepented and unforgiven sins are the commonest causes of fear and anxiety. Many neurotics, who profess no religion, do not realize that their troubles are due to a hidden guilt. To deny the existence of our past sin is as serious to a soul as the denial of an existing cancer is serious to the body. An uneasy conscience is always anxious as to the future—just as an embezzler who is presently stealing from a bank lives in dread of being caught. The mere denial of the concept of sin does not relieve our guilt: the conscience of man will not be bribed so easily, nor fobbed off with a shallow denial of the moral law which is engraved in all our natures. The only real escape from the anxiety of guilt is to restore oneself to union with Divine Righteousness through penitence. The past is blotted out by His forgiveness, and worries over a future reckoning disappear. Hence Sacred Scripture gives us this sound psychiatric advice: "Love drives out fear, when it is perfect love." (I John 4:18.) In the case of Mary Magdalene, Christ's fullness of love wiped out her sin, her fear, and even the punishment due to sin. "And so, I tell thee, if great sins have been forgiven her, she has also greatly loved." (Luke 7:47.)

Repentance for sin is inseparable from love. Our hatred of sin is a measure of the deepness of love. God would not be good unless He hated evil, nor can any of us claim to value the Divine Love unless we avoid all that would wound that Love. To love a fellow creature we must first know him—but in the case of God the reverse is true, and to know Him we must love Him first. If we love, we shall want to separate ourselves from anything that might be harmful to that love. For love always seeks to be with the one loved; love always seeks to please the one loved; love is ready to suffer for the one loved; love hates what hurts the one loved; love never feels that it can do enough for the one loved. The laws of all love apply here, too, and Our Lord in His teaching told us how we might express our love for Him in many ways. For instance, we are to repay evil with good. "If a man strikes thee on thy right cheek, turn the other cheek also toward him; if he is

ready to go to law with thee over thy coat, let him have it and
thy cloak with it." (Matt. 5:39.) He also wishes us to overcome our self-will by charity to our neighbor. "If he compels
thee to attend him on a mile's journey, go two miles with him
of thy own accord." (Matt. 5:41.) We are to love our enemies.
"Love your enemies, do good to those who hate you, pray for
those who persecute and insult you, that so you may be true
sons of your Father in heaven." (Matt. 5:44.) And all this is
to be done with joy. "Again when you fast, do not shew it
by gloomy looks, as the hypocrites do. But do thou, at the
times of fasting, anoint thy head and wash thy face, so that
thy fast may not be known to men, but to thy Father Who
dwells in secret; and then thy Father, Who sees what is done
in secret, will reward thee." (Matt. 6:16–18.)

The effort to apply these laws of love eventually brings us
to a higher kind of repentance, in which some souls do
penance, not only for their own sins, but for the sins of others.
Deeply loving souls are conscious of their unity with all mankind and wish to satisfy for the guilt of others as their own.
Their mission in life is to make pardon available to those too
blind to ask for it themselves. In the moral order, this is as if
the comparatively healthy—seeing the injuries from which
others suffer—should offer to bind up their wounds. If love, in
the face of physical misery, tries to relieve the pain of others,
then love, in the face of sin, is even more concerned to cure
the guilt of others. This is the work Our Lord performed in
the Garden of Gethsemane when He took the iniquities of
all upon His Soul, as if He had wrought them—into His blood,
as if He had experienced them. It was the horror of our sins
which caused Him to burst into a sweat, in which His blood
crimsoned the olive roots of the Garden.

Our Lord's first follower and emulator in this high mission
of Redemption was the Blessed Mother, who claimed no im-
munity, no *noblesse oblige* from the vocation of suffering from
sin. Although she had no personal guilt requiring satisfaction,
she allowed her heart to be pierced by the swords of evil
done by other men and women. She too, in Her more limited
way than His, would share the world's guilt as Her own. The
same high mission is continued today in the contemplative
orders of the Church: the Trappists, Carmelites, Poor Clares,
and dozens of other gifted souls renounce the world, not because they want to save only their own souls, but because
they want to save the souls of others. The cloistered religious
are like spiritual blood banks, storing up the red energy of
salvation for those anemic souls who sin and do not atone. It
is possible that these souls, praying and fasting in secret, are
alone holding back the arm of God's Wrath from a rebellious
and a blasphemous age. As ten just men could have saved
Sodom and Gomorrah, so a scattered few of these consecrated
victims may save a nation or the world. Their merits overflow
to others who have made no contribution to goodness, as the
benefits of electricity come to many of us who have never
put a screw into a dynamo. The communicability of merits
in the Communion of Saints is one of the most beautiful and
consoling truths taught by the Church. Love between its members does not operate only on the horizontal plane—between
one person and another—but resembles a triangle; a sacrificial
prayer breathed on earth is lifted up to Our High Priest, Christ
in Heaven; He transubstantiates it with His merits and sends
it down to earth again to enrich the sinful soul in need. As it
is possible to graft skin from one part of the body to another
to heal a burn, so it is possible in the Mystical Body to graft a
prayer; as it is possible to transfuse blood from one healthy

person to another to cure him of his weakened condition, so it is possible to transfuse sacrifice. Because sacrificial souls love God and long to undo whatever has offended Him, they see other people's sins as their own, as works of evil they are called to set aright by sacrifice and prayer. The saint believes that to know of another's sin is to be obliged to do penance for it—God, he feels, has made him clear-sighted about another's sin only in order that he may undo the damage. He does not scold the sinner for not doing the work himself. Tolerance says: "He is as good as I am." Charity says: "He may be far better than I." By this the saint means that if the other man knew God's love as he knows it, the present sinner might love Him much more fervently than the saint. The fully Christian soul not only forgives others; it suffers for others, takes on others' sins as its sins. The best men and women never consider that they are good; they feel constantly in need of Divine Mercy for their own failures to love perfectly; to merit it, their hearts overflow in mercy and kindness to others. The sinful conscience is cruel and cynical; the repentant conscience is kind and filled with Charity.

Reparation, like self-discipline, depends on love of God. It does no good to tell people to stop doing certain things, unless they can be given something else to do that they will care for more. An alcoholic will not be persuaded to give up the liquor he loves unless he is made to love something else. For evil can never be thrown out; it must be crowded out. When finally a Perfect Love is found, there is less adhesion to other things; when a soul responds to the limit of its capacities to that love, there often follows a longing to take on others' burdens as one's own, that they may not miss the glory of an intimacy with Love, for which they were intended.

St. Catherine of Siena once said:

"Lord, how could I be content if any one of those who have been created in Thy image and likeness, even as I, should perish and be taken out of Thy hands. I would not in any wise that even one should be lost of my brethren, who are bound to me by nature and by grace. Better were it for me that all should be saved, and I alone (saving ever Thy Charity) should sustain the pains of hell, than that I should be in Paradise and all they perish, damned; for greater honor and glory of Thy Name would it be."

At another time her prayer was:

"Lord, give me all the pains and all the infirmities that there are in the world to bear in my body; I am fain to offer Thee my body in sacrifice and to bear all for the world's sins, that Thou mayest spare it and change its life to another."

Though such an ideal is transcendent to most of us, it is still well for the world to have some souls dedicated to ideals which the mass of men will never practice. The illiterate in a village will point with pride to the one man who can read and write; through him, they derive their education vicariously. The saints fulfill such a spiritual role in humanity—through them, some satisfaction is made vicariously for the failings of us all. As soldiers offer their lives that the non-combatants can preserve political freedom in time, so these soldiers of Christ sacrifice their lives that others may enjoy their spiritual freedom in eternity.

20

Hound of Heaven

THE two greatest dramas of life are the soul in pursuit of God and God in pursuit of the soul. The first has less apparent urgency, for the soul that pursues God can do it leisurely, as Peter followed the Saviour from afar. But when God pursues the soul, He proves a Relentless Lover, Who will never leave the soul alone until He has won it or been conclusively denied.

One of the most beautiful descriptions of God in pursuit of the soul is that of Francis Thompson in the poem, "The Hound of Heaven." The Hound is God, rapid is His pursuit, and there is nothing new in such a name for Him. Sophocles in one of his dramas speaks of "Heaven's Winged Hound"— as a Punic inscription speaks of *Kelbilim*, the Hound of Divinity.

There are eight distinct situations described in Thompson's masterpiece; five describe the flight of the soul from God, and three, the chase of God after the soul. As the rabbit runs into its hole to evade the hunter, so the soul tries to escape into five lairs: these are the unconscious mind, sex, science, nature, and humanism. These five substitutes for God are chosen in an effort to preserve the ego or the I intact, to save it from the shattering contact of Divinity.

The effort to escape from God into depth psychology is common now. The modern soul is probing into the lowest depths of his mind, from which he hopes to draw a new and refreshing elixir of life. He is tired of living on a single, horizontal plane. He hopes that by plunging into the great wells of the unconscious, he may discover some new mystery about himself that will "solve" his life and bring him peace.

In the days of faith, men lived in a three-dimensional universe. Heaven was above, hell below, and the earth between the two was a mere vestibule—an anteroom in which we stayed long enough to say "aye" or "nay" to our eternal salvation.

But about two centuries ago, as men began to lose the faith in God, the other great eternal verities also slipped away; morality went into a decline, and men no longer saw themselves as inhabitants of the universe of three dimensions. They reduced life to a single dimension, that of the flat surface of the earth; they felt that, thanks to science and evolution and inevitable progress, it would be possible for everyone to become a kind of god and to enjoy his Heaven here.

Their dreams were not realized; they could not be. Wars, depressions, and fears of further war finally made men despair of realizing any hope on earth. But they had meanwhile lost their hope of Heaven. The result was that they were driven, more and more, into themselves, until finally many of them were tightly locked into their own minds. Some false "scientists" now attempted to restore the three-dimensional universe that they had lost—but they placed it *inside* the mind. Instead of a heaven and an earth and a hell, they offered, as substitutes, a conscience, a consciousness, and an unconsciousness—a super-ego, an ego, and an id. The prophets of the cavernous depths felt that if they could dig, explore, analyze, plunge into the wells of unconsciousness, they might unearth new mysteries which men had never penetrated, and that out of this subliminal self they might stir up new energies, new powers, which would bring peace and salvation to the world.

But individuals had tried, before, to find salvation within the self, and they had always failed. The poet, Thompson, tried it, too, and he speaks of the fears and glooms encountered in "the labyrinthine ways of my own mind." God still pursued him in the midst of all the fears his unconscious mind threw up into consciousness.

> I fled Him, down the nights and down the days;
> I fled Him, down the arches of the years;
> I fled Him, down the labyrinthine ways
>   Of my own mind; and in the midst of tears
> I hid from Him, and under running laughter.
>   Up vistaed hopes I sped;
>   And shot, precipitated,
> Adown Titanic glooms of chasmed fears,
>   From those strong Feet that followed, followed after.
>   But with unhurrying chase,
>   And unperturbed pace,
>   Deliberate speed, majestic instancy,
>   They beat—and a Voice beat
>   More instant than the Feet—
>   "All things betray thee, who betrayest Me."

The search for peace within the self is always doomed to fail; the two loneliest places in the world are a strange city and one's own ego. When a man is alone with his thoughts, in false independence of the Love Who made him, he keeps bad company. No amount of psychoanalysis can heal the uneasiness that results, for its basis is metaphysical, its source the tension between the finite and the infinite. Such a mind may attempt to shut out Divinity, but Thompson pictures God as the "Great Disturber," with His message that all results in misery if Mercy is left out.

Nothing except man can ever become less than its nature. A monkey cannot become less than a monkey; a cauliflower cannot become less than a cauliflower; an orange cannot become less than an orange; but a man can become less than a man, as he can also become more than a man. He can become less than a man by acting like a beast. He can become more than a man by becoming a child of God. But although a man descends to the beast-level, he never loses the Divine imprint on his soul, is never released from his craving for the Infinite.

Thus, in the very moment that anyone denies God, he affirms Him—for Godlessness means nothing unless one admits a God. The atheist feels the pull of Divinity at the very time that he is drawing away from it. A man without God is very much like a frightened new sailor on a ropeladder, trying to climb to the crow's-nest. Suspended midway between the crow's-nest, which is his present destiny, and the deck below, to which he might fall, he is panic-stricken. Modern man, who is not yet with God, and who has not yet fallen completely into Hell, is in this midway condition of anxiety.

The Hound of Heaven would remind every soul that self offers no escape. To settle down inside our own minds is to imprison ourselves. There is no great mystery inside of the psyche that has not already been explored; men have lived too long with agile, thinking minds for it to be likely that in this twentieth century there is still hidden some other salvation within us than God Himself. When a ship is sinking, we do not stop to analyze the chemistry of the water that pours into the holes. Pawing over our past blunders, like a ragpicker, will never reveal to us the Pearl of Great Price; for that is to be found beyond ourselves. No mind is creative of its own salvation, and other distracted minds cannot solve our distraction. Salvation will come by breaking the circle of our egotism, allowing the Grace of God to pour in. That is what the Incarnation made possible for us—it was a Divine invasion. The Incarnation of Our Blessed Lord split time in two. And as He entered time to link it to eternity at Bethlehem, so, as the Hound of Heaven, He would now enter the "labyrinthine ways" of our mind to link it with His Truth and Life and Love.

A second escape by which souls try to find fulfillment without God is sex. If the word "sex" is defined to mean erotic lure, then it may be called the false ideal of the ego. If "love" is used in its classical sense, it is the proper ideal of the I, or personality. An age of religious anarchy is always a licentious age, and a period of political confusion, too: this is because a rebellion against the Divine Law affects both society and man. When a people have lost sight of the meaning and purpose of life, they then attempt to find compensation in the intensity of their experiences, either revolutionary or personal. The "thrill" is sought for itself. *Real* love attaches itself to a single, unique personality and remains loyal, nontransferable; but sexual enjoyment, if it is a goal in itself, leads to promiscuity.

The ego can never love anything but itself; it "loves" another person only so long as he or she is a source of selfish pleasure. Illicit love affairs are a very common method of trying to escape from God. The state of being in love is an attraction upward toward Love Itself, but unlawful, erotic love is merely another effort to find self-fulfillment without relinquishing the ego as our primary concern. It is bound to fail.

The poet describes the erotic escape; he sees it in terms of a romantic but illicit love he pressed. He describes the windows of his lady's cottage, which were casements cut in the shape of a human heart:

> I pleaded, outlaw-wise,
> By many a hearted casement, curtained red,
> Trellised with intertwining charities;
> (For, though I knew His love Who followed,
> Yet was I sore adread
> Lest, having Him, I must have naught beside.)

This last line of Thompson's describes the situation of many men who fear that if they give in to God, they will "narrow" their personality—as if, by giving up the arc for the circle, one could lose the arc! The assumption that Love of God is inimical to human love is a fallacy—it is only the men who love God foremost who can ever really love as husbands or as friends. Later the poet was to learn that, in having Him, he will have everything. But first:

> But, if one little casement parted wide,
> The gust of His approach would clash it to;
> Fear wist not to evade, as Love wist to pursue.

Just as the ego assured itself that it had completely escaped from God, the spirit of God blew closed the casement window. No human fear of Him is canny enough to escape His love, for He knows how to outrun the soul He made.

Carnality is no answer to man's search for lasting happiness, for the simple reason that we are more than animals. If man were simply an animal, he would not ask sex to give him more than it can possibly provide—infinite, lasting joy—nor would he suffer the satiety that comes with its overindulgence. Other sins are less seductive, for they do not promise to cure our loneliness and emptiness, as illicit love in its first stages seems to do. The body is finite; the soul is infinite. The loneliness of the one can be satisfied—but not the aspirations of the other. This disproportion between the lasting ecstasy one had hoped to enjoy and the finite, short-lived pleasure actually given begets sadness and, ultimately, despair. The Hound of Heaven does not permit the soul to find a lasting peace in such a sin.

It is also possible for a man to fly to nature (which God made) in an effort to hide there from His pursuit. As we can read a book, forgetting the author, so it is possible to see and even become an "authority" on God's world in total forgetfulness of its Creator. The poet now describes how He "drew the bolt of Nature's secrecies"—threw himself into a torrent of scientific truths pouring from the storehouse of the natural world.

> I knew all the swift importings
> On the wilful face of skies;
> I knew how the clouds arise
> Spumed of the wild sea-snortings;
>   All that's born or dies
> Rose and drooped with; made them shapers
> Of mine own moods, or wailful or divine;
>   With them joyed and was bereaven.

I was heavy with the even,
When she lit her glimmering tapers
Round the day's dead sanctities.
I laughed in the morning's eyes.
I triumphed and I saddened with all weather,
Heaven and I wept together,
And its sweet tears were salt with mortal mine;
Against the red throb of its sunset-heart
I laid my own to beat,
And share commingling heat. . . .

Science, valid and necessary as it is as a human pursuit, could
not completely satisfy the soul's hunger. For scientific man
remains a spectator of reality, its copyist and chronicler; but
the soul is never satisfied until it can find union with a greater
Personality. The language of nature is not the language of the
human heart; unless the silence of the spheres awakens the
heart to God, it is a violent disturber of the mind. Nature is on
God's side—when Peter denied His Lord, the cock crowed.
Nature will never let us rest, content, in her arms if we try to
love her without loving her God.

In vain my tears were wet on Heaven's grey cheek.
For ah! we know not what each other says,
These things and I; in sound I speak—
Their sound is but their stir, they speak by silences.
Nature, poor stepdame, cannot slake my drouth;
Let her, if she would owe me,
Drop yon blue bosom-veil of sky, and show me
The breasts o' her tenderness:
Never did any milk of hers once bless
My thirsting mouth.

Because the ego is still restless in its scientific knowledge, still discontented with the half truths it has found, the Hound of Heaven still pursues:

> Nigh and nigh draws the chase,
> With unperturbed pace,
> Deliberate speed, majestic instancy;
> And past those noised Feet
> A voice comes yet more fleet—
> "Lo! naught contents thee, who content'st not Me."

Far commoner than study or research as an escape is nature— the effort to run away from God by changing the environment. Speed, too, has its attraction for the ego in full flight. Some people try to travel away from God by an intellectual movement—fantasy, daydreams, alcoholism, sleeping tablets, or dope. Describing this evasion of the Hound—this wild retreat from reality—the poet writes:

> Across the margent of the world I fled,
> And troubled the gold gateways of the stars,
> Smiting for shelter on their clanged bars;
> Fretted to dulcet jars
> And silvern chatter the pale ports o' the moon.
> I said to Dawn: Be sudden—to Eve: Be soon;
> With thy young skiey blossoms heap he over
> From this tremendous Lover—
> Float thy vague veil about me, lest He see!

But speed and change of scene cannot deter the Hound of Heaven. The mind itself—no matter what fast wings we try to give it by this stimulant or that—is slower than He. All of the things of earth were made by God, and all of them remain

his faithful "servitors," whom we cannot suborn away from
Him:

> I tempted all His servitors, but to find
> My own betrayal in their constancy,
> In faith to Him their fickleness to me,
> Their traitorous trueness, and their loyal deceit.
> To all swift things for swiftness did I sue;
> Clung to the whistling mane of every wind.
> But whether they swept, smoothly fleet,
> The long savannahs of the blue;
> Or whether, Thunder-driven,
> They clanged his chariot 'thwart a heaven,
> Plashy with flying lightnings round the spurn o' their feet:
> Fear wist not to evade as Love wist to pursue.
> Still with unhurrying chase,
> And unperturbed pace,
> Deliberate speed, majestic instancy,
> Came on the following Feet.
> And a Voice above their beat—
> "Naught shelters thee, who wilt not shelter Me."

When man has despaired of finding happiness in any sen-
sual pleasure, or in the mere accumulation of facts, he may still
have a fond fallacy that he can discover contentment without
God in humanitarian enterprise. Such dreamers hope that if
they work for the "brotherhood of man," they need take no
cognizance of the Fatherhood of God. Thompson described
this last flight from the Divinity in terms of the love of
children:

> I sought no more that after which I strayed
> In face of man or maid;

> But still within the little children's eyes
>> Seems something, something that replies,
> *They* at least are for me, surely for me!
> I turned me to them very wistfully.

But even in this last and best of all his earthly loves, the poet finds that the children, who come from God, continue to belong to Him:

> But just as their young eyes grew sudden fair
>> With dawning answers there,
> Their angel plucked them from me by the hair.

Francis Thompson now describes the three stages through which a soul—defeated in its other searchings—advances from the ego-level to the I, from selfishness to Divine love. These are marked by a sense of emptiness, a later fear of the Cross, and an ultimate surrender to its appeal.

The emptiness which moves the soul to begin, in earnest, its honest search for God may be physical loneliness, after the loss of a beloved husband, wife, or relative; it can be moral emptiness, as when there is a deep sense of guilt and remorse for the past; or it can be spiritual emptiness, where there is a vague dissatisfaction with the mediocrity of one's life. But none of these alone would be enough: there is also emptiness in hell. Loneliness begins to be redemptive and creative only when the personality feels itself opposed by another Personality. A soul does not become ready to be converted because it realizes that it has broken a code, a law, or a commandment, but rather because it sees that it has broken a relationship with Love itself. Saul felt this stunning fact as he neared Damascus, when the Heavens were opened and Our Lord asked, "Why persecutest thou Me?" Augustine felt it

when he heard a voice that was not only in his mind. Whenever anyone suspects that a personal God may, after all, exist,
he knows that if He *is*, He must be sought and found, and all
sin and guilt exposed to Him:

> Naked I wait Thy love's uplifted stroke!
> My harness piece by piece Thou hast hewn from me,
>   And smitten me to my knee;
>   I am defenseless utterly.

Then, recalling that Samson had pulled the pillars of the
temple upon himself, he sees his life a ruin, his personality
buried beneath the wreckage of a disillusioned self:

> In the rash lustihead of my young powers,
>   I shook the pillaring hours
> And pulled my life upon me; grimed with smears,
> I stand amid the dust o' the mounded years—
> My mangled youth lies dead beneath the heap.
> My days have crackled and gone up in smoke,
> Have puffed and burst as sun-starts on a stream.

All the past pleasures of life now seem ruinous wastes. The
dreams vanish. The earth, which he had thought that he, as
an artist, could swing like a trinket from the wrist, now adds
itself to the burden of his emptiness. Poetry itself is not
enough:

> Yea, faileth now even dream
> The dreamer, and the lute the lutanist;
> Even the linked fantasies, in whose blossomy twist
> I swung the earth a trinket at my wrist,
> Are yielding; cords of all too weak account
> For earth with heavy griefs so overplussed.

Even though one is convinced of the emptiness of life and
suspects that God might fill that void, there is still a great
obstacle to be surmounted on the road to peace; and that
obstacle consists of self-discipline, mortification, and penance.
"If any man has a mind to come my way, let him renounce
self, and take up his cross daily." (Luke 9:23.) This sounds
like an austere and frightening invitation: Our Lord is always
forbidding to those who see Him only from a distance. In
this, He reverses the ways of the world; pleasures of the flesh
are often greater in anticipation than in realization, while the
joys of the spirit are always greater in realization than in
anticipation. The poet still shrinks back from Christ, because
he falsely thinks He will allow no other loves, no natural joys:

> Ah! is Thy love indeed
> A weed, albeit an amaranthine weed,
> Suffering no flowers except its own to mount?

His analogy is of the legendary flower which kills every
other plant near it. The poet is fearful that Our Lord will
tolerate no other affection but His Cross; and he pictures Him
as putting each of us through a Calvary before we may share
in a Resurrection. The figure that he uses is that of wood
which must be thrown into the fire before it can become an
artist's charcoal:

> Designer infinite!—
> Ah! must Thou char the wood ere Thou canst limn with it?

Thinking of his past youth as wasted water and as pulp, he
dreads old age:

> My freshness spent its wavering shower i' the dust;
> And now my heart is as a broken fount,

Wherein tear-drippings stagnate, spilt down ever
   From the dank thoughts that shiver
Upon the sighful branches of my mind.
     Such is; what is to be?
The pulp so bitter, how shall taste the rind?

At the moment when he feels drawn to surrender to the
Crucified, there comes before him, once again, a fear of sub-
mitting to the tortures of the Cross:

I dimly guess what Time in mists confounds;
Yet ever and anon a trumpet sounds
From the hid battlements of Eternity;
Those shaken mists a space unsettle, then
Round the half-glimpsed turrets slowly wash again.
     But not ere him who summoneth
     I first have seen, enwound
With glooming robes purpureal, cypress-crowned;
His name I know, and what his trumpet saith.
Whether man's heart or life it be which yields
     Thee harvest, must Thy harvest-fields
     Be dunged with rotten death?

God still pursues; and, as the Apocalypse says: "His voice
is like the sound of water in deep flood." The things of earth
have failed the poet at every turn—he begins to understand
that it is because he has rebelled against their God, has tried
to use earth's benefits without Him:

     Now of that long pursuit
     Comes on at hand the bruit;
That Voice is round me like a bursting sea:
     "And is thy earth so marred,

> Shattered in shard on shard?
> Lo, all things fly thee, for thou fliest Me!"

Finally, in the moment of surrender, the poet understands that love is what he desperately wants—and that of and by himself, he is unlovable. God gives him then the assurance that none of the pain and sacrifice have been in vain: He never closes a door, but that He opens a window; He never creates an emptiness, but in order that He might fill; He never humiliates an ego, but that He might elevate a personality: the trials and crosses, bereavements and sadnesses of life were only the shadow of His hand, stretched out for an embrace:

> Strange, piteous, futile thing!
> Wherefore should any set thee love apart?
> Seeing none but I makes much of naught (He said),
> "And human love needs human meriting:
>   How hast thou merited
> Of all man's clotted clay the dingiest clot?
>   Alack, thou knowest not
> How little worthy of any love thou art!
> Whom wilt thou find to love ignoble thee,
>   Save Me, save only Me?
> All which I took from thee I did but take,
>   Not for thy harms,
> But just that thou might'st seek it in My arms.
>   All which thy child's mistake
> Fancies as lost, I have stored for thee at home:
>   Rise, clasp My hand, and come!"
> Halts by me that footfall:
>   Is my gloom, after all,
> Shade of His hand, outstretched caressingly?

"Ah, fondest, blindest, weakest,
I am He Whom thou seekest!
Thou dravest love from thee, who dravest Me."

Those who have never had any experience of intimate union with Divine Love sometimes deny the reality of the experience recounted in the Hound of Heaven. There are some things which have to be experienced to be known: the happiness of falling head over heels in love with God is one of these. As there are two ways of knowing chastity—by studying about it from a book, and by living purely—so there are two ways of knowing God—by studying about Him, and by incarnating His Truth in our lives.

Cardinal Newman wrote: "Not all the possible descriptions of headlong love will make me comprehend the delirium, if I never had a fit of it; nor will ever so many sermons about the inward satisfaction of strict conscientiousness create in my mind the image of a virtuous action and its attendant sentiments, if I have been brought up to lie, thieve and indulge my appetites." Those whose only interest is a music that imitates the tom-tom of the jungle often regard the love of classical music as a pose: the music we love is the music we have already in our souls. There is an expectancy of taste in all of us—a blueprint of what we shall like and approve whenever we meet it; the reality we welcome is the reality that corresponds to our inmost hope. Everyone carries his unrealized ideal; the day that he discovers its counterpart in the romantic order is the day he "falls in love." But the higher loves, which will perfect us, have to be cultivated. Many who love classical music now once considered Bach and Brahms a bore. For good music, like all the best things of life, must be won and conquered. The music lover once exposed himself, forced himself to listen to good music; he made an intellectual effort to grasp it; finally, with growing knowledge, there came love, and with love, sympathy, and with sympathy, joy. The love of the best in painting or in poetry requires a similar effort. But those who have never read Vergil or Sophocles are foolish indeed if they say that the interest the scholar takes in them is unreal.

Even the taste for God must be acquired. When one reads the testimony of a convert who describes the transition from sin to grace as like emerging from a prison to the light, the statement is not to be dismissed as an illusion or a pose. The honest response of a listener to such a remark should be that there is at least the probability of a Reality which aroused this love, as there is a reality to the woman who claims the love of a devoted husband. Love does not spring into being without an object, nor do men and women bind themselves for life by strict monastic vows because of some idle imagining.

Yet such a tremendous Reality is hard to prove to some. Suppose that everyone in the world were blind except three persons. These three really saw, not only the sun, but also things under the sun. Their unique claim to a thing called "sight" might become a very interesting problem to a group of blind psychologists bent on investigating the existence of vision. These psychologists would probably start with the assumption that, since they are blind, everyone else is also blind. Before making any tests at all, their minds would be already closed. When the three with vision claimed that they could see the sun and things under the sun, the psychologists would call it a delusion; belief in the objective existence of the sun would be traced back to Persian mythology, and left there. A second group of psychologists might arise to suggest that belief in the sun was basically a complex, based on a curious and morbid wish for light.

The psychologists would always assume that, because they were groping in the dark, therefore everyone else must be in the dark. And this is the attitude of those who live in sin, unhappiness, and agony and who call the love of God a superstition and a myth. If one of the three persons in our story who could see was so ridiculed by those who could not that he finally plucked out his eyes, it would correspond to abandoning one's Faith because of the scorn the world gives to the lover of the Saviour and His Church.

Scripture says: "How gracious the Lord is! Taste and prove it!" Do not attribute the belief in the True God to emotion or to sentiment. The experience of God is real and can be tried. If it were an illusion, it would not inspire the sacrifice, the purity of morals, the humility, the sublimity of learning, that it has inspired for twenty centuries. "Taste and prove it."

But one cannot "taste God" so long as the ego holds first place in the heart, causing it to reject anything that is non-ego. Thus many people go through life defrauding themselves of anything that threatens their egregious pride. They have never either lived or loved. They love themselves, it is true—but there is no joy in throwing one's arms around his own ego. What such people call "falling in love" is only a projection of their own ego onto someone else; their enjoyment is not the *Thou* of the other person, but their own ego in that Thou. They marry, not to love, but to be loved; they are never in love with a person, but with a nerve ending. And as soon as the other person ceases to pamper and praise them, they leave and marry again. Those who have never loved at all are on the level of the ego, with everything to learn. The I-level knows the reality of selfless, human love. But it has still to learn the sublime experience of loving God.

The love of God has three characteristics. First, it is inexhaustible. Human love can be understood, explained, run down to its source like a mountain stream which can be traced to a spring in the rocks. But Divine Love is Infinite. If we start with the stream—in Holy Communion or in prayer—we soon discover that it runs into the Ocean of inexhaustible delights. What we know about Love is a minute drop in that Ocean. God's Love existed before the world began; it will exist after we go; our hearts can hold only its merest particles, as in such loves as Romeo's for Juliet or Dante's for his Beatrice. Love eludes our greatest poets' words, and even the mystics' writings do not capture it.

Love of the Lord is greater in realization than in desire. Here, again, it differs from worldly love, which is greater in anticipation than in realization. All the popular love songs tell us: "How happy we *will* be!" Divine Love, on the contrary, does not look at all enchanting or ecstatic before we have it: the Cross frightens us; the sacrifice of selfishness and sin seems like a little death; non-sensual love appears as lovelessness. But after one makes the surrender, gives up the field to win the pearl, then one is possessed of a joy that is ineffable, that beggars all description. The discovery makes one act so differently that his friends think he has lost his mind; but actually, he has found his soul, which the believer would not now give up for anything in all the world.

The love of Our Lord is not affected by suffering. He who loves the Tremendous Lover sometimes finds, indeed, that pain adds fuel to the Flame. Sorrow remarries the soul to God.

St. Theresa called each trial that came to her "a little present from God." Persons in adversity taste and find the Lord is sweet. An elderly woman with arthritis, her limbs twisted like olive trees in the Garden of Gethsemane, pours out her oil of prayers in fifty rosaries a day; a young bride writes in her diary: "Keep me O Lord, close to Thy Kingdom that I may sanctify the flesh and make it the chariot running its course to the supernal crown of the spirit"; Bishops in China pushing wheelbarrows through their dioceses, preaching in one city and then another as the Communists burn their churches and schools, rejoice that they can suffer for their Lord; a young husband with an unfaithful wife, who is consecrated and dedicated to continence, eats daily of the Bread of Life so that the bride may one day return to both the home and the Faith; religious women in convents offer prayers of thanks to God when told they are mortally ill, so that they may offer their lives as soldiers on the battlefield of Faith in reparation for the evil of the world; soldiers returning from the battles of a World War enter a religious life that they may now win the battle against the powers of darkness through a life of silence and penance; a young woman, heroine of the war, rescuing soldiers, feeding the diseased, and then contracting their malady herself, says: "All I want really—*is to love God more*"; a Jewish psychiatrist leaves a good practice to enter one of the strictest orders in the Church to pray for his own people; a woman in the world promises to fast from meat and fish for life, in order to bring fallen-away Catholics back to the embrace of the Master.

Boundless love alone can explain these surrenders! For these are happy people, all of them—it is a joyous thing to live on the Divine-level. Religion does not seem pleasant to those who have never climbed high enough, by a renunciation of selfishness, to glimpse its vistas; but a Divine Religion with the Holy Eucharist is much more pleasant to those who experience it than the world is pleasant to those who sin in it. It is possible that a true lover of God may have tasted both worlds, both lives, if he is a convert or a penitent. But the man who has lived only for the flesh, pleasure, and profit has no experience whatever of the thrills of the spirit. Since he has never tasted, he never can compare.

Many know the anxiety of a bad conscience; few know the peace of a good conscience lifted to the Divine level. If God's displeasure is so terrible that it keeps the guilty awake at night, think of the joys that beckon in His Pleasure! If it is misery to be under His wrath, then it is ecstasy to be under His Love! As St. Augustine asked:

"But what do I love, when I love Thee? Not beauty of bodies, nor the fair harmony of time, nor the brightness of the light so gladsome to our eyes, nor sweet melodies of varied songs, nor the fragrant smell of flowers, and ointments and spices, not manna and honey, not limbs acceptable to embracements of flesh. None of these I love, when I love my God; and yet I love a kind of light, and melody, and fragrance, and meat, and embracement, when I love my God, the light, melody, fragrance, meat, embracement of my inner man: where there shineth unto my soul, what space cannot contain, and there soundeth, what time beareth not away, and there smelleth, what breathing disperseth not, and there tasteth, what eating diminisheth not, and there clingeth, what satiety divorceth not. This it is which I love, when I love my God."

Lift up your heart: the search for pleasure is a sign of emptiness which the Divine alone can fill. Everyone who is not in love with Love is hunting for an artificial paradise; and would he look so hard for Heaven if he were not intended for Heaven? Inside his heart is a terrible void. Every sin he commits is an attempt to fill that void. All lovers without God are disappointed lovers.

Only God can love Himself, because He is Perfect; an ego cannot be satisfied with self-love, because it is so imperfect. That is why human beings love one another—to complement their own want of perfection, for what is loved in others is often what is lacking in self. But in the love of every other human being, there is a paradox that robs the love of its perfection. For say that I love and I am loved. If the one who loves me does so totally and with complete surrender, then he ceases to exist: I dominate, possess, and subjugate him to such an extent that, as a God-image, he no longer exists of and by himself, but only for me. In that case I have no one left to love. But if he does not love me totally and to the point of surrender, then he is not devoted; then he does not satisfy my needs, for I am made for infinite love and he does not love enough.

Thus in loving others, and in being loved by anyone but God, there is both a hunger and a satiety—a hunger because no creature can love enough; a satiety because he loves too much. The escape from this paradox is the Love of God. In Him there is no hunger because there one possesses the ecstasy of Perfect Love. *Voluptas cordium.* In Him there is no satiety, because it takes a never-ending eternity to begin to sound the depths of Love Divine. God is Love, and love is what we want and need. Love is our destiny.